ADIRONDACK COMMUNITY COLLEGE
LIBRARY
DISCARDED
BAY ROAD
QUEENSBURY, NY 12804

P9-APR-179

R
E
A MILES DAVIS
D
E
R

A MILES DAVIS READER

Edited by
Bill Kirchner

Smithsonian Institution Press
Washington and London

© 1997 by the Smithsonian Institution
All rights reserved

Copy editor: Aaron Appelstein
Production editor: Duke Johns
Designer: Martha Sewall

Library of Congress Cataloging-in-Publication Data

A Miles Davis reader / edited by Bill Kirchner.
     p.   cm.
   Includes index.
   ISBN 1-56098-774-X (alk. paper)
   1. Davis, Miles.   I. Kirchner, Bill.
ML419.D39M55   1997
788.9'2165'092—dc21   97–12802

British Library Cataloguing-in-Publication Data is available

Manufactured in the United States of America
04 03 02 01 00 99 98 97   5 4 3 2 1

☉ The paper used in this production meets the minimum requirements of the American
National Standard for Information Sciences—Permanence of Paper for Printed Library
Materials ANSI Z39.48-1984

For permission to reproduce illustrations appearing in this book, please correspond directly
with the owners of the works, as listed in the individual captions. The Smithsonian Institution
Press does not retain reproduction rights for these illustrations individually, or maintain a
file of addresses for photo sources.

Contents

Preface

A Miles Davis Reader continues a series of Smithsonian Institution Press jazz anthologies conceived by the late Martin Williams and inaugurated by *A Lester Young Reader*, edited by Lewis Porter. This volume has been several years in the making and could not have happened without the assistance of the following persons: Mark Hirsch (American studies acquisitions editor for Smithsonian Institution Press), series editor Scott DeVeaux of the University of Virginia, managing editor Duke Johns, copy editor Aaron Appelstein, Lewis Porter, Peter Shukat (attorney for the Miles Davis Estate), Dan Morgenstern and the staff of the Institute of Jazz Studies, Samuel Floyd and Marsha Reisser of the Center for Black Music Research, Gerald Early and Elizabeth Kellerman of Washington University, Bob Belden, Michael Cuscuna, and all of the authors and publishers who consented to have their works included here. And a "without whom" to my wife, Judy Kahn, for her invaluable support, suggestions, and encouragement.

I had only one brief contact with Miles Davis, but I'd like to recount it for the historical record. In the spring of 1981 Davis was preparing to emerge from a nearly six-year retirement, and he spent several consecutive Monday nights visiting the Village Vanguard in New York and listening to Mel Lewis and the Jazz Orchestra. During the last of those visits (at which, to my good fortune, I was present), Lewis persuaded Davis to sit in with the band. Lewis kicked off one of his orchestra's staples, Thad Jones's

"The Second Race," and Davis, borrowing in succession all four trumpets from the band's trumpet section, played an extended blues solo to the delight of everyone in the club. Since he was playing borrowed horns and was still getting his chops back after years of inactivity, Davis sounded rusty, but *what* he played could have come only from him.

During the next break, I was sitting at a table with one of the band's trumpeters, Joe Mosello. Suddenly, Davis approached our table and crouched down next to us. He placed his left hand on my right knee, looked straight at Mosello, and said in his famous raspy voice, "You know, you shouldn't drink beer on the gig—it dries you out."

He was right.

Introduction

Warning: this is a book about Miles Davis the musician, and therefore about the music of Miles Davis. Readers who are interested in Davis "the man," the media figure, the Prince of Darkness, the sartorial style-setter, the sexually provocative presence will need to look elsewhere.

And there are plenty of places to look. Unlike many, even most, major jazz figures, Miles Davis has been the subject of several biographies, including those by (in order of appearance) Bill Cole, Eric Nisenson, Ian Carr, and Jack Chambers. And, of course, there is Davis's own *Miles: The Autobiography* (1989), written in collaboration with Quincy Troupe. Other biographies will no doubt appear in the future, and at this writing a movie is purported to be in the works.

So there is no shortage of interest about Davis's life, and with good reason. Along with Leonard Bernstein and Frank Sinatra, he is among the most compelling personalities in the history of American music. And there are pieces in this volume where his arresting magnetism and unflinching honesty come out in full force: his own "Self-Portrait," revealing portraits by Pat Harris, Marc Crawford, Chris Albertson, and Sy Johnson, and the oft-quoted "Blindfold Tests." But the focus of this book, and the foremost motivation for all of the interest in him, is the music itself. In his autobiography Davis, with the directness and economy typical of his speech as well as his playing, summed up his career and influence in one sentence: "I've changed music five or six times."

Indeed he did. From the time that Davis, then eighteen, arrived in New York in the fall of 1944, he gravitated toward the standard-bearers of the jazz advance guard of the era: Charlie Parker, Dizzy Gillespie, Coleman Hawkins, Eddie "Lockjaw" Davis, and others. It must have been evident to all of these musicians that this youngster, unseasoned as he was, had something unique to offer. Within a year, Davis was Parker's regular trumpeter, eventually playing on some of the great saxophonist's finest recordings. At his best, young Davis, to quote critic Martin Williams, "was sometimes so good a lyricist as to be able to follow, for example, Charlie Parker's superb solo on 'Embraceable You' without sounding a hopeless anti-climax."

However well he managed to thrive in the virtuoso atmosphere of the Parker quintet, Davis quickly realized that his brand of lyricism required a different kind of showcase. In essence, he spent the rest of his career searching for, assembling, perfecting, and jettisoning a series of such showcases. The best of them, as Davis declared, changed music: the 1948–50 *Birth of the Cool* nonet, the 1955–60 quintets and sextets, the orchestral collaborations with Gil Evans, the 1963–70 quintets, and the *In a Silent Way/Bitches Brew* "electric" bands. In each case Davis provided focus and impetus for developments that became major parts of the jazz *and* popular mainstream.

There were many other achievements as well, in a career that spanned almost a half century and idioms ranging from bebop to varied fusions of jazz and rock. For the record I should state my own view of Davis's career, especially of his post-1968 work; the reader deserves to know the editorial viewpoint behind a project such as this. Although my enthusiasm for Davis's electric incarnations is not as consistently high as for his earlier work, it does exist. The 1969 quintet (discussed in this collection by Peter Keepnews) was a phenomenal group that, except for one track, "Sanctuary" on *Bitches Brew*, was never recorded in a studio. Bootleg recordings of this band are virtually the only testimonials to its excellence, including live performances of *Bitches Brew* material that, in my opinion, are far superior to the studio versions—more riveting and energetic and less cluttered. For that matter, and for the same reason, most of my favorite electric Miles recordings come from concerts; notable exceptions are *A Tribute to Jack Johnson* (1970) and *Aura*, his 1985 orchestral collaboration with the Danish trumpeter-composer Palle Mikkelborg.

If the contents of this book do not fully reflect my rather catholic view of Davis's work, there are two reasons. One is what was available for inclusion here, and the other is that serious writing about his music of the '60s, '70s, and '80s is not exactly voluminous. Much work remains to be done in analyzing all periods of Davis's career, most of all concerning the later developments.

In any case, I am pleased to present the contents of this volume, all substantial works: some well known and frequently quoted but long out-of-print, and others obscure. Individually and collectively, they give us a many-faceted view of one of the most fascinating musicians of the twentieth century.

Editor's Note

In compiling this volume, I have edited all historical information to conform with recent research. Obvious typographical, grammatical, and factual errors have been corrected silently, and all articles have been edited for stylistic consistency with respect to spelling, capitalization, punctuation, number and date style, treatment of titles, footnote and list formats, and so on. The "flavor" of each author's writing style has not been touched. In those articles with music examples, references to and placement of examples have been modified to improve the integration of music and text and to accommodate layout. Each author is responsible for the accuracy of his music examples, but in a few cases I have corrected obvious errors in transcription.

Miles Davis

Self-Portrait

Originally published by Columbia Records Biographical Service, November 26, 1957. Reprinted by permission of Sony Music and the Miles Davis Estate.

Miles Dewey Davis III was born on May 26, 1926 (not May 25, as published in many earlier accounts), in Alton, Illinois, not far up the Mississippi River from East St. Louis. He was the second of three children. In 1927 the Davis family (Miles II, his wife, Cleota Henry Davis, and Miles III and his older sister Dorothy) moved to East St. Louis, where Davis *père* practiced dentistry. (A third child, Vernon, was born in 1929.)

In his autobiography Davis described his father as "one of the pillars of the black community in East St. Louis, because he was a doctor and got into politics." The Davis family was by all accounts highly prosperous, although Miles's parents had a troubled marriage that broke up about 1944, when young Davis was still in high school. (His account in "Self-Portrait" of receiving a trumpet instead of a violin at age thirteen is thus tinged with more than a little sarcasm.)

"Self-Portrait" is an unusual example of a press release that took on a long life. Compiled from a taped interview with Davis conducted by George Avakian, then Davis's producer at Columbia Records, the release appeared in several jazz publications, including *Down Beat*, and in an anthology called *The Jazz Word*. Three points of clarification: Davis's early trumpet instructor was Elwood Buchanan; the band known as the Blue

Devils was led by Eddie Randle and was based at the Rhumboogie Club in downtown St. Louis; and Charlie Parker and Dizzy Gillespie came to St. Louis in 1944 with the Billy Eckstine orchestra, with which Davis played as a substitute.—Ed.

You want me to tell you where I was born—that old story? It was in good old Alton, Illinois. In 1926. And I had to call my mother a week before my last birthday and ask her how old I would be.

I started playing trumpet in grade school. Once a week we would hold notes. Wednesdays at 2:30. Everybody would fight to play best. Lucky for me, I learned to play the chromatic scale right away. A friend of my father's brought me a book one night and showed me how to do it so I wouldn't have to sit there and hold that note all the time.

My mother wanted to give me a violin for my birthday, but my father gave me a trumpet—because he loved my mother so much!

There was a very good instructor in town. He was having some dental work done by my father. He was the one that made my father get me the trumpet. He used to tell us all about jam sessions on the Showboat, about trumpet players like Bobby Hackett and Hal Baker. "Play without any vibrato," he used to tell us. "You're gonna get old anyway and start shaking," he used to say, "no vibrato!" That's how I tried to play. Fast and light—and no vibrato.

By the time I was sixteen, I was playing in a band—the Blue Devils—in East St. Louis. Sonny Stitt came to town with a band and heard us play one night. He told me, "You look like a man named Charlie Parker and you play like him too. C'mon with us."

The fellows in his band had their hair slicked down, they wore tuxedos, and they offered me sixty whole dollars a week to play with them. I went home and asked my mother if I could go with them. She said no, I had to finish my last year of high school. I didn't talk to her for two weeks. And I didn't go with the band either.

I knew about Charlie Parker in St. Louis, I even played with him there, while I was still in high school. We always used to try to play like Diz and Charlie Parker. When we heard that they were coming to town, my friend and I were the first people in the hall, me with a trumpet under my arm. Diz walked up to me and said, "Kid, do you have a union card?" I said, "Sure." So I sat in with the band that night. I couldn't read a thing from listening to Diz and Bird. Then the third trumpet man got sick. I knew the book because I loved the music so much I knew the third part by heart. So I played with the band for a couple of weeks. I had to go to New York then.

My mother wanted me to go to Fisk University. I looked in the *Esquire* book, and I asked her, "Where's all of this?" Then I asked my father. He said I didn't have to go to Fisk, I could go to big New York City. In September I was in New York City. A friend of mine was studying at Juilliard, so I decided to go there too. I spent my first week in New York and my first month's allowance looking for Charlie Parker.

I roomed with Charlie Parker for a year. I used to follow him around, down to 52nd Street, where he used to play. Then he used to get me to play. "Don't be afraid," he used to tell me. "Go ahead and play." Every night I'd write down chords I heard on matchbook covers. Everybody helped me. Next day I'd play those chords all day in the practice room at Juilliard, instead of going to classes.

I didn't start writing music until I met Gil Evans. He told me to write something and send it to him. I did. It was what I played on the piano. Later I found out I could do better without the piano. (I took some piano lessons at Juilliard, but not enough.) If you don't play it good enough, you'll be there for hours and hours.

If you can hear a note, you can play it. The note I hit that sounds high, that's the only one I can play right then, the only note I can think of to play that would fit. You don't learn to play the blues. You just play. I don't even think about harmony. It just comes. You learn where to put notes so they'll sound right. You just don't do it because it's a funny chord. I used to change things because I wanted to hear them—substitute progressions and things. Now I have better taste.

Do I like composing better than playing? I can't answer that. There's a certain feeling you get from playing that you can't get from composing. And when you play, it's like a composition anyway. You make the outline. What do I like to play? I like 'Round About Midnight. In fact, I like most any ballad. If I feel like playing it.

What do I think of my own playing? I don't keep any of my records. I can't stand to hear them after I've made them. The only ones I really like are the one I just made with Gil Evans (*Miles Ahead*), the one I made with J. J. (Johnson) on my Blue Note date about four years ago, and a date I did with Charlie Parker.

People ask me if I respond to the audience. I wouldn't like to sit up there and play without anybody liking it. If it's a large audience, I'm very pleased because they are there anyway. If it's a small audience, sometimes it doesn't matter. I enjoy playing with my own rhythm section and listening to them. I'm studying and experimenting all the time.

I know people have some rhythm and they feel things when they're good. A person has to be an invalid not to show some sign—a tap of the finger even. You don't have to applaud. I never look for applause. In Europe they like everything you do. The mistakes and everything. That's a little bit too much.

If you play good for eight bars, it's enough. For yourself. And I don't tell anybody.

Michael Ullman

Miles Davis in Retrospect

Originally published in New Boston Review *6, no. 3 (May/June 1981).* *Reprinted by permission of the author.*

When "Miles Davis in Retrospect" appeared in spring 1981, Davis was only weeks short of ending his nearly six-year sabbatical from public performance. The piece thus provided a perceptive and fair-minded overview of Davis's career through 1975, when he went into seclusion. During the trumpeter's long hiatus, there was intense interest both in and beyond jazz circles about when—or if—he would resume his career, and "Retrospect" subtly reflects that curiosity.

Author Michael Ullman's jazz criticism has appeared in a number of publications, including the *Atlantic Monthly*, the *New Republic*, the *Boston Globe*, and the *Boston Phoenix*. He also is the author of *Jazz Lives* (1980) and coauthor (with Lewis Porter and Edward Hazell) of *Jazz from Its Origins to the Present* (1993). Ullman teaches music and English at Tufts University in Medford, Massachusetts.—Ed.

Few musicians have brought as many new sounds and sights to the jazz world as Miles Davis. An intense, ambitious musician, he has managed to make a limited instrumental technique suggest infinite possibilities. As one of the great leaders in jazz, Davis, like Ellington and Charles Mingus, consistently assembled groups that sound remarkably better than their individual parts. In the 1950s the trumpeter changed the manners in jazz performance when he turned his back on audiences and refused to announce his tunes. No Louis Armstrong stage tricks for him. (But when asked a leading question about Armstrong, he lavishly praised the older man's playing: it was impossible for a trumpeter to play things Armstrong hadn't already done, he asserted.) Later Davis helped improve working conditions for jazz artists when he insisted on playing only a couple of sets a night; previously musicians were expected to play forty minutes and take twenty off for as many as six hours.

Davis's accomplishment is all the more impressive given his gruff and withdrawn manner, even among his musicians. Bassist Miroslav Vitous told me that Davis spoke to him only once in the many weeks that he played with him during the early 1970s, and that was to ask his young sideman to rush another group offstage so that the trumpeter could play and go home.

Davis's early development had been swift. When in 1945 at the age of nineteen he first recorded with alto saxophonist Charlie Parker, Davis seemed a somewhat bumbling, insecure stylist without the agility or panache of Dizzy Gillespie, who indeed took over Davis's trumpet for the virtuoso performance of Parker's "Ko Ko." But Davis's tentative phrases contained the germ of an idea: two years later he would record for the same company four of his own tunes, and this time Parker would be a sideman on tenor saxophone. Clearly the twenty-one-year-old who could make a tenor player out of Charlie Parker knew what he was doing. Unable to play as fast or as high as other bebop trumpeters, Davis developed an intimate, round, almost vibratoless tone as far from the brash, extroverted sounds of Louis Armstrong and Roy Eldridge as from the bright fluidity of the bopsters. And he found the proper setting for that sound on compositions like "Milestones" and "Sippin' at Bell's." Darker in texture than comparable Parker arrangements, Davis's pieces reflected his simpler strengths. He seemed intent, serious, restrained: "cool" is what the critics called him, and a series of 1949–50 recordings led by Davis with arrangements by Gil Evans, Gerry Mulligan, John Lewis, and John Carisi was dubbed *Birth of the Cool.*

In his memoirs Dizzy Gillespie warmly describes Davis's approach in the late 1940s: "Miles ushered in an innovation that the press immediately smeared with the term 'cool' jazz. . . . The record was called *Birth of the Cool* because the guys in California sort of played not hot but 'coolish.' They expressed less fire than we did, played less notes, less quickly, and used more open space, and they emphasized tonal quality. . . . I liked to fill up a bar myself—the Charlie Parker school—to take advantage of every space that's there instead of just leaving it to go over into the next bar. Miles had wide open spaces."

Wary of other members of the cool school, Gillespie praised Davis for the guts in his music, for his ability to play the blues. And Davis acknowledged in a typically backhanded way the influence of Gillespie: "He could teach anybody, but me. No, man—the shit was going too fast. I mean that was a fast pace, man. . . . Freddie Webster and I used to go down every night to hear Diz. If we missed a night, we missed something. We'd go down to Fifty-Second Street to hear Diz and get our ears stretched." Trumpeters Webster and Davis could play a game while listening to Diz: one of them would throw a coin in the air, and the other would have to identify the note Gillespie was playing when the coin hit the bar. Davis said that he couldn't learn from Gillespie, but later he contradicts himself. "My style wasn't any different [from Gillespie's], I just played in a low register."

Davis's developing style was something more than Gillespie's played lower or slower. Soon, Davis could do some things Gillespie shied away from. By the 1950s his blues had a rich, down-home quality: on cuts like the 1951 "Bluing" (reissued on *Chronicle*), Davis manages to sound sophisticated while suggesting a chaste intimacy unparalleled in modern jazz. "Miles is deep," Gillespie has said—deeper into the blues than Gillespie himself. Dizzy was once criticized for his thin tone; from the beginning Davis's was vibrant and intense. Gillespie is for many listeners an acquired taste, while Davis's music seems to arouse instant passion. Gillespie's trumpet, one might say, dances before your eyes, and Davis's breathes down your neck.

As critic Martin Williams has pointed out in *The Jazz Tradition*, many artists would have been sufficiently content with the *Birth of the Cool* to have spent the rest of their careers copying that achievement. Davis has maintained the outlines of his early trumpet style, but he has repeatedly transformed the size and sound of his groups until in the 1970s he would, to the dismay of older fans, attach his trumpet to a wah-wah pedal and lead something like a rock band. While fans talked darkly of coercion by CBS president Clive Davis, the trumpeter simply announced that he would assemble "the best damn rock band" in the world. The rock-influenced *Bitches Brew* sold half a million copies in its first year, and Columbia's public relations office started calling Davis "the Prince of Darkness."

A critical reaction was inevitable. In his history of jazz, James Lincoln Collier reproaches Davis for the paradoxes in his career, calling him "a man who possessed only a relatively modest natural gift, but who by dint of intelligence and force of personality made himself one of the major figures of jazz." Besides lacking Beiderbecke's sense of musical line, Lester Young's rhythm, and Armstrong's drama, Davis is, according to Collier, "a limited instrumentalist with a poor high register and a tendency to crack more notes than a professional trumpet player should." (I am reminded of Whitney Balliett's description of Armstrong's early style, which he asserts is typified by the trumpeter's tendency to fluff every fifth note.)

Those of us who find Davis's cracked notes more electrifying than other trumpeters' ringing tones should be thankful that so many of the recordings remain readily available. *Chronicle: The Complete Prestige Recordings, 1951–1956* begins with some sessions showing Davis still toying with the cool sound and ends with Davis's most celebrated quintet, featuring John Coltrane on tenor sax, Red Garland on piano, Paul Chambers on bass, and Philly Joe Jones on drums. Never before assembled in a single package, these recordings include some acknowledged classics in modern jazz: the two takes of "Bags' Groove" and "The Man I Love," the "Walkin'" and "Blue 'n' Boogie" session. Recordings from this period also introduced to a wider public some of the brightest names in the music: Sonny Rollins, John Coltrane, John Lewis, Thelonious Monk, Jackie McLean, Milt Jackson. They demonstrate Davis's uncanny ability to create the perfect context for his improvisations.

Despite the seeming informality of these early dates, Davis was concerned with the quality of the overall sound. In his notes to an album recorded in 1971 by pianist Joe Zawinul, Miles Davis comments admiringly on the Austrian pianist's arrangements: "All these musicians are set up. Joe sets up the musicians so that they have to play like they do, in order to fit the music like they do. In order to fit this music you have to be 'cliché-free.' " One can never prevent determined sidemen from playing clichés, but Davis makes it difficult, both by his example and by the explicit demands he makes on his musicians.

These recordings from the 1950s demonstrate his concern for group sound. Uncomfortable with pianist Thelonious Monk's irregular accompaniments, Davis had Monk lay out during the trumpeter's solos. A renewed feeling of intimacy with the listener, appropriate to Davis's sound, resulted. Davis instructed pianist Red Garland to imitate the lightweight touch and chic harmonic sophistication of Ahmad Jamal—and Garland's reward was his feature "Ahmad's Blues" (reproduced on *Chronicle*). The blend in the quintet first recorded in 1955 was ideal: Garland's feathery strokes were offset by drummer Philly Joe Jones's aggressive polyrhythms. Bassist Paul Chambers held steadily to the beat behind the two horns, Coltrane and Davis. Where Davis might play one note, bend and develop it, finding a pulse within a single tone, Coltrane would surge up and down a scale in a heroic attempt to play everything at once. A striking contrast, engineered purposely by the trumpeter.

But if Davis resisted musical clichés, he also, like Louis Armstrong before him, had a penchant for redeeming the banal. In *Chronicle* one can hear him work his magic on songs like "It's Only a Paper Moon" and "Surrey with the Fringe on Top." The foolishly jogging rhythms of the latter open up deliciously when Davis runs through and over them, and he makes "It's Only a Paper Moon" round and elegant while paying more than casual attention to its melody. In the 1960s when he performed many of his hits night after night, his method was to increase the tempos. A hackneyed phrase at a moderate tempo might become a tour de force when speeded up.

Many of the *Chronicle* cuts are marred by bad moments: on his second date with Davis, Sonny Rollins's interesting contributions are cut short by a squeaky reed. The reunion of Davis and Charlie Parker—the latter again on tenor saxophone—was weakened by Davis's moodiness and Parker's drunkenness. (After entering the studio, Parker reportedly downed a quart of gin and promptly fell asleep. When he woke up he felt sluggish, but as producer Ira Gitler noted, only Parker would have awakened. Davis complained, and Parker responded, "Lily Pons, beauty must come of suffering," identifying Davis with the sweet, light voice of a popular opera singer.) *Chronicle* is indispensable, however, for Davis's playing of blues and ballads, and for incomparable solos such as Monk's eerily timed choruses on "Bags' Groove." In *The Jazz Tradition* Martin Williams announced that everything came together for Davis in 1954. Certainly Davis and his groups became more consistent about that time, but several of my favorite performances—"Bluing," "It's Only a Paper Moon"—come earlier.

Davis signed with Columbia in 1955, although he taped a few more sessions for Prestige. The most celebrated of his CBS recordings remain in print, including the seminal *Kind of Blue* recorded in March and April 1959—a collection of five sketches, primarily modal, filled out stunningly by Davis with Cannonball Adderley, Coltrane, Chambers, drummer Jimmy Cobb, and pianists Bill Evans and Wynton Kelly. (The choice of the lyrical Evans is instructive. From Garland to Evans to Herbie Hancock, his pianist from 1963 to 1968, Davis has shown a preference for pianists with a light, even fragile touch.) Experimental though it was, *Kind of Blue* sounds as natural as breathing.

Davis shifted toward rock gradually. The quintet of the 1960s included Wayne Shorter, whose lazy melodies with their infrequent harmonic changes often lacked a second theme or bridge. The languorous sound and monolithic quality demanded new rhythmic energy in the drums and new textures, soon provided by an electric piano. Davis was used to being in the vanguard of music, but jazz was being left behind in the rock-oriented 1960s and 1970s. Davis wanted to make more money—he has one of the most flamboyant lifestyles in the business, buying expensive sports cars, it would seem, only to crack them up. And surely he saw more than economic possibilities in rock rhythms and electronic sounds. Rock may have piqued his longtime interest in salvaging the banal.

The transitional *Miles Smiles*, with three Shorter compositions, was deservedly well received: not so some of the later recordings, which alarmed critics while delighting larger and younger audiences. Onstage in the early 1970s, Davis was a sight: stalking about, wolflike and thin, dressed extravagantly—a family of four could survive for a year on what he's spent on sunglasses—he remained in perfect control, calling out rhythms to a variety of percussionists, an electric bassist, a couple of guitarists, and occasionally to as many as three electric keyboardists. In fact, this was a difficult music to record, and few of the heavily edited records that CBS released captured the excitement of the Miles Davis show. In 1975, amid speculations about his health, wealth, and possible dissatisfaction with his music, Miles withdrew at what seemed the height of his popularity. He hasn't reappeared since; nor has he stated the reason for his apparent retirement.

Unable to offer more current recordings by their jazz star, Columbia Records has been searching its vaults for Davis material. *Circle in the Round* and *Directions* collect primarily unissued recordings dating from 1955 to 1970. Most come from the transitional period of the late 1960s. Certainly the most satisfying material does: after one listens to the awkward " 'Round Midnight" on *Directions*, one knows why other versions were preferred. *Circle in the Round* is valuable for its side-long title cut, for the 5/4 blues "Splash," and for a wrenching nine-minute version of Wayne Shorter's "Sanctuary." A less important release, *Directions* includes a short addition to the Davis-Gil Evans canon, "Song of Our Country"; "Fun" and "Water on the Pond" by the Shorter-Hancock-Carter-Williams quintet, joined by guitarist Joe Beck on the latter; and a spacious recording of Joe Zawinul's floating "Ascent," featuring three electric instruments (two pianos and a bass) played by Herbie Hancock, Chick Corea, and Dave Holland.

By the time he retired, Davis's solos, seemed a series of disjointed gestures, dramatic and striking in themselves but not the patient constructions of earlier years. Nevertheless, during this period he was much praised for his impact on younger musicians. The man who had allowed John Coltrane to explore and develop, who had defended Philly Joe Jones's aggressive drumming, in the 1970s promoted the work of young, white saxophonists Dave Liebman and Steve Grossman, pianists Chick Corea, Herbie Hancock, and Keith Jarrett, and guitarist John McLaughlin. Davis may not have talked to Miroslav Vitous, but he—albeit unconsciously—helped the bassist's career. After the stint with Davis, says Vitous, his phone would not stop ringing. Davis's spare but passionate playing has influenced trumpeters from Detroit's Donald Byrd to Tokyo's Terumasa Hino. Less beneficial has been the impact of his image. Impressed by the Davis lifestyle, Tony Williams and Herbie Hancock formed aesthetically uninteresting fusion bands in an attempt to reproduce Davis's financial success. Hancock and Chick Corea told Leonard Feather that Davis discouraged them from practicing: both realized later that the advice was harmful.

And what of Davis's own achievements? Can we, with Collier, pass off the Davis recordings as the inspired ramblings of a "limited instrumentalist"? All musicians have limited techniques, and all artists adapt in some way their art to their technique. More important, in the late 1940s the trumpet players who imitated the virtuosic Dizzy Gillespie simply flattered him; the few who recognized that he was inimitable paid him a realer kind of tribute. Davis was neither intimidated by nor envious of Gillespie. He knew he had to do something else, and from the time of his first sessions with Charlie Parker, we see him working to find a new music appropriate to his talents. Davis is, as Collier implies, one of the great opportunists in jazz. But he has never been one to simply adapt to changing trends in music. When Davis assembled a band in the 1970s that included a British rock guitarist, an Indian tabla player, and a Fender bassist straight out of rhythm and blues, he was creating for himself and for his players new musical problems. These newly issued recordings contain some of his solutions from the past, and they sound as fresh and original as when they were first recorded.

Pat Harris

Nothing but Bop? "Stupid," Says Miles

Originally published in Down Beat, *January 27, 1950, 18–19. Reprinted by permission of Maher Publications.*

If this is not the very first published interview with Miles Davis—it probably is, but I can't say for sure—it's surely among the first, and a good one. Written by the Chicago-based *Down Beat* writer Pat Harris—the Chicago area, then as now, was the magazine's home base—the article gives a detailed account of Davis's early life and career. Harris generally gets the facts right, with three notable exceptions: Davis was never legally married to Irene Birth, mother of three of his children; he left Juilliard in the fall of 1945; and he used trombonist Michael Zwerin, not Ted Kelly, at his second booking at the Royal Roost.

Harris, incidentally, was a woman and a quite capable journalist. I mention this because *Down Beat* in the 1940s and early 1950s was a decidedly male-oriented publication with lots of cheesecake photos of girl singers. (Many of these singers literally *were* girls still in their teens.) To have been a female jazz writer at that time must have been an interesting challenge.

The piece ends on a rather ominous note. What isn't said is that Davis had recently become a heroin addict; he would remain one for four years.—Ed.

"I don't like to hear someone put down Dixieland. Those people who say there's no music but bop are just stupid; it just shows how much they don't know." This was Miles Davis speaking, and he rose to defend the universality of jazz while decrying the much less than universal respect given the jazz musician.

Miles, whose definitely modern trumpet has been heard for the last month at the Hi-Note here, is a mild, modest, quiet young man of twenty-three, and he has a lot of respect for his elders.

Not So New

"Sidney Bechet—we played opposite him at the Paris jazz festival last year—played some of the things Charlie Parker plays, particularly a riff on 'Ko Ko.' We talked to Bechet for some time over there and asked him where he had gotten the riff. He told us it was from an old march and had been transposed from a flute or clarinet part. I've heard Parker do a lot of things that show a Bechet influence, and Johnny Hodges, too."

Need Foundation

"No, I never played Dixieland myself. When I was growing up I played like Roy Eldridge, Harry James, Freddie Webster, and anyone else I admired. You've got to start way back there before you can play bop. You've got to have a foundation."

Miles himself started early. Not as early as his three-year-old son, Gregory, who is already blowing a horn ("he has a natural rhythm," Miles reports proudly) but shortly after his thirteenth birthday. "I was expecting a violin for a birthday present, and my father came home with a trumpet and the trumpet teacher."

The teacher, Elwood Buchanan, was a good friend of Miles Sr., a dentist, and came around to all the grade schools in East St. Louis, Illinois, once a week and taught daily classes in the high school there. Miles was his pupil until he graduated from high school and left for New York and two years at Juilliard.

Lots of Competition

"There was a lot of competition, and we all learned to play very quickly," Miles remembers. "The teacher would say, 'Brown, you played that line very well,' and the next day we'd all be trying to play better than Brown. In four months we were playing marches."

He didn't stick with marches, of course. When he was fifteen, Miles had his union card and was gigging around town and playing with Eddie Randle's big band in St. Louis, across the river. He was a good friend of Clark Terry, still one of his favorite trumpet players, and of Sonny Stitt. The Randle band, a Savoy Sultans-styled outfit, played shows at the Rhumboogie in St. Louis, and Sonny heard Miles there. He tried to get Miles to join the Tiny Bradshaw band, but Miles's mother refused to let her sixteen-year-old leave home.

He also had a chance to join Illinois Jacquet and McKinney's Cotton Pickers, whose trumpet playing manager, A. J. Sulliman, tried his best to pull Miles out of East St. Louis.

Sitting In

Miles worked part of one summer with a Creole band in Springfield, Illinois. Guitarist Adam Lambert was the leader, and Stanley Williams played drums. Pay was good, $100 a week, but the job lasted only two weeks. One night the Billy Eckstine band came to town, and Miles, who had heard of Dizzy Gillespie from Stitt, went to hear the band. They lacked a trumpet player, and Miles just happened to have his horn with him. He sat in, after assuring Gillespie (Eckstine's music director at the time) that he had a union card, and was started on his way. That night he first heard Charlie Parker.

When Miles went to New York and to Juilliard in 1944, 52nd Street was in its heyday. Coleman Hawkins was working on the Street, and Joe Guy was with him on trumpet. But half the time Guy didn't show up, so Miles sat in. He was working pretty steadily, without pay, and going to school all day.

Then his wife (he married [*sic*] at seventeen) came to New York, and Miles had to look around for a job that would include a paycheck.

For Loot, Now

First one he found was at the Spotlite, with tenorist Eddie Davis; Rudy Williams, alto; Ernie Washington, piano; Leonard Gaskin, bass; and Eddie Nicholson, drums. He had been playing there anyhow on the nights Guy did show up for Hawkins, so just moved in on a business basis. This job lasted a month.

Most of the bands Miles has worked with were similar units, and the jobs were none too steady. He ruefully describes his life as months of no work, interspersed every quarter year or so with a two-week job.

"I've worked so little," Miles says, "I could probably tell you where I was playing any night in the last three years."

Noncommercial

It doesn't seem to bother him very much, though. He likes to play what he believes is noncommercial bop, a middle-register horn, subdued and soft, with a many-noted complexity few other trumpeters can match.

"I play high when I work with a big band," Miles says, "but I prefer not to. A lot of trumpeters, Gillespie is one, have trouble controlling their tone when they play low. I don't want to have that trouble."

After the Spotlite, Miles read that Bird would be at a jam session at the Heatwave. He showed up and, renewing his friendship with Parker, worked with Charlie at the Three Deuces. The band had Al Haig, piano; Curley Russell, bass; and Stan Levey, drums. They moved over to the Spotlite after three weeks, with Sir Charles Thompson on piano, Leonard Gaskin, bass, and Levey, drums. Dexter Gordon joined them after the first two weeks of the five-week job.

Back Home

Davis worked at Minton's with Sir Charles and a drummer for a short time and also played, for pay this time, with Hawkins. Then, two years [*sic*] after he went to New York, Miles quit school and went home to East St. Louis.

Benny Carter was playing the Riviera in St. Louis, and Miles joined him for the trip to the West Coast. Parker was on the coast then. Miles and Charlie are very close friends, Charlie having lived with the Davises for a while in New York in 1945. Miles says that when he plays with Parker or with Lee Konitz, "it sounds like one horn."

He worked with Carter a month. Most of the band's book was of ancient vintage, except for a few arrangements by Bob Graettinger, Neal Hefti, and Carter himself, and Miles was not too happy with it. The Carter band was playing at the Orpheum theater in Los Angeles, and Parker was working at the Finale club. Miles doubled jobs for a week and was roundly fined by the union for it.

Long Time No Work

Miles stayed on the coast for seven months without a job. He joined Billy Eckstine's band, heading east, and was with the band five months. Hobart Dotson was playing lead trumpet ("he didn't miss a note in five months," Miles says), and Gene Ammons, Art Blakey, and Doug Mettome were also in the outfit. "Me and Art Blakey got Doug in the band in Detroit," Miles remembers. Miles missed the last date with the Eckstine crew because of illness.

In the spring of 1947 Miles again joined Parker, this time at the Three Deuces in New York. Max Roach was on drums; Tommy Potter, bass; and Duke Jordan, piano. They worked together until mid-1948, off and on at the Deuces and in Detroit and Chicago.

When the Royal Roost opened, Miles went in with Allen Eager, Kai Winding, Tadd Dameron, Roach, and Curley Russell. His second date at the Roost was with a ten-piece band, including Konitz, Mulligan, Roach, Al McKibbon, Lewis, Junior Collins, trombonist Ted Kelly [sic], and Bill Barber on tuba. Pancho Hagood sang with the unit. The first Roost date lasted eight weeks; the second, two.

Capitol Contract

The Capitol recording contract followed, with eight sides cut. Those issued already are "Move"/"Budo," "Godchild"/"Jeru," and "Boplicity"/"Israel." Fourth release, "Venus de Milo"/"Rouge," will be out soon. On Miles's first recording, a blues with Herbie Fields, he says, "I couldn't be heard, 'count of I played into a mute and was frightened." He's recorded a number of sides with Parker, including a couple of albums, and some things including "Milestones" and "Half Nelson" under his own name on Savoy.

On the Parker "Ko Ko," Dizzy Gillespie was playing piano and had to double on trumpet for Miles because Miles said he was too nervous to play. The label has Miles's name on it as trumpeter and has caused some confusion.

The Eckstine band, he believes, was the best of all modern units, with the possible close second of Claude Thornhill's band when Gil Evans was writing for it and Lee Konitz was in the reed section.

"The Greatest"

"Thornhill had the greatest band of these modern times," Miles says, "except for Eckstine, and he destroyed it when he took out the tuba and the two French horns. It was commercially good and musically good. For the Capitol records I made last year, I wanted to get a band as close to the sound Evans writes for as I could.

"I'm going to try to get Evans to do four more arrangements for our next record date with Capitol, and have John Lewis and Gerry Mulligan do some writing, too. I'll use the same instrumentation, and the same men."

Favorites

Miles's favorite musicians, who form a huge, formidably heterogeneous group, include John Lewis, whose composing and arranging skill he greatly admires; Evans; Will Bradley, "who writes like Stravinsky"; Parker; Konitz; Freddie Webster; Vic Coulsen (who worked with Hawkins before Joe Guy and is now out of the business); Fats Navarro, whose ability to play high and fast and still sound pretty he finds amazing; Bechet; Billie Holiday; Louis Armstrong; Gillespie, who Miles says is still progressing; and on and on. In fact, it would be difficult to find a musician for whom the easygoing Miles wouldn't have a good word.

He has nothing good to say, however, about band promoters ("look what they've done to Dizzy") and club operators—nightclub operators especially. "They don't treat musicians with enough respect," Miles complains. "They think all jazz musicians are irresponsible drunkards."

Like Paris

"What I would like to do is to spend eight months in Paris and four months here. Eight months a year where you're accepted for what you can do, and four months here because—well, it's hard to leave all this." Like a great many jazz musicians who have been in Europe, Miles feels that's the only place to bring up his two children and to live freely as a man himself.

Until then, he can count on another year with Capitol and maybe a little work. During the last year he worked a couple of weeks at Soldier Meyers' in Brooklyn, played the Paris jazz festival with Parker, four one-nighters around New York, and a month at the Hi-Note. When he closed here, nothing very substantial was in sight.

André Hodeir

Miles Davis and the Cool Tendency

Originally published in Jazz: Its Evolution and Essence, *trans. David Noakes (New York: Grove Press, 1956; rev. ed., New York: Grove Press, 1979), 116–36. Reprinted by permission of Grove/Atlantic, Inc.*

The French composer André Hodeir has been one of the most formidable of jazz critics, and *Jazz: Its Evolution and Essence* is a landmark volume of jazz criticism. It was published in the United States in 1956, two years after its initial publication in France as *Hommes et problèmes du jazz*. The late Martin Williams, certainly no slouch himself as a critic, paid tribute by remarking that even when he felt that a Hodeir viewpoint was wrongheaded, "Hodeir remains a true critic in that one cannot deal with his position without arriving solidly at one's own."

"Miles Davis and the Cool Tendency" is a classic evaluation of Davis's first major musical achievement, and the value of Hodeir's remarks is not diminished by the occasionally dated, early-fifties tone. Also, as Hodeir implies, European jazz critics, no matter how gifted, usually are at a disadvantage in having to form so much of their opinions solely on recorded evidence. This was even more true, of course, in the fifties than it is now, but Hodeir overcame that problem by the sheer quality of his insights.—Ed.

A New Feeling

Once past its great periods of classicism, it is not unusual for an art to lose its unity. What happens then is a division into branches of what was a single trunk. Factional differences, which are no longer the expression of conflicts traditionally opposing one period to its predecessor, begin to spring up among the members of a single generation. Modern jazz seems to be caught in this pattern. The conflicts have not yet assumed an aggressive character, but they exist. The bop movement, which we have just been examining as represented by its foremost creator, is only one part of postwar jazz—the most important, perhaps, but not the only one. While the influence of the Minton's group was emerging triumphantly, another tendency was taking shape among jazzmen who were scarcely younger than Gillespie and Parker. It took root in the art of Lester Young. In this way, a musician whose conceptions were so original that he might have seemed impossible to put in any category turned out to be a precursor. His influence, though it merely touched Charlie Parker and his disciples lightly, is evident today, above and beyond bop, in the work of a whole group of young saxophonists who regard the "President" as their spiritual father. Lester's mark has even extended well beyond the saxophone's domain. For a long while, Young was believed to have given the tenor sax a new style; actually, what he did was to give birth to a new conception of jazz.

This new style has been labeled "cool," undoubtedly in allusion to the "hot" jazz of 1925 to 1935. Chronologically, the cool movement represents the furthest point reached to date in the evolution of jazz. Among its representatives, which include both white and colored musicians, are renegades from the movement headed by Parker, such as trumpeter Miles Davis, trombonist J. J. Johnson, and pianist John Lewis; disciples of Lester Young, such as tenor saxophonists Herbie Steward, Al Cohn, Allen Eager, Gene Ammons, Stan Getz, and Wardell Gray; or declared "progressives," such as Lee Konitz, Lennie Tristano, and Billy Bauer.[1] It is too early to judge the value of the work created by these musicians. Moreover, the European critic, who must rely on recordings, is not always in a position to form a valid judgment on the most recent evolution of jazz; he may lack some essential bit of evidence. It is still permissible to observe that up to now the cool tendency has not produced a body of creations that can compare in quantity and quality with what we were given by bop in its most brilliant period (1945–47). Personally, I can credit the movement with only two incontestable masterpieces, "Israel" and "Boplicity," both by the Miles Davis band. That may seem very little, but it is enough to encourage the greatest hopes for a conception that has given such proof of vitality.

In any case, it is both necessary and exciting to study the cool tendency, inasmuch as it is the most up-to-date expression of jazz. Apart from Lester Young, who was more a precursor than an animator, this movement has not been dominated by one man as bop was dominated by Parker or preclassical jazz by Armstrong, although it has been more homogeneous than might appear. Nevertheless, Miles Davis seems to be a kind of leader. After collaborating for some time with Charlie Parker, this young colored trumpeter, the most gifted of his generation, took the initiative and produced straight off the most representative of the new school's works. More than any other, his art attests the accomplishments and the promise of today's jazz. It seems reasonable, therefore, to recognize his role as more or less predominant throughout this chapter.

We haven't yet defined the cool style. In a very general way, it represents a striving toward a certain conception of musical purity. This effort, which implies a rejection of the hot way of playing and its most typical procedures, finds its justification in the new element it contributed, a kind of modesty in musical expression that was not to be found in jazz before. Even when the performer seems to be letting himself go most completely (and cool musicians, as we shall see, cultivate relaxation), a sort of reserve, by which we do not mean constraint, marks his creative flight, channeling it within certain limits that constitute its charm. It may be said that the cool musicians have brought a new feeling to jazz. With them, jazz becomes an intimate art, rather like what chamber music is by comparison with symphonies. Analytically speaking, their conception shows three principal characteristics: first, a sonority very different from the one adopted by earlier schools; second, a special type of phrase; and finally, an orchestral conception that, without being essential to the style, is not its least interesting element. We are going to consider each of these aspects in turn.

The Cool Sonority

At the very core of classical jazz, a reaction was forming just when a disciplined but violently colored sonority was being established by the masters of all kinds of instruments, from Eldridge to Wells and from Hawkins to Hodges, as the ideal way to express jazz. Benny Carter, Teddy Wilson, and Benny Goodman were among the first exponents of a new conception that was more sober, more stripped. Carter tended to underplay attacks, Wilson's touch was unusually delicate, and Goodman replaced his predecessors' thick vibrato with a more discreet timbre. Sharp attacks, rough timbre, hard touch, and vibrato had for a long time been regarded as essential characteristics of the Negro's sonority, whereas they were actually just characteristics of the hot idiom. Lester Young deserves the credit for showing that it is possible to avoid almost all these features and still produce authentic jazz. Young's veiled sonority and his almost imperceptible vibrato, which tends to disappear completely in quick tempos, brought into being an unprecedented musical climate, the first fruit of the revolution begun by men like Carter, Goodman, and Wilson. But the indefinable charm that is all Lester Young's own comes chiefly from his astonishing muscular relaxation. Good jazzmen have always had to be supple, but Lester has gone beyond being merely supple to achieve a kind of relaxation that has become something of a cult among his disciples.

In trying to achieve a maximum of relaxation, the cool musicians at first were merely taking advantage of Lester Young's example. However, it seems that the young saxophonists went further than their model. In place of Lester's cloudy sonority, they substituted a still more wispy sound. They realized that they could do almost completely without vibrato and sharp attacks and still manage to create as beautiful a quality of sound, in spite of the apparent indifference shown by it, as that produced by the most violently expressive vibrato. Miles Davis did something similar on the trumpet. Doesn't he seem to reject haughtily all exterior ornaments in order to concentrate on giving his tone a serene, undeniably noble resonance? He achieves this by maintaining a constant breath pressure and by "placing" the sound well (just as a singer may be said to "place" his voice forward).[2] He rarely plays forte, even in the upper register. Moreover, he rarely plays in this register. The logic behind his "introspective" style makes him avoid everything that his predecessors indulged in with abandon. Such effects are, in fact, one of the main things cool musicians have given up.

Modern jazz's opponents won't fail to point out that what we have here is a return to the European conception of "purity of sound," and will cite as an argument in their favor the presence of a large proportion of white players among the cool musicians. Their error is understandable. Miles Davis's playing does have fleeting resemblances to the way trumpets are used in symphonies—imperceptible vibrato, the manner in which notes are strung together, and so forth. But a fair examination of what there is to say on the other side is enough to establish, in our opinion, how little weight these comparisons have when brought into opposition with the outstanding feature of the modern jazzman—his relaxed manner, which very few symphonic soloists have. Thanks to this characteristic, one conception differs very markedly from the other in tone production, in legato, and in the way passages are played in the upper register. By the same token, Lee Konitz has obtained from the alto saxophone a diaphanous sound that no soloist in the European tradition has. It is not unthinkable that some use might be made of this sonority in a symphony orchestra. Pierre Boulez, for whom I played some of Konitz's recordings, would like to see European saxophonists get around to adopting it; and I subscribe to this opinion all the more willingly because the conception imposed by Marcel Mule and his disciples has led me personally to avoid using the saxophone except in my jazz pieces. To date, though, the cool sonority exists only in jazz, so there is every reason to conclude that it really is a jazz sonority.

The Phrase: Melody and Rhythm

Whereas the evolution of the cool sonority is of considerable interest, it is in certain respects somewhat disappointing to study the cool phrase. Ignoring what bebop had achieved, the cool musicians generally adopted outmoded melodic and rhythmic conceptions. With a few exceptions, they preferred Lester Young's example to Charlie Parker's; and, though Young was a prodigious innovator for the classical period, Bird obviously went much further. This choice has resulted in a kind of backtracking that may be only temporary but is nonetheless one of the most disquieting signs in the history of jazz.

In the field of melody, the cool soloists seem to stick more closely to the theme, which is often taken from the most commonplace part of the repertory. They are not always concerned, as the better bop musicians were, about creating a common stockpile by means of boldly paraphrasing the old standards. Is it because they like to or is it for extramusical reasons that Stan Getz records "Pennies from Heaven" or that Herbie Steward sticks scrupulously close to the melody in "My Last Affair"? It wouldn't be so bad if, following the example of Lester Young in "These Foolish Things," they had sense enough to abandon these weak themes after stating them; but, far from showing any conviction that their raw material needs to be renewed, they sometimes delight in this melodic indigence and become guilty of the most regrettable error their seniors ever committed.[3] Similarly, their variations are less rich and bold than those of their immediate predecessors. They have a definite melodic charm, but all too rarely do they have that spark which brightens the choruses of Parker or even those of Gillespie on his better days. Without question, the best improvisers in the cool movement are those who have been influenced by the bebop spirit of research. Miles Davis, who strikes me as being by far the most interesting cool soloist, played with Charlie Parker for a long time. Still, Lee Konitz on the alto sax and Gerry Mulligan on the baritone show undeniable originality. That Davis had these two sensitive musicians as the principal soloists with him in the band he organized in 1948–49 accounts in part for the exceptionally successful recordings he made then.

The cool idea of rhythm differs from the bop idea as much by the way in which phrases are shaped as by the role of the accompaniment. Bop's polyrhythmic aspect is scarcely to be heard in the cool musicians' work, and they seem also to have cut out of their vocabulary the Afro-Cuban elements that Dizzy Gillespie introduced into the language of jazz (but they are hardly to be blamed for doing this). Their idiom is purer, perhaps, but also poorer. No cool soloist seems to have made good use of the prodigious enrichment that Charlie Parker brought to jazz rhythm. Miles Davis is the only one this criticism doesn't apply to. His phrasing, which was formerly based on accenting the weak part of the beat ("A Night in Tunisia," "Billie's Bounce," with Parker), has infinitely greater relief than most cool musicians'. Is his work with Bird responsible, in this area also, for his being the most advanced creator of his group? It may very well be.

In the intelligent and allusive style of many of his solos, the young trumpeter shows a concern for alternation and contrast that augurs well for what he may create in the future. It would be well if more of the musicians we consider, rightly or wrongly, as represented by him were to follow his lead. Davis's phrasing has a variety that must be called rare. It is made up of two complementary kinds of phrase. The first is characterized by mobility and abundance. In moderate tempos Davis uses short notes—eighths and even sixteenths. Not infrequently there occurs in such phrases a note that might be called a *resting note*. Coming at the end of a period, it serves as a sort of calm zone between two agitated phrases. Curiously—even paradoxically—the less vibrato the resting note has, the more it stands out. The second kind of phrase, which contrasts with the first, is based on a rhythmic and melodic discontinuity of the kind we observed in Parker's work. Like Bird, Miles Davis likes to put together a lot of little melodic fragments separated by rests. The beginning of his chorus in "Move" (ex. 1) constitutes a remarkable example of this conception, which is reflected in most of his quick-tempo solos in the

1949 period. A reasonably attentive study of this brief fragment shows how well Davis knows, consciously or unconsciously, how to vary rhythmic figures within a single phrase. The three-note motif that fills the first four bars of this chorus, repeated in a symmetrical, scalewise descent, has a central accented note. This note, which is longer than the ones around it, appears three times, like the motif itself, and each time it has a different time value—first it is a quarter note, then a half, finally a dotted quarter. Similarly, first it falls on the second beat, then on the third, and finally on the second half of the third. This asymmetry produces great rhythmic freedom. In that respect, Miles Davis seems more like a bopper than a cool musician.

EXAMPLE 1

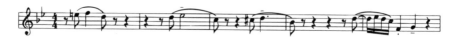

In both kinds of phrase, the soloist occasionally introduces one or more detached, stressed notes that stick out in their context as an antithesis. They would undoubtedly hurt the music's swing if they weren't played with perfect rhythmic precision. Don't they come directly from Lester Young's vocabulary? In his more recent works, Davis tends to make a more general use of detached notes ("S'il vous plaît").

At the same time, Davis's essential contribution consists in a variant of the second kind of phrase. This variant is based on a new conception of the long note, the *dancing note,* of which there are abundant examples in the chorus of "Godchild," between the ninth and twenty-fourth bars. Usually begun on the weak part of a beat, the dancing note—almost always the next to the last one of a motif—finds its resolution in a single note played on either a strong or a weak beat. But what gives it all its value is not so much its syncopated character as the vibrato that enlivens it—a discreet vibrato, though a very perceptible one, which pulsates in a strictly measured way (four oscillations per beat) that has the effect of making the rhythm of the phrase rebound. Besides, this treatment is reinforced by a variation of intensity that puts the note "off center." This rhythmic manipulation of a note taken in its structural unity seems to me a completely new swing phenomenon. Thus Miles Davis, who so willingly does without vibrato, takes it up again and gives it a rhythmic—and accordingly very important—function just when its chances for survival in jazz were becoming doubtful.[4] In the diversity of rhythmic values that make it up and by virtue of the resting and dancing notes it has contributed, Miles Davis's phrase goes further, in some cases, even than Parker's. The only regrettable thing is that these tendencies should be, as they seem to be at present, strictly personal.

The perfectly relaxed playing of cool musicians would call for an equally supple phrasing, a construction of phrases following some precise but rigid idea of rhythm. The truth is that most of the new school's adherents lack rhythmic imagination. Lester Young's phrase represented definite progress, fifteen years ago, because it tended to get away from the bar line. In this direction his disciples do not seem to have bettered their master's accomplishments. Their phrase always fits into the contour of strong and weak beats. It is true that they got away from a minor tyranny— that of the dotted eighth plus sixteenth, which gives Armstrong's and Hawkins's phrase its characteristic aspect. But they weren't responsible for this liberation, which dates from before the war and was already demonstrated by Lester Young in the first Basie records. Such highly gifted soloists as Stan Getz, Al Cohn, and Zoot Sims have not renewed either the rhythmic or the melodic language of jazz. Herbie Steward is the one who seems to have understood Parker's lesson best; his phrase shows a use of rests and suggested notes that gives it a more intense life. Gerry Mulligan, an artist of exquisite sensitivity, has to his credit above all the emotional impact of his solos, which are sometimes particularly successful melodically. As for Lee Konitz, who also has brilliant gifts, he is more an explorer than an inspired artist; although he occasionally tries to use a technique of accentuation rather like Bird's, he falls back at the first opportunity into a regular pattern in which the strong beats are like immovable posts. There is a hundred times more rhythmic richness in Parker's solo based on "What Is This Thing Called Love (Hot House)" than in the version that Tristano's partner has given of the same theme ("Subconscious-Lee").

Just what has the cool style brought to rhythmic infrastructure?[5] Here again there seems to be a kind of backtracking. An ardent defender of the cool musicians, Henri Renaud, after noting that "the same accompanists are found in both styles" (bop and cool), recognizes that "drummers have a general tendency [in the cool style] toward a greater rhythmic continuity," because, he adds, "the cool soloists' phrases, which are more legato than Parker's, call for a more sustained support."[6] This implied disavowal of Kenny Clarke's contributions, supplementing a general disavowal of Parker's rhythmic ideas, would in most cases bring us back to Count Basie's rhythm if the modern accompanists didn't strive for a kind of complete relaxation that makes actual performance cast a different light on the basic meaning behind what they do. Whereas the classical rhythm section joined punch to flexibility, played somewhat nervously, and made the hearer feel, just when everything was swinging along most smoothly, that the tempo was being accelerated, the cool rhythm section performs similar figures in a completely different spirit. The tempo may be equally strict in both cases, but the drummer's perfectly relaxed manner of playing in today's jazz is enough to modify the whole rhythmic perspective; in this case, the listener will have a vague feeling that the band is slowing down, though not swinging any the less for that. This new manner, which was already perceptible in certain bop works of 1947, is one of modern jazz's principal contributions.

The Miles Davis Band

Is the cool style appropriate for bands of the size reached by those at the end of the classical period? Probably not. The ten brasses and five saxes in Hampton's 1946 band had one object—to create maximum shock power. The sound aimed at by the band that Miles Davis organized in 1948, on the contrary, was a kind of unified half-tint. It was essentially a "chamber orchestra" by virtue of both its composition and the style imposed on it. Its melodic section consisted of six instruments: trumpet, trombone, French horn, tuba, and alto and baritone saxes. It was a rejection of the hot idiom that permitted use of the French horn, which had for a long time been excluded from jazz bands. Similarly, Davis reintroduced the tuba, which had been highly rated by the old-timers but eliminated during the preclassical period. It wasn't brought back, be it noticed, simply to turn out rudimentary basses, but rather to be included among the melodic instruments. This plebeian was becoming an aristocrat. To the usual distribution of ranges, with two middle voices balanced by two high and two low ones, was added a distribution of timbres, with each instrument supplying a special color that still blended harmoniously into the whole. The rhythm section was limited to three basic elements—piano, bass, and drums. Davis didn't keep either the guitar, which would be difficult to manipulate in the harmonic and rhythmic climate he had in mind, or the bongo drums, which provided an element of exterior coloration that would be out of place in this intimate music. Accordingly, the band had no more than nine men, just one more than King Oliver's.

What remained to be done was to give the group a basic homogeneity. Did Miles Davis manage to do this by a careful choice of collaborators—arrangers and instrumentalists—or did the initiative come from Gerry Mulligan and Gil Evans, as Barry Ulanov leads us to understand?[7] Was it these two musicians who foresaw Davis as the leader of a band that was really their idea and for which they had composed scores even before it was actually organized? In any case, the problem for these arranger-composers was to write music that the performers could play in the same spirit as they would have improvised solos. Evans and Mulligan were joined by John Carisi and John Lewis. All of them had participated, as improvisers, in the cool movement, so there was every reason to hope that the music they conceived would be profoundly impregnated with that spirit. The instrumentalists themselves were chosen among the young school's most remarkable improvisers. It was vitally important that they should express themselves naturally in a common language. The presence of an outside element, even a valuable one, would have weakened the band by destroying its unity. As it happened, only Bill Barber, on tuba, was not one of the movement's leaders, and he showed great flexibility, fitting into his new surroundings very well.

Although the Miles Davis band played in public on several occasions, it owes its fame to records. Nevertheless, it recorded very few sides. Its reputation was made by eight pieces recorded during two sessions in New York in 1949.[8] In the first, the band included seven white musicians (Kai Winding, Junior Collins, Lee Konitz, Gerry Mulligan, Al Haig, Joe Shulman, and Bill Barber) and two colored ones (Miles Davis and Max Roach). In the second, this proportion was almost reversed, since Winding, Collins, Haig, and Shulman were replaced, respectively, by J. J. Johnson, Sanford Siegelstein, John Lewis, and Nelson Boyd. Furthermore, Max Roach was replaced by Kenny Clarke, so only Davis, Konitz, Barber, and Mulligan remained. It is hard to compare the work of the two groups. One thing is certain: the second plays in a more relaxed way than the first. The two most successful sides, "Israel" and "Boplicity," both come from the second session. It should be noted, however, that the first group, which perhaps had less practice, had to handle arrangements that were trickier to perform.

Since some of the pieces ("Budo," "Move," "Venus de Milo") are interesting almost exclusively for the playing of the soloists and the rhythm section, we shall consider only four sides in this brief study of the cool orchestral language. Two of them, "Jeru" and "Godchild," arranged by Gerry Mulligan, were recorded during the first session; "Boplicity," arranged by Gil Evans, and "Israel," John Carisi's work, come from the second.

What do these two records bring us? They seem to offer not merely the promise but the first fruits of a renewal that has a twofold significance, first for what the music represents in itself and second for the conclusions it permits us to draw about certain conceptions demonstrated in it. To begin with, let us limit ourselves to a consideration of melody, harmony, and orchestration. The convergence of a fairly special orchestral combination and the cool style of playing created an absolutely new sonority, which is what was meant by calling it a *fresh sound*. The term is a good one. It gives a fairly accurate definition of this music's special climate and obviates certain misunderstandings on the part of listeners [for] whom its small quota of the hot element might have led [them] to speak in [comparative] terms of "straight" jazz or even of "sweet" music. There is no justification for making such comparisons. Both "straight" jazz and "sweet" music, which are commercial products, make use of a sonority and a melodic and harmonic language that are exaggeratedly sugarcoated. The work of the Miles Davis band, on the contrary, boasts excellent melody and expresses it, as we have observed, by means of a sonority that is to be admired precisely because it forgoes all ornament; and if the firmness of its harmonic language is sometimes veiled by an apparent indistinctness of timbres, analysis shows it to be there nonetheless. Davis uses some of the same clusters as Gillespie, although the latter made them seem more aggressive because of their violently expressionistic context. Elevenths, thirteenths, and polytonal chords alternate with more consonant combinations; the successions are generally more supple, less mechanical than in Gillespie's work. Frequently—and this is one respect in which the new works fit into the jazz tradition—the harmony develops in the form of chord clusters garnished with acid dissonances. Judging by ear (naturally, I haven't had a chance to look at the scores), I'd say that the rather special character of these dissonances comes less from the actual notes than from the orchestration. Since the most dissonant note is more often than not assigned to the French horn, which has a less penetrating timbre than the other instruments, the result is an equilibrium in the superposition of timbres and intervals that is not the smallest charm of "Godchild" and "Boplicity." This sort of interpenetration of instrumentation and harmony would repay closer study, with the scores in hand.

Generally speaking, the arrangements played by the Miles Davis band treat each section as a unit. Nevertheless, as we have just observed, the diversity of timbres among the winds adds a great deal of freshness. Moreover, the arrangers have shown a certain amount of flexibility, occasionally dividing this section. The voices are not yet really independent, but they are clearly moving in that direction. The writing of the middle voices in "Godchild" and the attempted polyphony of "Israel" are evidences of an effort to achieve some still vague goal, which I would define as a worked-out counterpoint in which each voice is conceived as if it were improvised. Such music would require its creators to study a lot and to make a great effort of adaptation; but what possibilities a kind of jazz based on this principle would have! Miles Davis's beautiful passage in the second part of the central bridge in "Boplicity," which imitates so delicately the ascending melodic figure stated a few bars earlier by the clear voices of the band, gives a cautious glimpse of what an orchestral language based on this conception might be.

Other details of orchestration and melody are worth noting. Octave doubling, a holdover from bop's unisons, is fairly frequent, notably in the central bridge of "Boplicity" and in the exposition of "Israel" and "Godchild." On this last side, the exposition, which is assigned to the tuba and baritone sax, begins in a very low register; the color of the sound becomes brighter as the melody rises; then, in a second phase, the theme is taken up by the whole wind section. The gradation is skillful, and George Wallington's nimble theme lends itself nicely to such treatment. In terms of melodic analysis, the piece contains in the fifth bar a figure in triplets that is typical of the classical period; on the other hand, the central bridge of "Boplicity" begins with a phrase obviously inspired by bop. Except for these two relatively minor reminiscences, the melodic language expressed by the themes and the arrangements would seem to account in large part for the originality of these works. On this score the most remarkable side is probably "Israel," which offers a rather astonishing renewal of the blues.

"Israel" is an example of blues in a minor key, like Ellington's "Ko-Ko." Combining the minor scale and the scale used in the blues results in a scale like the mode of D. With true musical intelligence, John Carisi has played around with this ambiguity, extending the modal color of his composition by making fleeting references to other modes and by using defective scales. The most significant passage in this respect is the end of the trumpet solo (fourth chorus), in which a countermelody in parallel fifths accompanies Davis's improvisation. Since the soloist, too, has caught the modal atmosphere of the piece perfectly, the combination of his melody and the underlying harmony is an exceptionally happy one. It should be added that the blue notes, which figure naturally in each of the modes employed, help to make the piece sound like the blues but do not have the kind of expressive singularity that makes them stand out from the other degrees in the regular blues scale. Finally, "Israel" suggests two other observations, one concerning the melody, which moves chiefly by scale steps at some times and largely by leaps at others, and the other concerning the orchestral language, which curiously heightens the effect of the lower voices by making them very mobile (particularly in the second and seventh choruses, which are the most polyphonic of all).

Is Modern Jazz Opposed to the Four-Bar Unit?

Broadening our horizon, let us now consider the second part of what has to be said about the Miles Davis band. The problems posed here touch upon the very essence of jazz. A double challenge seems to be hurled at the jazz tradition by these works, a challenge that has scarcely been formulated so far but that will undoubtedly become acute sooner or later and that throws into question the two aspects of jazz that have up to now been regarded as unshakable—its four-bar unit of construction and its $4/4$ time. Actually, the challenge to the four-bar unit is not the first of its kind. Duke Ellington, in "Concerto for Cootie," had made a bold break with this tradition. We know that Ellington, however, even when he conceived a seven-bar phrase,[9] didn't completely follow through with it and used a kind of transitional figure to reestablish a certain equilibrium, winding up with an even number of bars. Gerry Mulligan, as we shall see, goes much further.

In "Boplicity," Gil Evans begins an attack on the tradition by making the last phrase of his theme run into the following chorus; however, here as in "Concerto for Cootie," there is a compensation. Mulligan doesn't begin his solo before the end of the first bar, so that there are still thirty-two bars in the exposition and sixteen in the baritone sax chorus. Nonetheless, the melody's final rebound, which has an exquisite musical effect, seems to show its resistance to being tied down to a rigid framework. This resistance shows up again during the second chorus, where the first part of the bridge extends over six bars (instead of four), giving the two voices, which play in octaves at first, time enough to split up in an attractive counterpoint before coming back together. The last part of the phrase, in which the trumpet evokes the figure just played, covers only four bars. It introduces a particularly successful paraphrase of the theme, which remains in suspense and blends very smoothly into the following chorus, in which each eight-bar period is treated in a different way, like a series of variations. We should call attention here, even at the price of being taken away from our subject, to the astonishing musical quality of the first eight bars of this final chorus, in which the dialogue between the soloist (Miles Davis) and the band is worthy of Ellington at his best. Mention should also be made of the gradual leveling off of sound that begins with the paraphrase at the end of the second chorus. First there is the whole band, then Davis accompanied by the winds, then the rhythm section alone, then just the piano; and finally the initial theme is taken up again by the band in a decrescendo that one might wish more pronounced. "Boplicity" is enough to make Gil Evans qualify as one of jazz's greatest arranger-composers.

The admittedly rather weak challenge to traditional structure that an analysis of "Boplicity" reveals is strengthened, in "Godchild" and "Jeru," by a much more sensational challenge to the unity of the bar. If my recollection is accurate, it is the first time in the history of jazz that the permanence of the 4/4 bar becomes doubtful. Will this revolutionary attempt bear fruit? It is much too early to tell. All the analyst can do is record facts. The exposition of "Godchild" drastically "reconsiders" the traditional structure of this classical thirty-two-bar theme with bridge. The addition of first two beats and then four to the initial phrase makes the first period cover seventeen and a half bars instead of sixteen. The bridge, on the other hand, is half a bar shorter than customary. Only the final phrase keeps its original structure in the exposition. "Jeru" is still more revolutionary. It includes four choruses in all. The exposition begins in the traditional way with a double eight-bar phrase. That the bridge has twelve bars would not be surprising in itself if five of them—from the fourth to the eighth—were not in 3/4 time.[10] The reprise covers nine bars. Here, then, is an exposition with an uneven number of bars and of beats. The same is true of the final reexposition. Only the second chorus, which is set aside for Davis's improvisation, is brought back to the customary proportions. The third has thirty-two bars also, but two of them, the fourth and the twelfth, are in 2/4.

It is apparent that the traditional four-bar unit of construction meets a definite check in this composition. The most interesting innovation is undeniably the 3/4 bars in the first and last choruses. They do not, in reality, seem so much a change of measure as a suspension of meter. The question that inevitably arises is, Does the music continue to swing? A decisive answer is hard to give. Certainly, listening to this passage creates an incontestable annoyance, a feeling of floating around; but neither effect is enough to destroy the impression of swing established by the preceding phrases. There is a kind of momentum that could be modified only by brake pressure, and what the listener feels is that there is not more control but less. Moreover, even if the attempt were a total failure, that would not rule out certain possibilities. Who could be surprised if a jazz musician, accustomed to playing 4/4 rhythms, were to be thrown for a loss by the sudden appearance of 3/4? But Davis and Mulligan's attempt, precisely because it is neither an unqualified failure nor an unqualified success, authorizes us to wonder whether it hasn't actually become possible to express swing using other bars besides 4/4 and 2/4. The experiment had never been given a fair trial. Before the war Benny Carter had recorded—if I remember correctly—a "Waltzin' the Blues" that was entirely in 3/4, but he did so under poor conditions and without the help of a band made up of real jazzmen. As far as I am aware, no one since then had tried to follow up his attempt, so it could not have much effect. We must hope that good jazz musicians will pursue the experiment begun in "Jeru" with enough perseverance to make possible some definite conclusion, favorable or not. But Davis and Mulligan deserve credit for having made it possible to ask the question. "Jeru" and "Godchild" show a determination to get away from the four-bar unit that may soon spread from arrangers to improvisers.

As we said, it is too early to draw up a balance sheet on what the cool musicians have done. All we can do is modestly give our impressions, which are contradictory. Cool jazz presents a mixture of reassuring and disquieting elements. The very artists who repudiate Parker and go back to Young are looking, sometimes timidly but with a certain persistence, for a way to renew jazz. They make music for music's sake, scorning even the most remunerative of spectacular effects. Many of them who are as good as any professional musicians would rather hold another job on the side than have to make commercial concessions. This attitude speaks well for their conscientiousness and their sincerity, both of which are attractive qualities, but valuable works are not necessarily the result of either one or the other. To date, the cool musicians have brought us more promises than results. But isn't the existence of these promises the essential thing, however uncertain the path in which they seem to involve jazz may be? Quite apart from their value as pure jazz, sides like "Boplicity" and "Godchild" direct jazz toward a language that seems to hold great potential riches; "Israel" shows a fertile determination to investigate polyphonic writing; "Jeru" boldly calls for a reexamination of form, construction, and meter. Men like Evans and Mulligan seem to have understood that the principal objective of the arranger should be to respect the personality of each performer while giving the group a feeling of unity. There may well result from all this, sooner or later, a completely renewed jazz that, without renouncing its tradition, would find its justification in a new classicism, which bop no longer seems capable of bringing about. True, it is also possible to believe that music so essentially intimate and excessively polished may lose some of jazz's essential characteristics and cease to be anything but a devitalized successor. Only time will tell which of these two hypotheses corresponds to what the future actually holds.

Notes

1. The musicians in this last group remain somewhat in the margin of the movement because of an otherwise praiseworthy concern for musical research that sometimes takes them away from jazz. The recorded work of Lee Konitz, nevertheless, ranks him among the best alto sax soloists.

2. It will be profitable to read, in this connection, Jean Ledru's interesting study "Le Problème du saxophone-ténor," *Jazz-Hot*, October and December 1949 and July 1950.

3. It must be acknowledged that, melodically, certain themes of Raney, Wallington, Gryce, etc., come off very well. Nonetheless, the spirit behind them does not seem to be so revivifying as the one that animated theme composers of the bop period.

4. True, many other soloists use a measured vibrato, but its rhythmic function is not so evident anywhere else as in Davis's dancing note.

5. What the author means by *infrastructure* is explained in chapter 12, pp. 197 ff.—D. N.

6. Henri Renaud, "Qu'est-ce que le jazz cool?" *Jazz-Hot*, April 1952.

7. Barry Ulanov, "Gerry," *Metronome*, April 1951.

8. A third session took place the following year. "Rocker," "Darn That Dream," "Deception," and "Moon Dreams" were recorded then but not released until much later.

9. Cf. chapter 6, pp. 82–83.

10. Gerry Mulligan, who wrote the arrangement, will surely excuse me if my description does not correspond exactly to his manuscript. I have no way of being absolutely sure just how to divide the forty-three beats in the bridge.

Bill Kirchner

Miles Davis and the Birth of the Cool: A Question of Influence

Originally presented on April 8, 1995. Published by permission of the American Culture Studies Institute at Washington University.

The next chapter can be viewed as a sort of sequel to the foregoing Hodeir piece. Using citations from Hodeir and other authors, plus my own discographical research, I aim to demonstrate that the influence of the *Birth of the Cool* has been far wider than has generally been acknowledged.

This paper was presented at the "Miles Davis and American Culture" Conference held at Washington University in St. Louis, Missouri. It was supported by a grant from the National Endowment for the Humanities, an independent federal agency.—Ed.

The Miles Davis *Birth of the Cool* nonet is an anomaly. It recorded only a dozen pieces for Capitol and played in public for a total of two weeks in a nightclub, but its recordings and their influence have been compared to the Louis Armstrong Hot Fives and Sevens and to other classics by Duke Ellington, Count Basie, and Charlie Parker.[1] Although its personnel changed frequently, many of the nonet's members and composer-arrangers became jazz musicians of major stature. Most notable were Davis, trombonists J. J. Johnson and Kai Winding, alto saxophonist Lee Konitz, baritone saxophonist and arranger Gerry Mulligan, pianist and arranger John Lewis, pianist Al Haig, drummers Max Roach, Kenny Clarke, and Art Blakey, and arrangers Gil Evans and John Carisi.

These accomplishments notwithstanding, the *Birth of the Cool* band has been controversial. Consider these remarks by two prominent critics:

> Heard now, the nonet recordings seem little more than primers for television writing. What the recordings show us, though, is that Davis, like many other jazzmen, was not above the academic temptation of Western music. Davis turns out to have been overly impressed by the lessons he received at Juilliard, when he arrived in New York in 1944. The pursuit of a soft sound, the uses of polyphony that were far from idiomatic, the nearly coy understatement, the lines that had little internal propulsion: all amount to another failed attempt to marry jazz to European devices.[2]

> ... the descendants of Miles Davis' *Birth of the Cool* sides include the Tijuana Brass and the background music of any number of well-crafted TV commercials. I'm not sure whether it's fair to hold Davis, Gil Evans, et al. accountable for the fact that their musical ideas are being used to sell chewing gum and life insurance, but the transition to *kitsch* has been easy enough to raise doubts about the value of the originals. Either form *can* be separated from content, or, more likely, "Jeru," "Boplicity," and "Moon Dreams" never had that much content in the first place.[3]

The second comment is more readily addressed. In this century, with its massive developments in media, the separation of form and content has been honed to at least a low art. Musical underscoring of films and television is a notable example. More than a half century ago, Oscar Levant wryly commented on the already widespread generification of European concert works in film scoring. Levant mentioned such pieces as Stravinsky's *Petrushka*, Richard Strauss's *Till Eulenspiegel's Merry Pranks*, Dukas's *The Sorcerer's Apprentice*, and other works by Delius, Handel, Ravel, Debussy, and Rimsky-Korsakov as frequent objects of dissection and recycling.[4] If the *Birth of the Cool* music and other jazz works, such as Duke Ellington's "It Don't Mean a Thing (If It Ain't Got That Swing)," have endured a similar fate, we have the dubious consolation that they are in good company. We should not, however, be blinded to the intrinsic value of the originals.

In responding to the first comment, I need to invoke first a short historical survey. As Max Harrison has pointed out, "There has always been cool jazz."[5] Some performers of a more subdued—though not necessarily less intense—music include Leon Roppolo, Bix Beiderbecke and Frankie Trumbauer, and Red Nichols and Miff Mole in the twenties, as well as Benny Carter, Teddy Wilson, Red Norvo, and Lester Young in the thirties. This "cool" tendency was also reflected in certain ensembles, including the various recording units led by Nichols and Mole and, later, the John Kirby sextet and the Red Norvo and Claude Thornhill orchestras. Of particular interest here is the Thornhill band, with its unique sonority based on clarinets, French horns, tuba, and a generally subdued approach. The Thornhill band's most venturesome arranger was Gil Evans, whose postwar scores included treatments of such bebop anthems as "Anthropology," "Yardbird Suite," and "Donna Lee." In the course of arranging "Donna Lee," Evans met the theme's composer, Miles Davis.

During the late forties Gil Evans lived in a one-room apartment on West 55th Street in Manhattan, and this informal setting served as the gathering point for many of the most important jazz musicians of the day, including Charlie Parker, Davis, Gerry Mulligan, John Lewis, Max Roach, John Carisi, and George Russell. In the winter of 1947–48, Evans and Mulligan began discussions about forming a different kind of rehearsal band. The instrumentation they arrived at—trumpet, alto saxophone, French horn, trombone, baritone saxophone, tuba, piano, bass, and drums—was a reduction of the Thornhill one. As Evans put it: "This was the smallest number of instruments that could get the sound and still express all the harmonies the Thornhill band used. Miles wanted to play his idiom with that kind of sound."[6] Davis himself added, "I always wanted to play with a light sound, because I could think better when I played that way."[7]

The emphasis that both Evans and Davis placed on "sound" is no accident. As André Hodeir explained:

> The convergence of a fairly special orchestral combination and the cool style of playing created an absolutely new sonority, which is what was meant by calling it a *fresh sound*. The term is a good one. It gives a fairly accurate definition of this music's special climate and obviates certain misunderstandings on the part of listeners [for] whom its small quota of the hot element might have led [them] to speak in [comparative] terms of "straight" jazz or even of "sweet" music. There is no justification for making such comparisons. . . .
> The work of the Miles Davis band, on the contrary, boasts excellent melody

and expresses it . . . by means of a sonority that is to be admired precisely because it forgoes all ornament; and if the firmness of its harmonic language is sometimes veiled by an apparent indistinctness of timbres, analysis shows it to be there nonetheless. Davis uses some of the same clusters as Gillespie, although the latter made them seem more aggressive because of their violently expressionistic context.[8]

Both Evans and Mulligan give Davis credit for being the driving force behind the nonet. In Mulligan's words, Davis "took the initiative and put the theories to work. He called the rehearsals, hired the halls, called the players, and generally cracked the whip."[9] Davis also led the band in its only public appearance, two weeks at New York's Royal Roost in September 1948,[10] as well as obtained its Capitol recording contract. Above all, Davis was the group's principal soloist and its lead ensemble voice; these dual demands were prodigious and would have overwhelmed a lesser player.

Davis, though, did none of the arrangements. Seven were written by Mulligan ("Jeru," "Godchild," "Budo," "Venus de Milo," "Deception," "Rocker," and "Darn That Dream"), two by Evans ("Boplicity" and "Moon Dreams"), two by Lewis ("Move" and "Rouge"), and one by Carisi ("Israel"). In addition, Lewis wrote two arrangements ("Why Do I Love You?" and "S'il vous plaît") that are heard only on recordings of broadcasts from the Royal Roost.[11]

These writers could hardly be described as "academics." Evans and Mulligan were autodidacts who had gained most of their experience writing for big bands. To a lesser extent this also applied to Lewis and Carisi, although Lewis had attended the University of New Mexico and the Manhattan School of Music, and Carisi was studying with composer Stefan Wolpe. All four were experienced big-band professionals who sought to apply the lessons of orchestral jazz, along with the melodic, harmonic, and rhythmic advances of bebop, to this strikingly different format.

Except for passages in "Israel" and "Moon Dreams," little in the music could be described as polyphonic. What one *does* hear frequently is an independence in the inner voices that was uncommon in previous orchestral jazz (though, as Mulligan points out, it was a technique he heard used by Ellington and Billy Strayhorn).[12] Again, André Hodeir goes to the heart of the matter: "The voices are not yet really independent, but they are clearly moving in that direction. The writing of the middle voices in 'Godchild' and the attempted polyphony of 'Israel' are evidences of an effort to achieve . . . a worked-out counterpoint in which each voice is conceived as if it were improvised."[13]

As for Crouch's notion that these lines "had little internal propulsion," a Max Harrison remark about the 1957 *Miles Ahead* album applies equally to the *Birth of the Cool* music: "Complaints that these Davis/Evans collaborations produced unrhythmic music were due to faulty hearing. . . . Despite its richness, the orchestral fabric is constantly on the move, horizontally and vertically. . . ."[14]

The *Birth of the Cool* sides were recorded in three sessions on January 21 and April 22, 1949, and March 9, 1950. Issued initially as single 78s and eventually in various LP collections, these recordings had an enormous impact on musicians and the jazz public. Principally, they have been credited—or blamed, depending on one's point of view—for the subsequent popularity of "cool" or "West Coast" jazz. Indeed, composer-arrangers such as Mulligan, Shorty Rogers, Marty Paich, Lennie Niehaus, John Graas, and Duane Tatro were inspired by the *Birth of the Cool* instrumentation and approach. A good deal of their music, though, was more aggressive and rhythmic than some critics would lead us to believe—the frequent presence of such impeccably swinging drummers as Shelly Manne and Mel Lewis alone insured that.

But the *Birth of the Cool* influence extended far beyond West Coast jazz and frequently appeared in all sorts of unexpected places. In the fifties East Coast composer-arrangers such as Gigi Gryce, Quincy Jones, Benny Golson, and Teo Macero produced recordings using this approach, as did traditionalist Dick Cary, who used the style in orchestrating a set of Dixieland warhorses. Thelonious Monk, with arranger Hall Overton, used an almost identical *Birth of the Cool* instrumentation for his famed 1959 Town Hall concert. The format was proving to have all sorts of possibilities for creative jazz writing.

Gil Evans spent much of the rest of his career expanding on the innovations of his Thornhill and *Birth of the Cool* scores. The most obvious examples, of course, are his famed orchestral collaborations with Davis, but there are others where the connection is even more direct. In the fifties these included arrangements Evans did for Mulligan, Teddy Charles, Hal McKusick, and Don Elliott, as well as his own *Gil Evans & Ten* album. Of his later work, the most *Birth of the Cool*–oriented writing appeared on *The Individualism of Gil Evans*, with the concept expanded by the use of mixed woodwinds, including flute, bass flute, English horn, bassoon, and tenor saxophone.

The other writers for the Davis nonet, John Lewis and John Carisi, both produced works that expanded, in different ways, on their *Birth of the Cool* pedigree. In 1956 Lewis produced "Three Little Feelings," a tripartite work with featured soloist Miles Davis. Carisi wrote two of his best pieces, "Moon Taj" and "Angkor Wat," for an eleven-piece band recorded under Gil Evans's name in 1961.

In the sixties a number of diverse recordings displayed a *Birth of the Cool* approach. Among the most surprising came from an expanded edition of Art Blakey and the Jazz Messengers, with arrangements by Wayne Shorter, Cedar Walton, and Curtis Fuller. Another was an album of originals by Los Angeles avant-gardist Horace Tapscott for bop saxophonist Sonny Criss, pointedly titled *Sonny's Dream: Birth of the New Cool.* Herbie Hancock did one of his finest recordings *(The Prisoner)* with a nonet, and pianist-arranger Mike Abene scored two unheralded but inventive albums for an eleven-piece New York studio group led by trumpeters Burt Collins and Joe Shepley.

In the seventies and eighties, Lee Konitz, one of the stars of the Davis nonet, led one of his own, which, in addition to playing original music, re-created some of the *Birth of the Cool* pieces. Others, such as New York arrangers David Matthews and Bob Belden, formed ensembles (complete with French horn and tuba) that were larger versions of the Davis nonet concept, but with contemporary innovations.

The movement came full circle in 1992 when Gerry Mulligan re-recorded the twelve Capitol pieces. What began as a bold experiment in 1948 had become firmly established as a flexible, enduring tradition in orchestral jazz, and the originals that launched it all had not lost their luster.

Notes

1. Nat Hentoff, in Jack Chambers, *Milestones: The Music and Times of Miles Davis* (New York: Beech Tree Books, c1983–c1985; reprint, New York: William Morrow, Quill, 1989), 129.

2. Stanley Crouch, "Play the Right Thing," *New Republic,* February 12, 1990, 31.

3. Larry Kart, review of *Collins-Shepley Galaxy: Time, Space and the Blues, Down Beat,* February 5, 1970, 19.

4. Oscar Levant, *A Smattering of Ignorance* (Garden City, N.Y.: Garden City Publishing Co., 1942), 136–40.

5. Max Harrison, *A Jazz Retrospect* (Boston: Crescendo, 1976; London: Quartet Books, 1991), 132.

6. Nat Hentoff, "The Birth of the Cool," *Down Beat,* May 2, 1957, 16.

7. Leonard Feather, "Miles Davis: Miles and the Fifties," *Down Beat,* July 2, 1964, reprinted March 1995, 38.

8. André Hodeir, *Jazz: Its Evolution and Essence,* rev. ed., trans. David Noakes (New York: Grove, 1979), 129–30.

9. Gerry Mulligan, liner notes to *Miles Davis and His Orchestra: The Complete Birth of the Cool,* Capitol M-11026.

10. There has also been mention of a short engagement in 1950 at the Clique club (later reopened as Birdland), but there is no recorded evidence, nor can either Gerry Mulligan or Lee Konitz remember the engagement.

11. Over the years these arrangements have been attributed in various combinations to Mulligan, Lewis, Evans, Carisi, and Davis. The arranging credits listed here were supplied to the author by Mulligan in a February 25, 1995, conversation.

12. Gerry Mulligan, conversation with author, February 25, 1995.

13. Hodeir, *Jazz,* 130–31.

14. Harrison, *A Jazz Retrospect,* 140.

Discography

Belden, Bob. *Treasure Island.* Bob Belden Ensemble. Sunnyside SSC 1041D. 1989.

Blakey, Art. *Art Blakey and the Jazz Messengers Play Selections from the New Musical "Golden Boy."* Colpix CP 478. 1963.

Carisi, John [for Gil Evans]. *Into the Hot.* Impulse A-9. 1961. (Includes: "Moon Taj," "Angkor Wat," and "Barry's Tune")

Cary, Dick, and Johnny Plonsky. *Dixieland Goes Progressive.* Golden Crest CR 3024. 1957.

Collins, Burt, and Joe Shepley. *Collins-Shepley Galaxy: Time, Space and the Blues.* MTA NWS 2. 1969.

———. *Lennon-McCartney Live.* MTA NWS 4. 1970.

Criss, Sonny. *Sonny's Dream: Birth of the New Cool.* Prestige 7576/Original Jazz Classics OJC-707. 1968.

Davis, Miles. *Birth of the Cool.* Capitol CDP 7 92862. 1949–50.

Evans, Gil [for Gerry Mulligan]. *A Profile of Gerry Mulligan.* Mercury MG 20453. 1955–56. (Includes: "La Plus que lente")

——— [for Teddy Charles]. *The Teddy Charles Tentet.* Atlantic 1229. 1956. (Includes: "You Go to My Head")

——— [for Hal McKusick]. *Jazz Workshop.* RCA LPM-1366. 1956. (Includes: "Blues for Pablo" and "Jambangle")

——— [for Don Elliott]. *Jamaica Jazz.* ABC-Paramount ABC(S) 228. 1957.

———. *Gil Evans & Ten.* Prestige 7120/Original Jazz Classics OJC-346. 1957.

———. *The Individualism of Gil Evans.* Verve V-8555/833 804-2. 1963–64.

Golson, Benny. *Benny Golson's New York Scene.* Contemporary C-3552/Original Jazz
    Classics OJC-164. 1957.
———. *Take a Number from 1 to 10.* Argo LP 681. 1960–61.
Graas, John. *Jazzmantics.* Decca DL 8677. 1957.
Gryce, Gigi, Duke Jordan, and Hall Overton. *Signals.* Savoy SJL-2231. 1955.
Hancock, Herbie. *The Prisoner.* Blue Note BST 84321. 1969.
Konitz, Lee. *The Lee Konitz Nonet.* Roulette SR 5006. 1976.
———. *The Lee Konitz Nonet.* Chiaroscuro CR 186. 1977.
———. *Yes, Yes, Nonet.* SteepleChase SCS-1119. 1979.
Lewis, John. *Music for Brass.* The Brass Ensemble of the Jazz and Classical Music
    Society. Columbia CL 941. 1956. Reissued as *The Birth of the Third Stream.*
    Columbia Legacy CK 64929. 1996. (Includes: "Three Little Feelings")
Macero, Teo. *What's New?* Columbia CL 842. 1955. (Includes: "Neally,"
    "Adventure," and "T. C.'s Groove")
Matthews, David. *Live at the Five Spot.* David Matthews Big Band. Muse
    MR 5073. 1975.
Monk, Thelonious. *The Thelonious Monk Orchestra at Town Hall.* Riverside RLP
    1138/Original Jazz Classics OJC-135. 1959.
Mulligan, Gerry. *Walking Shoes.* Capitol M-11029. 1953.
———. *Re-Birth of the Cool.* GRP-GRD-9679. 1992.
Niehaus, Lennie. *Vol. 2: The Octet.* Contemporary C-2517. 1954.
———. *Vol. 3: The Octet #2.* Contemporary C-3503/Original Jazz Classics OJC-
    1767. 1955.
Paich, Marty [for Mel Tormé]. *The Tormé Touch.* Bethlehem BCP 6042. 1956.
———. *Mel Tormé Loves Fred Astaire.* Bethlehem BCP 6022. 1956.
——— [for Art Pepper]. *Art Pepper + Eleven: "Modern Jazz Classics."* Contemporary
    C-7568/Original Jazz Classics OJC-341. 1959.
Rogers, Shorty. *Short Stops.* RCA/Bluebird 5917-1-RB. 1953–54.
———. *Way Up There.* Atlantic SD 1270. 1955. (Includes: "Wail of Two Cities" and
    "Baklava Bridge")
Tatro, Duane. *Jazz for Moderns.* Contemporary C-3514/Original Jazz Classics OJC-
    1878. 1954–55.
Taylor, Billy. *My Fair Lady Loves Jazz.* Billy Taylor Trio with Quincy Jones. Impulse
    A-72. 1957.

Max Harrison

Collector's Items

Originally published in Miles Davis: Collector's Items, *Prestige 24022.* *Copyright © 1973. Reprinted by permission of Fantasy, Inc., and the author.*

The gifted critic J. R. Taylor has described Max Harrison as "an iconoclast with a devastating wit and deep contempt for received opinion, [who] has . . . been among the most thoughtful and knowledgeable of jazz writers." Accomplished in both classical music and jazz criticism, Harrison began writing on jazz in 1955 for *Jazz Monthly* and has since written for the *Jazz Review*, the *Wire*, and other publications. He also authored the main entry on jazz for *The New Grove Dictionary of Music and Musicians* (1980; revised for *The New Grove Gospel, Blues, and Jazz*, 1987). His own books include *A Jazz Retrospect* (1976, 1991) and, with Charles Fox and Eric Thacker, *Essential Jazz Records*, vol. 1, *Ragtime to Swing* (1984).

"Collector's Items," the first of three Harrison pieces included in this volume, was originally a liner essay for a reissue of some Davis sessions recorded for Prestige in the early-to-mid-1950s. The music, musicians, and recording dates referred to in the text are as follows: "The Serpent's Tooth," "'Round Midnight," and "Compulsion" were recorded on January 30, 1953, with both Charlie Parker and Sonny Rollins on tenor saxophones, Walter Bishop Jr. on piano, Percy Heath on bass, and Philly Joe Jones on drums; "Nature Boy," "There's No You," "Easy Living," and "Alone Together" came from a July 8, 1955, session with trombonist Britt Woodman, vibraphonist Teddy Charles, bassist Charles Mingus, and drummer Elvin Jones; and "No Line," "Vierd Blues," and "In Your Own Sweet Way" resulted from a March 16, 1956, date with Rollins, pianist Tommy Flanagan, bassist Paul Chambers, and drummer Art Taylor.

The early 1950s were transitional but vitally important years for Davis, for both personal and musical reasons. He endured and finally triumphed over the scourge of his heroin addiction, and he formulated much of the aesthetic that he spent the rest of his life exploring. Harrison gives us an insightful look at that very personal aesthetic in the midst of its creation.—Ed.

One of the most vital factors in a jazz musician's equipment is tone, and all the genuinely creative improvisers—men such as Louis Armstrong, Lester Young, Charlie Parker, and Ornette Coleman—possess a sound that remains unique despite the widest imitation. It should not be imagined that this is merely some kind of lucky accident, for attempts to distinguish between technique and sensibility, form and content, style and idea are invariably artificial and misleading.

Thus, the hard, uncompromising tone, at once acid and richly sonorous, that Thelonious Monk draws from his instrument is not, as once was popularly supposed, a result of pianistic incompetence, but accords perfectly with the character of his musical thinking, and is also, one ventures to believe, a reflection of the attitudes of the man himself. Technique, even in the widest sense not only of instrumental command but of the ability to invent and organize musical material, is nothing by itself and only has meaning in relation to the vein of expression for which it is the vehicle. Established methods will suffice for the average jazz soloist, but an original has to forge an at least partially new technique and style that in essence will be an extension of his own musical sensibility and vision.

This can be a long process, and the generally poor quality of Miles Davis's earliest work, recorded in the 1940s, is an indication of this. As Gil Evans, with whom he has made so much fine music, once said, Davis "had to start almost with no sound, and then develop one as he went along, a sound suited to the ideas he wanted to express" (*Down Beat*, May 2 and 16, 1957). Receiving much encouragement from Parker, Davis quite naturally first responded by trying to play like him. Yet the trancelike stillness of his most personal early solos, which seem like an attempt to quiet the noise of the material world, to stop the unrelenting beat of time, always diverged sharply from the fury of the great altoist's lashing arabesques. Perhaps Davis could only develop freely after Parker's death in 1955, but the calm of his muted colors and fragmented lyrical extensions was never merely passive. From the fervor of bop, which remained intuitive despite its considerable technical sophistication, he distilled qualities of order, control, of rich sonority and lucid proportions.

The outward casualness of, say, the "In Your Own Sweet Way" theme statement is wholly deceptive for an inner tension asserts itself from the start, and this music, to misquote Charles Ives, is full of a sort of calm fury. In the rough-hewn ensembles of "The Serpent's Tooth" date, also, the mood may be that of the asphalt jungle, yet Davis's playing, especially, relates to a melancholy that is far more old; in fact, its desolate solitariness may remind us of the sorrow enshrined in Spanish flamenco—this being an affinity he exploited later in company with Evans. On performances such as "No Line" and "Easy Living," the trumpet is tightly muted, and this stifles the anger as well as the sonority, leaving it to etch a hard, dry, stoical line. Yet the Harmon mute and the closeness with which Davis holds his instrument to the microphone never deflect this music from its point: on the contrary, rather as Charlie Christian employed the amplification of his electric guitar to harden the edge of his blues-drenched phrases, to implement a new way of swinging, so the trumpeter uses electronics to suggest a violence beneath the surface of these improvisations. It is this, of course, that gives such jazz its power to disturb us, the cultivated purity of sound increasing the ambiguity.

In this connection a track like "Nature Boy," a kind of mood-fantasy spun from the melody, is of especial interest, appearing at once innocent and tense with apprehension.

This item comes from the middle of the three recording sessions represented here, each showing Davis at a different stage of his development, his music growing steadily in emotional insight and in the concentration of its utterance. Yet a piece such as "Nature Boy"—"Easy Living" is a further instance—can appear morose, excessively introverted. Perhaps, though, when he communes with himself in this manner, we should again think of Monk, whose unaccompanied versions of popular ditties usually sound as if they are played to himself, not to us. The extreme openness— not emptiness—of this jazz perhaps relates, also, to several other, seemingly quite different, elements in American music, typified by Aaron Copland; we feel its constituents to be somehow separated in time and space, wrapped in silence: emotion and silence, in fact, are held in balance, and hence, again, some of this music's power.

Certainly what may be termed Davis's melodic honesty pierces the facade of such items as "Easy Living" or "Nature Boy," finally shatters their bland pretences, and proves that the news of "a man walking on eggshells" was merely an inept phrase that could only hope to gain currency in the land of the deaf. His lyrical purity in meditative performances like these reminds us, also, of Milt Jackson, who likewise was first heard from during the unsettled days of bop in the 1940s; this is particularly apparent in the way both musicians place long notes within a phrase.

Even if Davis gradually supplanted the darting aggression of bop with supple and fluid lines, if heated virtuosity gave way to sophisticated introspection, he still remains an archetypal jazz figure, embodying that music's true spirit with its defiance of set patterns and established conventions. His antecedents, and at more than one level, are fairly obvious. The exactly pointed refinement of his phrasing and several aspects of his whole aesthetic stem, of course, from Lester Young, the most radical jazz innovator between Armstrong and Parker. Yet Benny Carter and Teddy Wilson, not to mention Bix Beiderbecke and Frankie Trumbauer before them, had already demonstrated the "cool" possibilities of the idiom, its potential for emphasis through understatement. From such exemplars, surely, derives Davis's ability to imply much, in terms of melody, color, feeling, with little, and in particular his gift for exploiting tensions between melodic simplicity and underlying harmonic complexity. Again, though in comparison with bop Davis's work may seem at first to be an undue reaction toward simplicity, it was paralleled by the way that in the late 1930s the massive directness of Count Basie's orchestra provided a viable alternative to virtuoso swing bands like that of Jimmie Lunceford. In listening to this music, as to any other, a feeling for the present is enriched by a sense of the past, and, along with Davis's adaptation of the asymmetries of bop phrasing, his admiration for Armstrong is apparent, rather as we can hear Coleman Hawkins in Sonny Rollins's playing as well as the influence of Lester Young.

Rollins, indeed, was an especially apt partner for Davis at several stages of his development, as their improvising works through distillation of given melodies, even if in quite different ways. This, like the best music of Monk or of John Lewis, is in exciting contrast to the essentially decorative approach of many earlier jazz players and produced results that are more complex both musically and emotionally. The 1953 version of Monk's "'Round Midnight" may be less harsh, less unsparing, than any by the composer himself, yet there is no doubt that this theme accords particularly well with Davis's haunted and astringent lyricism. His tonal control here is less perfect than it later became, but already we can hear him precisely weighing the expressive value of each note, and it is clear that neither he nor Rollins was in the least overawed by Parker's presence. No explanation has ever been offered as to why the master played tenor instead of his usual alto on this date, but it is striking that both the "Serpent's Tooth" and "Compulsion" themes relate to the suavely convoluted melodies—such as "Sippin' at Bell's"—that Davis composed for a session half a dozen years previous on which Parker also was heard on tenor. During his solos in all four performances done on this later occasion, we note the characteristic very fast alternation of tension and release in his phrases, although the larger instrument clearly did not suit him, and, as the first version of "The Serpent's Tooth" shows, his double-timing is less supple than usual.

It is, of course, instructive to compare the two performances of this piece. The first is in a very swinging medium groove, with the beat articulated with absolute precision yet unfailing flexibility by Philly Joe Jones and Percy Heath; Davis clearly finds his exchanges with the drummer a stimulus. The second attempt is faster, and the trumpeter uses some of the same melodic ideas, though in different ways; the phrases are more aired out with rests, and it is a comment on his long journey toward the mastery of his expressive means that this solo is both more adventurous and less successful, less of a complete entity, than that on take 1. Rollins, also, is not so good as on the earlier performance, and only Parker seems fully to profit from the occasion, turning in a solo that is more compact, wastes less effort, than before. In "Compulsion," too, the fast tempo suits him, despite the tenor, as does the enhancing commentary of Jones's drums.

As on "'Round Midnight," Davis in "Nature Boy" probes the meaning of each note in almost painful evaluation, this being an essential preparation for the extraordinary originality of his mature work. This was a somewhat unusual date for the trumpeter, shaped by Charles Mingus's characteristic attempts, which bore wonderful fruit in his own music later, to make each performance a whole, with further continuity imparted by Teddy Charles's gravely ringing tones. Mostly Britt Woodman is a subdued ensemble voice, but in "Alone Together" he produces a trombone figure that remarkably anticipates "Sonnet for Hank Cinq" from

Duke Ellington's *Such Sweet Thunder* suite of two years later. Here and on "There's No You" Davis traces his line more firmly, and the relaxation of Charles's "Alone Together" vibraharp solo ought not to disguise his fine combination of musical intelligence and feeling. Charles's accompaniments—to Woodman, for example, in "There's No You"—are interesting, also, and this session provides a good illustration of the flexibility of a pianoless ensemble and of the fullness of sound that can be drawn from a small group.

This last-mentioned track is jaunty without falling into blandness, and in "No Line," from the following year, Davis's playing is light, dancing, yet always has substance. Rollins also has grown more personal since we last heard from him, and on "Vierd Blues," a preliminary study for his "Blue Seven" masterpiece of three months later, his solo has something of that spontaneity reconciled with seeming inevitability that often marks the finest—but only the finest—jazz performances. Tommy Flanagan, likewise, takes one of his best recorded solos on this track. "In Your Own Sweet Way," a Dave Brubeck melody, is enclosed within two muted solos by Davis, the second having an aptly valedictory air. Once again we are moved by the acute sorrow that shadows the outward calm and are reminded of a comment by the English critic Michael James that "never before in jazz had the phenomenon of loneliness been examined in so intransigent a manner" (*Jazz Monthly*, February 1958) as by this musician. Davis had more to say, and found ways of saying it, yet by the time he made these recordings, he already had come a long way, and on a path nobody had traveled before.

W. T. Lhamon Jr.

They All Juggled Milk Bottles

Originally published in Deliberate Speed: The Origins of a Cultural Style in the American 1950s *(Washington and London: Smithsonian Institution Press, 1990), 169–78. Reprinted by permission of the Smithsonian Institution Press.*

In his book *Deliberate Speed*, cultural historian W. T. Lhamon Jr., a professor of English at Florida State University, takes a fascinating look at American popular culture in the 1950s, including developments in literature (Jack Kerouac, Thomas Pynchon, Ralph Ellison), painting (Jackson Pollock), poetry (Allen Ginsberg), photography (Robert Frank), jazz, rock 'n' roll, and the nascent Civil Rights movement. During this period, says Lhamon, "all of the elements of contemporary American culture were in the pot, swapping around, and affecting each other."

The chapter "They All Juggled Milk Bottles" (an image borrowed from William Inge's 1955 play *Bus Stop*) spotlights artists who were "pushing through poplore, absorbing it and its strategies into their work." One of them was Miles Davis, whose music receives an unusual examination as part of the zeitgeist of the mid-1950s.

As Scott DeVeaux points out, some of Lhamon's terminology is idiosyncratic. "Poplore," for example, underscores the variable folklike qualities of popular culture. The title of the book, though, comes from Chief

Justice Earl Warren's follow-up ruling to the landmark 1954 *Brown* v. *Board of Education of Topeka, Kansas* case. In May 1955 Warren ordered the desegregation of public schools "with all deliberate speed."

One elucidation: Lhamon mentions a blues composition known in various permutations as "Weirdo," "Walkin'," and "Sid's Ahead" and gives composer credit to Davis. The official composer of "Walkin'" is actually Richard Carpenter. In addition, the pedigree of this piece has been traced back to at least 1950, when it was recorded by tenor saxophonist Gene Ammons as "Gravy."—Ed.

You know what a miracle is . . . another world's intrusion into this one.
    —Jesús Arrabal talking to Oedipa Maas, in Thomas Pynchon's
                                                        The Crying of Lot 49

In the fifties, juggling poplore's artifacts substituted for the absent, embarrassing, or insufficient mentor. Such juggling maneuvered to compensate for and overcome the lonely, empty life that failing fathers bequeathed. Participating in the juggling of poplore linked the sons and daughters in distinct sibling gestures. These incorporations of poplore came at the moment the electronic media were discovering their increased power to tie together even distant isolates and their need for new content to broadcast. These factors complemented each other to create a sense sufficient to set off deliberately speeding culture from the high modernism between the wars.

Epochs establish a new lingua franca the way Latin linked earlier regional, national, and class cultures with a common language and a set of rituals, the way "literariness" provided a common set of signs to set apart elite culture and bind its participants. So too did the milk bottle jugglers aggressively dominating the arts in the fifties set up their own standards, signs, and rites, their own traditions and features that could link participants across cultures. Ellison's invisible man in his introverted hole, believing he was existentially alone even as he rediscovered his folk community, existed on one side of this new possibility. The extroverted Beat brotherhood, convening spur-of-the-moment parties from the left to the right coasts, confidently participated in a countercommunity of their own making. They walked just the other side of the possibility. The Beats were more aware of the networking capacity of radio, more attuned to the media and to continual coast-to-coast travel, able to find sustaining groups in San Francisco, New York, Denver, New Orleans, and Mexico.

Loneliness was one instigating common denominator. Finding a lore group to ease their loneliness was another. Ellison's youth acknowledged the continuation of his ethnic folklore in the city as he became a man. Kerouac turned thirty and reached his artistic maturity during the writing of *Visions of Cody*—recognizing, that is, the armoring use of poplore. Characteristically mocking his own serious attraction to this idea fifteen years later, Thomas Pynchon wrote many underground cults into *The Crying of Lot 49*. One of these cults called itself "a society of isolates"—no meetings, nothing face to face, but signs in common, congeniality, and mutual aid: "You get a phone number, an answering service you can call. Nobody knows anybody else's name; just the number in case *it* gets so bad you can't handle *it* alone." In Pynchon's case, "it," just like pop songs warn, is unrequited love: "That's the worst addiction of all." In the culture of deliberate speed, the media make impersonal connection especially possible. That way, people who loathe meetings can still be members of groups they never see. [. . .]

The point here, as in Kerouac and Ginsberg, as in Jackson Pollock and Miles Davis, as in Rauschenberg and Johns, as in Joseph Heller and Elvis Costello, is always the irrepressibility of the repressed. The theory of its disappearance was a modern dream. The fact of the repressed's persistence has therefore become a major theme for subsequent culture. It is a way for writers, muted trumpet players, and painters to represent their own status.

In *The Crying of Lot 49* the sign for the society of isolates is a muted post horn. For Pynchon the muted horn is a symbol of a culture struggling through opposition to announce itself, to surpass its suppression, just the way Jack in *Visions of Cody* thought "everything's waiting for me to understand it," "it seems to want to tell something intelligible to me." Can anyone say what the muted trumpet meant for Miles Davis, who played it persistently in the mid-fifties, even on up-tempo tunes when to stick with it surely was an impediment? Perhaps it stood for something abstract as it would later for Pynchon. Was it a way for Davis to implicate at once both the constraint and the openness he was yoking in the fifties wake of Charlie Parker?

Davis changed his life as well as his music in the mid-fifties. He began both again. Davis's addiction to heroin had reached infamous status by late 1953, when he was pimping, stealing friends' goods and

money, nodding through solos, and collapsing curbside—a clichéd veg-
etable of dependency. But during the winter of 1953–54 he regained
control of his life by locking himself in a guest house on his father's farm
near East St. Louis and sweating out his addiction. After a reentry recoup-
ment in Detroit, Davis returned to New York able to sustain concentration on the changes to emerge in his music commencing that summer of
1954, and continuing for the next five years.

By the end of the decade, with *Kind of Blue* (1959), Davis in one blow
consolidated avant-garde dissatisfaction with the elements of song form,
which were still vestigial after bebop's assault on them, and he popularized alternative structures. Instead of prescribed chord changes at prescribed bar intervals, *Kind of Blue* used modal structures. Davis was also
interested in free group improvising on this record, as Bill Evans's liner
notes emphasize. Davis had been heading toward this freedom for five
years. In the summer of 1954, recording "Oleo" (by Sonny Rollins), Davis
began to try soloing without piano accompaniment.

Like Gerry Mulligan, who first organized his West Coast quartet without a piano in 1952, Davis wanted a wider panoply of choices than was
available when a keyboard offered harmonies behind him. He would sometimes silence the piano during the next several years working with Horace
Silver, then Thelonious Monk, Red Garland, and on to Herbie Hancock.
That this was a stubborn intention comes clear in Davis's famous argument
with Monk while recording the "Bags' Groove" takes on Christmas Eve,
1954. Davis insisted on going it alone; Monk bristled at depreciation of his
role. This squabble over sound control continued between Davis and all his
pianists, in whom he favored extreme reticence and tact (the virtues he
heard in Ahmad Jamal and Bill Evans). Meanwhile, however, serious dis-
agreement among these players has not surfaced about the provenance of
their music. None of Davis's sidemen registered dissatisfaction with the
leader's important return, like so many advanced fifties artists in every
form, to the sustenance of poplore.

Davis was fully cognizant of working poplore into his art, rather than
stealing from and denying popular culture, as the modern boppers had
done. Let Parker stand in here as the quintessential jazz modernist,
performing art for art's sake—a plausible enough hypothesis when he was
with Savoy and Dial, 1944–48. As much as ever, Parker was then in control
of his music. How did he control it? He cued his reflexive composition off
pop tunes, using their chord changes but annihilating their surface
sound. To his cult audience, the way Bird metamorphosed melodies and

rendered standard structures unrecognizable was a brand of superiority that lifted bop above its smoky context of clubs and sweet tunes. In his original melodies, they say, Parker was responding to internal and autonomous cues in the music, not representing an exterior reality. They say his music was not subservient to an outside world it was trying to represent but pursuing lines of pure musical development.

Actually, there is no such thing as pure art. Parker's abstract flights represented an attitude if not an object. But because many in his crowd appreciated him as a pure artist, and tried to understand him in that way, he stood during his moment in relative contrast to Davis's path. Thinking his music was autonomous, Parker had few titles for his compositions, which were numbers to him and to the Dial studio people: "Klactoveedsedstene" was D-1112, for instance.

Thus, although cognoscenti were aware of the transformations on poplore material, their delusion was of a Yeatsian "out of nowhere" purity. "Usually, I dreamed up some kind of a title," reports Russell, who was then his producer, "when it was time to release the record." Bird's practice was much the same as Jackson Pollock's, who for an interval in 1948 resorted to exhibiting his paintings with numbers for titles, and who was too obsessed with painting and signing his works to name them at any time. That task fell to his wife, Lee Krasner, or to friends, although Pollock himself later said that the color of an eggplant in his garden or his fascination with night sounds or creepy-crawlies in the grass—or the energy in jazz itself—was what he was painting. No more than Parker was a pure musician was Pollock a pure painter. But Pollock's crowd also received him that way at the time—see any of Greenberg's reviews of his exhibits—and relative to, say, Rauschenberg's goat constructs, Johns's ale cans, and Warhol's multiple paintings of his patroness, Pollock seemed purist.

Unlike Parker and Pollock in the late forties—who used but sublimated their relations with lore—the fifties generation artists visibly or audibly affirmed their connection to poplore. If Miles Davis changed titles, for instance, it was mainly those of his own compositions so that he could rerecord them separately, as with "Weirdo," "Walkin'," and "Sid's Ahead." When he played George Gershwin *(Porgy and Bess)*, Cole Porter ("All of You"), Irving Berlin ("How Deep Is the Ocean?"), or Jerome Kern ("Yesterdays"), he always said so, insisting on the connection even when he had changed the songs until they occupied none of their original form and only slipped in allusions to their original melodies.

Davis's music was coming together strongly in 1954, with "Four" and "Walkin'" both recorded in the spring and "Bags' Groove," "Bemsha Swing," and "The Man I Love" that winter. But it was in mid-1955 that he put together the basis of his first steady quartet, appeared at that summer's Newport Festival playing a moving solo on Monk's "'Round Midnight," and incited the critical buzz that has since waxed and waned, but never abated, except for his six years of retirement between 1975 and 1981. A month before Newport, Davis went into the studio for Prestige and cut four tunes with the men who would remain with him for years. To Philly Joe Jones, who had been barnstorming with Davis and anchoring his pickup groups, he added pianist Red Garland, a southwesterner from Dallas (though a few years older than Ornette Coleman) with a tendency to chord sweetly with his left hand, and bassist Oscar Pettiford. These four became a quintet when he added John Coltrane and replaced Pettiford with twenty-year-old Paul Chambers before the next Prestige session.

The first session came out right after Newport, when critics were watching for Davis's new work. Its original title was *The Musings of Miles*, later appropriately renamed *The Beginning*. What's important about these records is that the spare, emotional music reconciled the avant-garde and funk developments that were ongoing and separate through the fifties. Davis's trumpet is lucid, piercing but generally soft. He phrases in mixtures of largely clipped, pure notes resting on a spicing of long notes that he suddenly kinks. Davis's sound is limpid. He runs the gamut on the blues "Green Haze"—from muted to crowing, sometimes breathy. Davis is seeking a voicing that will establish a place for his new fusion in the developing jazz scene, and for black music in the mainstream. He achieved it by choosing sidemen who would amplify the ambiguous aspects of his own personality—divisions in himself that matched those in jazz tradition. By emphasizing these parts and showing them together in the same group, pieces, performances, and albums, Davis used each to call attention to and correct the other. It was an important strategy that tucked in popular romanticism with avant-garde astringency.

Davis started both sides of his next record with tunes Ahmad Jamal had recorded in 1952, "Will You Still Be Mine?" and "A Gal in Calico." Especially with this last song, although perhaps Davis neither knew nor cared, he was participating in one of the earliest strategies of avant-garde art. Remarking the posturing dress, style, and attention of nightclub-goers reaching for fulfillment beyond their capacities is exactly the same strategy that Edouard Manet painted in the bars and cafés of Paris at the onset of high modernism. The strategy was to engage and place the congenial audience whose lore occasioned the art—those who sold the cloth by day and touchingly dressed in it by night.

Here is T. J. Clark on café-concert habitués in late nineteenth-century Paris:

> The most effective code name for these unfortunates—it appears repeatedly from the 1860s on—was the simple metonymy *calicot*. They were what they sold, the metonymy said, for all their wish to be something better; the word came into widespread use around the time that shopworkers were forming a union and going on strike, and its nearest equivalents in English are "draper's assistant" or "counter-jumper"—the latter perhaps to be preferred for its period flavour and less than affectionate snobbery. ("I don't want to see my daughter spinning round a public assembly room in the arms of any counter-jumper," as the dictionary quotes Miss Braddon in 1880.)

Beyond its connection to Hollywood's frontier West, where cowboys and cowgirls dressed in such cheap cotton, *calico* in American English had the same associations explicit in France and implicit in England. Webster's Second gives a jocose usage of the term to mean "a woman; a girl; womankind," a definition that Wentworth and Flexner's *Dictionary of American Slang* fulfills with the signification of "a flirtation; a love affair." Ab Snopes's daughters are dressed in calico in "Barn Burning" (1938), William Faulkner's study of class struggle in the rural South. James T. Farrell's collection of short stories *Calico Shoes* (1934) shows the term still in use among whites on the streets of American cities in this century. Duke Ellington demonstrates the idea in use among blacks, in July 1941, with his recording of "The Brown-Skin Gal (In the Calico Gown)"—interesting carnival lyrics by Paul Francis Webster. Therefore, the persistence of the *calicot* concept displays more than a remnant of the same social conditions from the last half of the nineteenth century still extant in the twentieth.

Within this persistence, the history of "A Gal in Calico" is a thicket in itself. Arthur Schwartz wrote it in 1934 (with different lyrics by Howard Dietz) for the radio series *The Gibson Family*. He then copyrighted it (with even more banal lyrics by Leo Robin), May 1946, for a remake of the 1929 junk Hollywood musical *The Time, the Place, and the Girl*. The song proved sufficiently popular for both Bing Crosby and Tony Martin to cover even before Jamal and Davis did.

These instances of the *calicot* concept illustrate how subliminal congeniality persists in poplore. It perseveres in codes that are both harmless and implicitly charged. These codes are easy to ignore yet ready, too, for a new calico chorus to decipher and reinvest with meaning. Men like Manet, Ellington, and Davis use and reactivate this perseverance in their art. So do men like Schwartz and Robin, Crosby and Martin. They touch and retouch it differently, but however they use it, they keep it cycling. The best of them allow the miraculous intrusion of another, riper world into the harmless, recreational one.

In between the Ellingtons and Crosbys exist performers like Ahmad Jamal. Martin Williams has said that at times "Jamal's real instrument is not the piano at all, but his audience." Jamal's consideration of audience emotion is manipulative, or congenial, as you wish, but it lingers nevertheless in the Davis quartet's rendering. The impressive part of Davis's recording of "A Gal in Calico" is the way he and Garland emphasize during Davis's solo the tension on which the young *calicot* thrives. Davis's trumpet and Garland's piano complement each other, broadening their response. Garland's solemnity in this instance undercuts Davis's willfully buoyant surface insistence. (The two usually worked the other way, Davis tersely spanking Garland's romance.) These ambiguous poles represent sympathetically the eager and unacknowledged stress of any gal or guy in calico. Neither the song nor the sympathy would be complete without either the sentiment or the seriousness.

Accumulated enthusiasts in calico are the avant-garde's public. Hardly ideal, this is nevertheless the root condition. *Calicots* encourage the music (or the painting, the writing), while they pose and strive for completion at night that their day jobs do not supply. This dependency between unfulfilling life and cultural satisfaction has held since the dawn of religion and tales; it existed in the café-theaters of Paris in the 1880s; it crops up in the jazz clubs and cocktail lounges of fifties cities in America. Davis's sentimentality simply acknowledges these facts. His music responds to and documents the tenuous support for the uncurated arts. They depend on such shifting and green publics. Material differences in the society and the turning lore cycle generate and combine these enthusiasts into publics who cannot long live the life, cannot survive the tension and the indeterminacy. So they constantly give way to other short-term publics to whom artists must each in turn extend sympathy and whatever snippets of their tradition they can contribute before the public dissolves, their calico skirts, shirts, and shoes bequeathed like their energy and club-going idealism to the next lot. The problem is not an absence of rigor or an edifying past, but the speedy turnover of audiences who ride by the tableaux offered them so quickly that they too seldom have time to extend or elaborate their meanings.

Audiences in general care nothing for these historical conditions that obsess performers and their critics. Indeed, one of the most vexing issues in cultural study is wonder at what makes individuals leap across from relatively passive participation in a public to active involvement with the edifying tableaux of any art, any rich lore. What turns a member of a public into a fan, a fan into a performer or critic who transmits the lot? There is a quick illustration of this gap in *The Crying of Lot 49*. Stumbling into a bar filled with participants in the cult-jammed underground she has begun to suspect props up contemporary history, Oedipa Maas confesses her budding connections to a man wearing a lapel pin of the muted horn. He says: " 'I never thought there was a history to it.' 'I think of nothing but,' said Oedipa."

Oedipa has proceeded from passive innocent to involved participant asking the tough questions of performers in the world. She suspects something of the tradition and puts its performers on the spot. You would not call her a laughing chorus—she is too surprised and perplexed for that. But she queries their conditions. She is a solemn chorus. In her way she, too, is acting on the lore that seems to her a miraculous intrusion. She, too, is recoding impulses and passing them on. Her drama is in finding meaning for the clusters of exhausted but still pregnable signs others bandy so carelessly.

For others the problem is not so much in finding these secret signs, kernels, and tokens as in delivering their structure. Like Jack Kerouac, Miles Davis used the history and attitude carried in the coruscating flashes of aggressionless assertion Lester Young practiced. Young's intelligence came down to Davis via Charlie Parker, who had himself digested Young's effect in Kansas City and reissued it in the pastiche flurries he sprayed where others played discrete notes. Working this tradition, Davis infused his own playing with the logical connections that Young had compressed into Basie's choruses and that Parker had pulled out into his brilliant three-minute miniatures. On those sessions, Davis was a sideman. But when he became a leader, Davis drew out the structure further and further.

The kernels of Davis's late-fifties compositions are organically delicate, an idea of melody, a hint of a relationship coded, say, in the sound of his muted horn whispering a centimeter from the mike's ear. He always had this attention to sound, even when in Parker's shadow he was aiming less to compose or arrange, much less beat the living legend, but simply trying to hang tight after the master's solo. His development through the fifties shows him learning to protect this kernel of himself. It is much the same story Kerouac played out between *On the Road* and *Visions of Cody*. Just as Kerouac had to learn to embed Cody's vulnerability in poplore's armature, so too did Davis have to learn how to use and structure his sound in relation to the congenial resources of deliberately speeding culture.

At barely twenty-one, Davis could not hope to equal Parker's dexterous flights, but he could and did learn from Bird's adaptation of the blues-toned waver, adding tones that imply a higher note beyond the chord as the sound settles to its place, flourishing like a mockingbird alighting on a wire. It is all there on the minute and a quarter of solo that Davis pulls off after Parker's legendary two minutes on "Embraceable You." It is there over and over in these early sessions, always most noticeable on the ballads, where Davis's protracted notes avoid vibrato but underscore that blues indeterminacy, thus compensating for and complementing in his own cunning way Parker's flurried demisemiquavers. Davis's notes project a man struggling to achieve his own sonority—his clatter and veering angst, his metallic hiss, brakes grabbing and rolling stock accelerating behind the repartee, all in a night's work, nothing to get hot about. Don't show or shout pain; admit it and clip it. Thus Davis threaded through the opening between his schematic intelligence and his developing fluency on the horn, standing nightly next to the fastest fingers and surest improviser in jazz. His was a kernel of precariousness out on its own.

As in "Weirdo" (recorded March 6, 1954, then repeated a month later as "Walkin'" and four years later as "Sid's Ahead"), the practice was to harry this precariousness until it took on viable life—then protect it. Think of Davis as scarifying the kernel of his sound to make it sprout, then improvising a precisely shaped cloche to house it. Here he is very like Kerouac, whose sketches were as tender as Davis's sonority. As the recording format opened up for Davis, and as Kerouac abandoned belief that his work would be published, so turned himself loose to write what he imagined, Davis's music and Kerouac's prose both became architectural from within. They held together by connecting internal tensions rather than fulfilling external expectations.

Here's Jack Duluoz, in *Visions of Cody*, admiring Davis's structuring:

> And meanwhile Miles Davis, like the sun; or the sun, like Miles Davis, blows on with his raw little horn; the prettiest trumpet tone since Hackett and McPartland and at the same time, to flash some of its fine raw sound, some

wild abstract new ideas developed around a growing theme that started off like a tree and became a structure of iron on which tremendous phrases can be strung and hung and long pauses goofed, kicked along, whaled, touched with hidden and active meanings; to come in, then, like a sweet tenor and blow the superfinest, is mowd enow [*sic*, for "more den enuff"]. I love Miles Davis because, send in your penny postcard [imitating Symphony Sid, the radio jazz deejay].

Duluoz summarizes significant aspects of Davis's style here, but more important is how the passage also webs Kerouac's own prose with the music. Acutely linking Davis's raw, pretty tone to Lester Young's "sweet tenor," Kerouac was also showing his own values. Like their music, his prose grew from riffs—penny postcard perceptions anyone might mail—into unusual iron structure, sufficiently strong to goof on, more than enough to protect the jelly of developing insights.

Amiri Baraka

Miles Davis: "One of the Great Mother Fuckers"

Originally published in The Music: Reflections on Jazz and Blues *(New York: William Morrow, 1987), 297–306. Copyright © 1987 by Amiri Baraka. Reprinted by permission of Sterling Lord Literistic, Inc.*

Imamu Amiri Baraka (né LeRoi Jones) has been prominent as a poet, playwright, and jazz critic since the late 1950s. His jazz writing has appeared in *Jazz Review, Jazz,* and *Down Beat* and in three books, *Blues People: Negro Music in White America* (1963), *Black Music* (1967), and *The Music: Reflections on Jazz and Blues* (1987). (The most recent of those volumes also contains poetry by Amina Baraka.) During the 1960s Baraka was an often controversial but always passionate advocate of "the New Thing" (as avant-garde jazz was then called) and his view of the black struggle in America.

In this excerpt from a chapter in *The Music* ("Miles Davis: 'One of the Great Mother Fuckers' "), Baraka insightfully discusses the enormous influence of the trumpeter's 1955–60 music, with emphasis on one of Davis's (and jazz's) greatest ensembles: the 1957–59 sextet with featured saxophonists John Coltrane and Cannonball Adderley.—Ed.

The appearance of Red Garland, Philly Joe Jones, and most importantly John Coltrane shaped the heaviest elements of "The New Miles Davis Quintet," formed in 1955, the same year Bird died.

In this period of rising black political consciousness, *soul* (blackness, negritude, etc.) and its expression *funk* (the heat, "odeur," of basic blues, and like jass also connected with *sex*) emerge. Jass (Jassm and Jism) is literally ejaculation music. "Funk" is the "smell" that goes with it, a piano drawling with blues reclaims its ancient "frenzy," the hard bopper (funky bopper, i.e., new and blue, and reemphasizing the rhythm almost at times to a back beat—you could dance with a tambourine to it) is the Preacher, driving the music and the congregation with the music into a mutual frenzy.

Blakey's Messengers were and remain a university of funk through which some of the hottest and bluesiest young musicians have passed. Especially people like Horace Silver, Bobby Timmons, Hank Mobley, Lee Morgan, Wayne Shorter. They were major influences. The incredible Brown-Rollins-Roach groups were perhaps the most sophisticated and heatedly lyrical of the bringers of the harder sound. This is a period of Rollins developing his long orderly logical extended improvisations and West Indian influences.

Miles's view that hard bop was the real New York music—the classic early bop a southwestern style—identifies the Caribbean, West Indian, Latino contributions, and the gospel inflection as part of an authentic New York style that emerged with Rollins, Blakey, Roach, and the rest.

Rollins's magnificent *Freedom Suite* reflected the stylistic and philosophical content of the times. Plus Max Roach's *We Insist! Freedom Now Suite* with Abbey and Max cooking at white-heat intensity and celebrating the intensifying African Liberation struggles. Mingus's "Fables of Faubus" took dead journalistic aim at real stuff as the times themselves spoke to the struggle against American apartheid. By 1954 *Brown* v. *Board of Education of Topeka, Kansas* supposedly ended 1896's "separate but equal," and by 1957 a new hero named Martin Luther King had transformed Rosa Parks's personal resistance to Montgomery bus segregation into a national democratic movement!

Monk's *Brilliant Corners*, with Monk in the red wagon behind the shades, drew together the earlier, more experimental bebop with the funky later music (Trane and Hawkins on the same sides).

Miles mentions the fantastic groups he worked with during the period. One particular stretch he worked with Trane and Rollins. "We did a con-

cert uptown for Paul Robeson. Doug Turner Ward [founder of Negro
Ensemble] helped put it together.

"I used to tell them, the bass got the tonic. Don't play in the same
register as the sax, lay out. Don't play."

These seem very appropriate stylistic caveats for the group that Miles
put together now that took the finger-poppin' urban funk blues of the
hard bop era and combined it with a harmonic placement conditioned by
Miles's need for a cushion, plus his gorgeous melodic invention. It was
called simply *Miles: The New Miles Davis Quintet.* It caused a sensation
among jazz people.

It was funky and sophisticated, swung hard, at the same time being
wispily lyrical. During the fifties years, Miles in a bop or hard bop context,
and finally in his symmetrically exquisite quintets and sextets with Trane,
later with Trane and Cannonball (1957–59), and in the fresh and lyrical
Gil Evans collaborations created music at a level very few people ever
approach, anywhere, anytime.

It is this music, from the raw funky and exhilarant sides like "Dig" or
the interracial experimentation of "Ezz-thetic" or the street-hip "Dr.
Jackle" to the exciting maturity of "Straight, No Chaser" or "Bye Bye
Blackbird," to the moody symphonic lyricism of *Porgy and Bess,* or the new
music minimalism of *Kind of Blue,* Miles created at a level and on a scale
that needs a Duke or Billie or Armstrong or Monk to equal for aesthetic
influence, length, and consistency.

This is also a period that Miles's own mystique gets somewhat
reshaped. In the postcool period Miles had begun to live hard in the
ghetto, a condition particularly depressing because he also addicted to
heroin.

From the drape-suited, gas-haired "cat," the Harlem music, particularly
"Dig" and "Walkin'" and "Dr. Jackle," complete with Miles in pulled-down
"black boy" hat and better-fitting Italian and Ivy threads, gives Miles the
"down" quality of the time. *Down,* the current parallel word for hip. Like
Robert Thompson has said of Kongo culture, it prizes "getting down,"
bending the knees and elbows. It also favors "cool" as subtle fire.

But now, too, the political sweep of the times meant one had to be
down with the people, to be in touch with one's roots. The gospels and
the blues were part of these roots. The music of this period is superbly
funky and bluesy.

Miles even had the unfortunate but spiritually "in tune" experience of
being jumped on by racist policemen outside Birdland when he tried to

take a "breather" in between sets. Black newspapers called it a "Georgia head whippin'," placing it squarely (1959) shoulder to shoulder with the beatings black civil rights marchers were receiving marching against segregation and "Jim Crow."

In a sense Miles embodied a black attitude that had grown steadily more ubiquitous in the fifties—defiance, a redefined, contemporary function of the culturally traditional *resistance* of blacks to slavery and then national oppression.

I stopped drummer Steve McCall, one of the elder statesmen of the new music, a few days after I'd talked to Miles. "What's Miles make you think of?" I asked.

"When I think of his influence, I think he's had a positive influence on black people in general. He transcended the slave mentality. I remember when he was setting all kinds of styles. The artist. He had class. Good taste. His music had a density."

So Miles was not only the cool hipster of our bebop youth, but now we felt he embodied the social fire of the times. All the musician-hippy stories about Miles told us he was "bad," that people, including the pó-lice, didn't mess with Miles.

We knew Miles went to the gym all the time and boxed. We had even been close enough a couple of times when the quintet opened at the Bohemia in the Village to hear the hipster foghorn bass that was his voice. That was the way Miles was supposed to sound. It was hip—somewhat mysterious with a touch of street toughness.

John Coltrane's tenure with Miles Davis helped produce some of the finest music played by anyone. Just the torrid classic *Cookin', Relaxin', Steamin', Workin'* sides and the amazing and beautiful *'Round About Midnight*—all these albums done in one year (October 1955–October 1956)—reveal Miles as a confident master having assembled a musical organization that was, during that period, without peers.

Trane, a rough-toned saxophonist from North Carolina, grew up, especially musically, in Philadelphia. The son of a tailor-musician, Trane later worked in Philadelphia factories and learned bebop in a Navy band. He had a background not only of spirituals and musical religious frenzy, but a more recent history of honking rhythm and blues, often while walking the bartops of Philly. He had played with Big Maybelle, 3 Bips and a Bop, and later Jimmy Smith and the Dizzy Gillespie big band. There is a fantastic flick of Bird and Miles on the stage at Birdland, while in the background a very young and slightly nervous-looking John Coltrane.

Miles's darting blue flashes and sometimes limpid lyricism were now placed in tandem collaboration with the big densely powerful song of Coltrane. If Trane's early efforts seemed crude and not quite articulate to some, the feelings and aesthetic bearing his playing carried caused quite a few hip people to pick up on Trane very early.

It was Philly Joe Jones who urged Trane on Miles as a replacement for Rollins. A vibes-playing roadie of mine in the early fifties had heard Trane somewhere and described him even pre-Miles as "a genius."

In some superficial ways Trane was similar to Rollins, except when Trane sounded most like Rollins he was just beginning to sound like his real musical self, which came a little later. Both possessed large dominating blues-filled honking tones, but Trane tore into the bulk of his sound to investigate ceaselessly the fundamental elements of timbre and harmony, combining complex rhythmic insistence with seemingly endless melodic and harmonic invention. John Coltrane was not just a great tenor saxophonist, he was an *innovator*.

That is the real secret of the classic quintet and sextet music of Miles Davis in the fifties and sixties—not only is there the Davis direction and innovation, but he carries with him as one part of his fantastic arsenal a "straight-out murderer," as we used to say, John Coltrane.

Trane gave Miles a balance that allowed his purple whispering lyricism to still touch the raw funky sidewalks. But Trane was not only "street," he was intense and searching. What Miles implied, the tension his silence and placement of notes created as an under feeling, Trane readily and openly proclaimed. Trane was a wailer—a throwback to Big Jay McNeely and Illinois Jacquet of the howling fifties. The sound of shouting and screaming, whooping and hollerin', crying and singing. Coon-hollers, yells, "Arwhoolies" were all in there, and low-down blues and gospel trembling. Plus, later, Trane carried it all back to its righteous source, the "East," Africa, the animist memory.

With the later addition of Cannonball Adderley, a Florida funk merchant in the keening tradition of a more simplified Charlie Parker. Along with Trane and Cannonball, Paul Chambers, bass, Red Garland, piano, and Philly Joe Jones make up the rest of the immortals, a band as heavy as Louis's Hot Five.

Miles, when I asked about that band, talked of Cannonball's coming with the group and reacting to the music, "This ain't no blues. Trane took Cannonball in the back and showed him what he was doin'. Trane be around there suckin' his teeth. I told Trane to show him and stop him from accenting the first beat.

"Bass got the tonic, don't play in the same register as the sax. Lay out. Don't play." The Milesian aesthetic for the group. Miles talked about people playing too many notes. He said when he listened to his own music, "I always listen to what I can leave out."

In one sense he is like Monk with his incisive blue pointillism, but Miles could not dig Monk's "comping" behind him for the same reasons. "Monk don't give you no support." No cushion or easily related-to pattern, for sure.

The quintet and sextet were the most popular jazz groups of their time. With them they carried the sound and image of the contemporary urban American intellectual and artist, one that was *Kind of Blue*. The *Milestones* and *'Round About Midnight* albums were great social events as well as artistic triumphs. They confirmed the astuteness of the listener. "Straight, No Chaser" was the state of (the) art—any art! *Kind of Blue* led us into new formal and intellectual vistas. (You remember "On Green Dolphin Street"?)

For me what the Trane-Cannonball groups represented and set up was the direction(s) the music has been moving for almost the last thirty years.

The two reed soloists each summed up certain stylistic tendencies in the music and revived these in more contemporary accents. The funky alto man had been a music teacher in Florida. And his expansive and rotund silhouette was the reason for his nickname.

Cannonball had the sky-highing piercing wail of Bird, but it was not the innovative rocket-sword "Yard" had. Ball's sound was stylistically like Bird, but not out of the deepest *understanding* of that aesthetic, it seemed to me, but a kind of appreciation.

It's what separates all the people who play "like" John Coltrane from really creating the emotional aura Trane did. They pick up the style, the form, but the philosophical and aesthetic mandates, which make that sound necessary, they often miss.

So that I thought much of what Ball played, certainly in contrast to Coltrane, seemed cruelly superficial. But at other times, Trane's thunder and lightning contrasted perfectly with the finally less complex but lilting melodic improvisation of Cannonball.

What is so heavy is that Trane and Cannonball, themselves the two opposing weights of saxophone balance in the classic Davis groups, are also two musical schools coming into being—first as key parts of the whole Davis vision, but later as musical (and philosophical) tendencies in the whole music!

From the Cannonball side of the Davis groups, one got the *pop* aspect of the funk/gospel hard-bop development. (A gospel *nightclub* opened briefly in New York during the same period!)

Ball's glibness and easy humor, coupled with a kind of swinging formalism and miniaturism, enabled him to create the kind of solos and compositions that would be commercially significant. (Although the *Somethin' Else* album with Miles under Cannonball's leadership is one of the hippest albums released in the period, it is Miles Davis-like music.)

Cannonball had several jazz hits with his own bands. He had a stylized glib gospel/funk kind of tune that really got over. "Jive Samba" (actually composed by brother Nat), Bobby Timmons's "Dis Heah" and "Dat Dere," Zawinul's "Mercy, Mercy, Mercy." What is seminal in this is that it is Cannonball and the characteristic music and musicians he developed that are the prototypes for the music later called *fusion!* The combining of jazz lines with rhythm-and-blues rhythms, or tuneful melodies with R & B bottoms.

Joe Zawinul, the major domo of the most successful fusion group, Weather Report, was a Davis/Cannonball sideman—in fact, the majority of the key musicians who created the cool-top blues-bottom music called fusion are alumni of one Davis group or another. Cannonball's bands were earlier practitioners of the form before it became a style.

The various funk miniatures Cannonball liked to play are one of the prototypes for what came to be known as fusion, a largely commercial music. But it is Miles who is the real originator of the form. The cool-top/R & B bottom sound, commercial version, is obviously given inspiration by Miles's general approach, particularly as interpreted by Cannonball and his bands.

On the other side of the bandstand of that great band was the great John Coltrane. The music Trane made and wanted to make with Miles's band and after was almost the exact opposite of what Cannonball was doing.

Where Cannonball seemed to treasure the glib artifact, Trane seemed with Miles always in the middle of creativity, sometimes driving Miles buggy because of the drawn-out length of some of his solos. And in these solos Trane searched and thrashed and struggled, always it seemed, looking for higher and higher levels of understanding and expression. Trane was the ceaseless experimenter—Cannonball the pragmatic miniaturist, creator of funky ready-mades.

So that Miles had two guns at his disposal, Trane the expressionist and Cannonball the formalist. These two horns marked the breaking off of two schools of jazz conception. But so powerful and broadly expressive was this classic Miles group that it contained the elements for establishing or redefining two significant jazz styles that have dominated to one degree or another the music for the last thirty years!

Both these styles make use of the blues in very definite but very contrasting ways. Cannonball was bluesy as form, Trane bluesy as essence. Hence Cannon thinking, when he first got to Miles's band, that what the group was playing wasn't the blues. That is, he was looking for the standard twelve-bar *form*. Miles on the other hand wanted the blues *expressed*, not just as form but as feeling and color. It was in Miles's band that both players developed as much more mature and forceful soloists.

Miles talked about the two directions Trane and Cannonball represented. In 1960 Miles's group, minus Cannonball, had done some eighteen concerts for Norman Granz in Europe. It was there that Coltrane had picked up the soprano saxophone, his later use of which, beginning with the big hit "My Favorite Things," revived the instrument among jazz players all over the world.

The chordal experimentation and chromatic lyricism Trane began to be identified with, even before he left Miles and which revolutionized the music, Miles casually accepts credit for laying on John. "I showed Trane all that," Miles averred. "Cannonball just played funk. But he could interpret any feeling."

What is important is that Trane's direction and legacy was to redefine avant-garde, to spread the social upsurge in society of the time, which somehow affected *him*, into musical revolution.

Cannonball's direction and legacy was to take the *form* of the fifties bebop, now hard-bop explosion, to include the "new" *gospel* awareness as jazz soul music and new emphasis on funk, and to repeat the classic form of a blues somewhat gospelized. Yet the reason for the upsurge of the blues was as a flag for the popular *social* feeling of the time. Its redefinition, as of that day, had to yet identify the *meaning* of the blues, which is alive and still with us. The *being* of the people, their minds and condition. The awful calamitous circumstance of their real lives.

Cannon's direction is more commercial because it freezes blues as blues form. This is the fusion phenomenon. Miles's "bottom" is a desired connection, with "America." It can be lush horns, strings, atmosphere, America will always dig *Birth of the Cool, Miles Ahead, Porgy and Bess, Sketches of Spain*, and *Kind of Blue* (black people and most intellectuals too). But the music that speaks most directly of the black urban experience are the forties Bird sides, "Billie's Bounce," "Now's the Time," "Ornithology," "Anthropology," "Donna Lee," "Scrapple from the Apple," etc.; or the fifties hard-bop gems and classic funk/cushion balancing standards "Morpheus," "Down," "Bluing," "Dig," "Tempus Fugit," "Weirdo," "Well, You Needn't," "Walkin'," "Airegin," "Oleo," "Bags' Groove," "Green Haze," "Dr. Jackle," "Ah-Leu-Cha," "Bye Bye Blackbird," "'Round Midnight," "It Never Entered My Mind," "If I Were a Bell," "On Green Dolphin Street," "So What," and "Straight, No Chaser." But the hugely successful pieces with Evans are symphonic tone poems, to a certain extent summing up midcentury American concert music. *Miles Ahead* was the giant step, replaying yet extending even further the Evans/Thornhill *Birth of the Cool* concept.

Miles's special capacity and ability is to hold up and balance two musical (social) conceptions and express them as (two parts of) a single aesthetic. The "cushion" Miles speaks of is the luxury, ease, mood, of sensuous well-being this society sports—its lushness and pretension. (How does access to all that sound?) Sometimes Miles's horn alone holds out for this warmth in the midst of fire, for example, with Bird or the hard boppers or the classic Coltrane/Cannonball sides. But by *Miles Ahead*, Miles understood enough about the entire American aesthetic so that he could make the *cool* statements at a level that was truly *popular* and which had the accents of African-America included not as contrasting anxiety or tension but as an equal sensuousness!

Sketches of Spain and *Porgy and Bess* are high American musical statements; their tension is between a functional impressionism, serious in its emotional detail, versus mood without significance. It is the bluesiness of the Davis conception even submerged in all the lushness that gives these moods an intelligence and sensitivity. There is yet a searching quality in Miles's horn, above, beyond, below, inside, outside, within, locked out of the lushness, the lovely American bottom. It is a searching, a probing like a dowser, used for searching out beauty. Miles's horn itself is so beautiful, except there is a feeling in us that maybe all of this is a dream. A film. An invisible pageant of feeling. *Miles Ahead, Sketches*, and *Porgy* are great movie music. But add them as well to a native U.S. impressionism brought here on Duke's back that is linked as well to Debussy and Delius and Ravel.

Kind of Blue is the stripped-down recombining of the two musical tendencies in Miles (the American and the African American) to where they feed each other like electric charges. Here the mood, the lush, the bottom is also *sketched.* Miles has discovered chords and the implied modal approach that link up object and background as the same phrase and note. *Blue* is not contrapuntal, it is pointillistic, yet its dots and its backgrounds are the same lines flowing together.

The harmonic bottom of Miles is sometimes translated as Eastern drone, what Trane later made even further use of. The drone here is that the chords link up, continue each other like a single modal insistence.

Miles's penchant for minimalism has gone back to his earliest music. It is the "fill-in" quality we remember with Bird. Only the essentials. Bird's ever-flowing elaboration must have consolidated in Miles the need to try to fill the "other" space (Bird did not fill). So that throughout Miles's playing days he has always cautioned his sidemen against playing "too much."

Miles says when he listens to his music he is listening for "what can be cut out."

Max Roach was as young as Miles during the bebop revolution. He was another of the genius teenagers to hook up with Charlie Parker to help create the explosion of bebop. Max's seriousness and integrity over the long haul are unquestionable. And while it was rumored back in the sixties that Max was critical of Miles, the master drummer responds directly and with no diversion, "Miles just shows several aspects of being creative. If you're being creative, you can't be like you were yesterday. Miles exemplifies it. The record industry keeps reading us out—but Miles will step out. Lester Young did that . . . always looking. It's the law of everything. Miles is that way . . . Ella and Miles breathed new life into the record companies. I think what Miles is doing is in keeping with our creative people today."

By 1960 Miles had created a body of music that could compare favorably with any in jazz. He had come in with bebop, innovated with cool, got down with hard bop, and put together his symphonic excursions into contemporary American music with *Sketches, Miles Ahead*, and especially *Porgy and Bess.*

It is fitting that *Kind of Blue* closed out those intensely creative years, because it sums up Miles's major musical tendencies as well as indicates what new roads exist not only for him but for the music generally. Bass great Reggie Workman calls Miles, "an important figure. He contributed a lot to our music. More than just stylistic." Laughing, Reggie goes on, "a typical Gemini. He's got strong convictions. You can hear in his art forms. He's a great person. A real wonderful person."

Both Coltrane and Cannonball left the band at this point. In Trane's wake, inspired by him, a whole raging avant-garde arose. People like Eric Dolphy, Pharoah Sanders, Ornette Coleman, Albert Ayler, John Gilmore, and thousands more arrived all lit up by Trane's search for a new sound and a new direction. A search that went on openly in Miles's classic bands.

The musicians that followed Trane, Cannonball, Chambers, Jones, Garland with the band reveal exactly in what direction the band, and Miles, were moving. After a series of Trane "replacements" (e.g., Hank Mobley, George Coleman, Sam Rivers), Miles moved to the next more stable period with Wayne Shorter, Herbie Hancock, Ron Carter, Tony Williams, and a music that, while not at the overall level of the Trane-Cannonball-Philly Joe years, is excellent music, the hip restatement of that classic period.

Just as Trane was identified with and inspired the screaming revolutionary players of the sixties and beyond, Cannonball's direction, as noted, was also significant and also a Miles by-product. Cannon put together a fairly stable quintet during the sixties and made some of the biggest commercial hits in the music—his "Sack o' Woe" and "Jive Samba." Joe Zawinul (an Austrian pianist, who later went on to head up the most successful fusion band in the business, Weather Report) while with Cannon's band contributed "Mercy, Mercy, Mercy" again in the formal soul/funk vein. It was one of the best-selling jazz records ever!

The Cannon/Zawinul approach was to take the surface or formal lines of the hard-bop funk/soul renaissance and make popular miniatures out of them. To emphasize the ensemble-arranged aspect of the music while deemphasizing the free improvisation.

What is interesting is that the Shorter/Hancock etc. band that was first noted for its further statements of the Miles classic fifties groups, by the late sixties became the vehicle for Miles's increasing use of the pop/commercial aspect of his own mind. But Miles's "cushion" or "bottom," the "handle" that he speaks of, was always a way for the music to be more accessible to himself as well as the people.

Miles went to Juilliard. Miles's father was a medium-sized land-owner and dentist. All that is in his life and to a certain general extent is in his art. But Miles is still tied to the blues, and that emotional aesthetic matrix.

Even in the American symphonic impressionism he created with Gil Evans, there is always an echo of the blues. At times, Miles's version of Duke.

After Trane and Cannonball left Miles in 1959–60, the best Miles bands were a restatement of that music. But Miles's classic small-group music of the fifties not only is the state of the art but a signpost of what is to come.

Max Harrison

Sheer Alchemy, for a While: Miles Davis and Gil Evans

Originally published in Jazz Monthly, *December 1958 and February 1960, and in revised form in* A Jazz Retrospect *(Boston: Crescendo, 1976; London: Quartet Books, 1991). Revised by the author in August–September 1994 and used by permission.*

Among the most important partnerships in American music—rivaled only by those of Duke Ellington and Billy Strayhorn, and Frank Sinatra and Nelson Riddle—was the partnership of Miles Davis and Gil Evans. Max Harrison's essay on the pair is the most detailed examination we have of their collaborations. The piece appeared in its original form in *Jazz Monthly*. Harrison revised the essay for inclusion in his *A Jazz Retrospect* and substantially revised and expanded it for this volume.

For the most part "Sheer Alchemy" speaks eloquently for itself, but a couple of points need to be added. One concerns Harrison's discussion of arranger credits for the *Birth of the Cool* music. Earlier in this volume (see my "Miles Davis and the Birth of the Cool: A Question of Influences"), I discuss findings from a February 1995 interview with Gerry Mulligan and have reason to regard Mulligan's statements on the matter as definitive.

Another point: two years after Harrison completed his latest revision, Columbia and Mosaic Records jointly issued *Miles Davis and Gil Evans: The Complete Columbia Studio Recordings*. Revelations in that collection include

alternate and rehearsal takes from the pair's 1957–60 dates, plus the previously unreleased music from *The Time of the Barracudas* (1963) and a
February 1968 date that yielded "Falling Water." A concert in April 1968
in Berkeley, California, went unrecorded by Columbia Records. Private
tapes, long rumored to exist, finally surfaced in late 1996.—Ed.

Neither of them was quite explicit as to when they met, although what
evidence we have points to 1947. Certainly in his autobiography Davis
repeated the oft-told story that begins with Evans wanting to score "Donna
Lee" for Claude Thornhill's band and assuming this theme was by Charlie
Parker because it had been recorded by Parker's quintet for Savoy in May
1947.[1] But like other small companies specializing in jazz, Savoy was as
offhand about composer attributions as about titles, and, though credited
to Parker on the label, the piece was actually by the quintet's trumpeter,
being the first composition he got recorded.[2] Based on the harmonies of
"Indiana" and even taking oblique glances at its melody, "Donna Lee,"
granted its rhythmic drive and passing syncopations, is a bit too symmetrical
to be typical of Parker, of bop themes in general, or indeed of what Davis
was to do later. And it is curious that so few people have noticed that it
starts with, and later repeats, a literal quotation from the trumpet solo on
"Ice Freezes Red," waxed by Fats Navarro and his Thin Men for Savoy the
previous January.[3]

Whether Evans knew this is impossible to guess, but Davis told him he
could use the theme provided he in return got a copy of the Thornhill
arrangement of "Robbins' Nest," which Evans had written. Whatever the
facts, this tale has a symbolic truth because Davis was not the only young
modernist intrigued by what Thornhill's band was playing, and "Donna
Lee" was not the first bop theme Evans had scored for it. His versions of
the Parker-Gillespie "Thriving on a Riff" (alias "Anthropology") was
recorded by Thornhill in September 1947, "Donna Lee" in November,
Parker's "Yardbird Suite" in December. And rather than being isolated
incidents, these were ventures characteristic of one who always followed
an independent path.

Evans was born, as Ian Ernest Gilmore Green, in Toronto on May 13,
1912, of Australian parents. The family moved around a good deal, and
this presumably contributed to his being entirely self-taught in music.

After periods in Montana, Idaho, Washington, and Oregon, they settled in California, in Berkeley, Burbank, and finally, from 1929, in Stockton for six years. There he finished high school and was in contact with an unusually musical family who had a piano and other instruments, a record player, and many records, jazz and otherwise. Perhaps it was here that Evans began to sense his life's direction, and certainly it was in Stockton that in 1933 he started his first band. Now becoming interested in arranging, he learned by adapting what he heard on records, the first being Red Nichols's "Ida, Sweet as Apple Cider" (1927), which featured Adrian Rollini. In 1936–37 his band was resident at the Rendezvous Ballroom, Balboa Beach, California, where fame later found Stan Kenton. By now Evans was too involved with writing to care about leading, so his band was in 1937 taken over by its singer, Skinnay Ennis, under whom it became more successful. So much so that a second arranger was soon needed. This was Claude Thornhill, who stayed until 1939 when he returned to New York to form his own band. Two years later he sent for Evans, who thus made the crucial move of his career.[4]

Since leaving Ennis, Thornhill had grown musically. It is usually said that he devised the "Thornhill sound," epitomized by his composition "Snowfall," first recorded in May 1941, but that it was Evans who knew what to do with it. In fact such pieces as "Portrait of a Guinea Farm," recorded in April 1941, six months prior to Evans's arrival in New York, show that Thornhill had further thoughts of his own. As Evans said, Thornhill's approach to writing for the band "didn't have anything to do with the way things were in the swing era." His were "very difficult arrangements that were more like a wind instrument transcription of the way you'd write for a chamber orchestra."[5] This was a result of Thornhill's emphasis on clarinets, on which all his saxophonists doubled, yet it was admittedly after Evans joined the band that changes were made to the instrumentation that proved so far-reaching. By the January 1942 Columbia date, two French horns and a bass clarinet had been added, and their effect can be heard in Evans's scoring of a lively Thornhill composition recorded the following July, "Buster's Last Stand." The true character of "Snowfall" also emerged in its second version, a Lang-Worth radio transcription issued on V-Disc.

But Thornhill was in the navy 1942–45, and Evans was in the army 1943–46 (where he met and played with Lester Young), and it was after the band re-formed in 1946 that it really took on momentum. Besides Evans, such players as Louis Mucci, Danny Polo, and Barry Galbraith rejoined. In the pivotal year 1947, Red Rodney, Lee Konitz, Joe Shulman, and Bill Barber were in the ranks, and along with Barber's tuba such instruments as piccolo and flute were added. Yet although Thornhill's accomplished and beautifully refined piano solos were always a major identifying factor, it was, again, Evans who turned the band into a force in jazz, and a highly independent one.

Obviously pieces like "Snowfall" indicated Thornhill's willingness to depart from swing or dance band conventions, and, quite apart from matters of instrumentation and Evans's technical procedures, the main point was the band's venturing into the expression of climates of feeling scarcely before met with in jazz. A good illustration is "La paloma," a tawdry wisp of musical Hispanicism that here, with the French horns coming into their own, evokes a hot summer night in Spain, a hint of flamenco lending to the nostalgia an epic quality, banishing sentimentality. This was Evans's first engagement with the "Spanish tinge" in jazz that Jelly Roll Morton had considered so important and that certainly was to have a significant role in Evans's collaborations with Davis. Already this music's elevation makes it hard to believe that the band survived by playing for dancers; and listen to "Arab Dance." Perhaps the reeds sound like those of Benny Goodman's band a few years before, and the brass are set against them in what at first seem rather obviously contrasting patterns. Yet the alternation of swinging and "eastern" sections glances forward to the interchange between what seem to be blues and Iberian themes in a piece we shall meet later, "Blues for Pablo." And this dialogue opens "Arab Dance" up to a climax that attains actual grandeur and is capped by a quotation from Ellington's "Ko-Ko." This last is reproduced with an accuracy few could then have matched, telling us something not just about the acuteness of Evans's ears but also about his grasp of larger musical realities.

Nothing else in Thornhill's output sounds like Ellington, yet this quotation signals the direction in which Evans was taking the band and subsequently his own music, namely, toward a higher integration of all elements in parallel with an entirely nonformulaic method of writing. The early goals are suggested by his extraordinary version of a movement from Mussorgsky's *Pictures at an Exhibition* piano suite, "The Old Castle," inexplicably retitled "The Troubador" either by Evans or by Thornhill. We can only regret that he did not undertake other movements from this work beyond the snatch of "Promenade" that prefaces "The Old Castle," for the sheer majesty achieved rivals and almost surpasses the famous orchestration by Ravel, given that Evans was confined to a modified dance band instrumentation dwarfed by the full symphony orchestra the French composer had at his disposal.

Mussorgsky's "The Old Castle," Tchaikovsky's "Arab Dance," and even Iradier's "La paloma" are ventures outside the dance band, or even swing band, repertoire at least as bold as the bop themes mentioned earlier, and their juxtaposition emphasizes factors in Evans's musical inclinations and artistic personality that, again, would be central to his collaborations with Davis. Treatments of pieces by Davis, Parker, and Gillespie were in line with those of other jazz themes Evans did for the band, including Trummy Young's "Sorta Kinda," "Sir" Charles Thompson's "Robbins' Nest," and several jazz-associated ballads such as "Lover Man" and "My Old Flame," both also recorded by Parker. We need to recognize that Evans's work for Thornhill was the basis of his entire achievement and something without which the heights scaled with Davis would have been unattainable to them both. It was often said that the sounds and textures Evans conjured out of the large jazz ensemble for *Miles Ahead*, his first major venture with Davis in 1957, were new to all music, but that was already true a decade earlier with the finest of his scores for Thornhill. And frequently their most inspired moments came in the introductions and codas. Often the former appear to start remote from the theme, as with "Lover Man," while the codas sometimes gaze toward horizons far off, as in the highly inventive end of "Yardbird Suite."

Consider the deft imagination shown in the introduction to "Sorta Kinda," a dialogue between piano and ensemble that continues into the announcement of the theme, the band's instruments mixed with an originality that is unemphatic yet still seizes our attention. The passage leading to the first vocal, as daring in harmony as in texture, mocks Gene Williams's wan singing, and the other ensemble passages are nearly as remarkable. "Robbins' Nest" goes further. An introduction by turns abrasive and sinuous leads to the theme from Thornhill, joined in the chorus's second half by the many-hued band. A clarinet solo is later enhanced in a similar way, and after a clarinet and tenor duet comes a composed ensemble passage that is a concentrated reflection on the theme. A perfectly integrated allusion to Kreisler's *Caprice viennois* cues in the leader with the theme, this winding the performance down to its close.

Thornhill's elegantly flowing pianism was never again heard to such advantage as amid the constant invention of Evans's orchestral textures, and in "Robbins' Nest," "Lover Man," or "Polka Dots and Moonbeams," the combination is quite magical. Yet it was the bop themes that made Evans most tellingly thrust into the future, activating his sensuous instrumental blendings with something of the rhythmic vocabulary of the new jazz. One member of the band, Ed Zandy, said that Evans "practically had to teach us to play bop,"[6] and as these themes were designed for small combos, it is instructive to observe how they were adapted for the rich-voiced Thornhill band. On two of them the bop ensemble sound was at first imitated, and in "Thriving on a Riff" Evans recalled that he had a unison "with all the trumpets in cup mutes, two altos and five clarinets."[7] But first comes an introduction featuring Thornhill that seems deliberately misleading, so that the arrival of the leanly convoluted Parker-Gillespie melody is a surprise. Trombone and tenor solos unrelated to the theme follow, then an ensemble that launches Konitz's first recorded solo. Another ensemble brings in Galbraith, then the theme again. Evans's most significant contributions are the two band passages, and these, although brief, are again of indelible originality.

Besides more aggressive playing by Thornhill, the introduction to "Donna Lee" contains several elements and passes kaleidoscopically through various brief phases on the way to Davis's theme. The bop ensemble texture is once more suggested, but the trombone and tenor solos are still unidiomatic. A densely eventful, almost noisy, passage by the whole band leads in its quietest voice, the guitar, and the restated theme gives way to Evans's best surprise thus far, a coda that obliquely condenses the introduction. Galbraith is on all three bop themes better attuned to Evans's ventures than the other soloists, Konitz included, and we find here an amusing reversal of the situation that often prevailed in big jazz bands. With Fletcher Henderson, for example, the most advanced music came from the soloists, while the written passages, unless they were by Don Redman, lagged far behind. But in Thornhill's music the improvising of individual players seldom approached the powerful imagination informing the finest scores. However, in "Yardbird Suite" the solos better respond to their setting, and Evans in turn has grown bolder. The introduction, again with Thornhill prominent, achieves something like the maximum unpredictability, and as further surprise Parker's theme is heard from the full ensemble. Its shape is considerably modified in its final eight bars to bring in Konitz, who is followed by excellent Rodney, by a further ensemble, and then Galbraith. We expect the theme again, but it is alluded to, much varied, instead of being recapitulated.

In fact Evans's freely composed ensemble passages in the most adventurous of his Thornhill scores are never merely transitions from theme to solos or links between one solo and another. Rather, they are brief developments or explorations of the themes that suggest fascinating perspectives unlike any being investigated elsewhere and constituting what—with due regard to Eddie Sauter and a few others—was then the sole entirely original departure in big band jazz aside from Ellington's work. Certainly those who played his music had no doubt of its emotional impact and intellectual content.[8] Rodney said that Thornhill's was "the only band I can ever remember playing in where you could play a second or third trumpet part and chills would run up and down your spine because they were beautiful melodies in themselves."[9] And Steve Lacy, speaking of work in a later Evans band, said that "when things jelled, I felt true moments of ecstasy; and recently, when a friend of mine who worked with the Claude Thornhill Band in the forties, when Gil was the principal writer, said that some nights the sound of the band around him moved him to tears, I knew exactly what he meant."[10]

Short though such freely composed ensemble passages might be in the Thornhill years, they seemed to demonstrate George Russell's later dictum that "a jazz writer is an improviser, too."[11] The richness and strangeness of the new world uncovered by Evans at such times, amply confirmed by his Tchaikovsky, Mussorgsky, and Iradier essays, were the chief point, not his use of bop themes. At a later stage of his career, Evans returned to bop material, but it was no more his main line than it was Davis's, even if the latter was at this time involved with that style at the top level with Parker's quintet.[12]

Evans's being self-taught fitted cozily into the notion of jazz as simply an emanation of the artist's personality, spontaneous and natural. So did his accounts of listening to broadcasts of big bands, and above all to Armstrong and Ellington, during the Stockton days. Yet it accorded less well with jazz mythology that he worked long and hard to acquire his skills, still less that he spent much time studying classical music. He emphasized this, however, saying that he bought his first records of Ravel's music in 1935 in Stockton and that when he reached New York he was always not merely taking many orchestral scores out of the public library but making complete copies of them better to absorb the music. He particularly mentioned the French impressionists (especially Debussy and Ravel), nineteenth-century Russians (Mussorgsky), and Falla and Bloch, above all the latter's *Schelomo*, which "had a tremendous effect" on him in the 1930s and which he spoke of forty years later as "really full of the blues, yet from another culture."[13]

Such recollections are important because they reveal significant aspects of the background to Evans's musical thinking. True, there were always a few conventional devices in his writing, such as the use of French horns on sustained chords in middle and low register. Yet even these instruments were employed to memorably original effect in, say, "Lover Man," and most of his work for Thornhill, let alone with Davis or subsequently, at first seemed without roots in earlier procedures. Of necessity this was a passing illusion because all real art grows out of the past into the future. In his music, wide interests, and conversation, Evans perfectly illustrated a point that should be self-evident, namely, that jazz and the classics are irreconcilable only in the inflamed fancies of jazz fans, writers on jazz, and, alas, some jazz players. As the above comment on *Schelomo* hints, for Evans an apparent bridge between the two was the folk song of many lands and further aspects of what is now called "world music," something of which emerged in his collaborations with Davis.

Unaffected by the dividing lines that lesser men suppose to be ruled across the musical terrain, Evans entered highly differentiated and, seemingly, mutually exclusive worlds of sound. Looking through his discography, we notice that he worked on items by Huddie Ledbetter and John Lewis, by Delibes and Monk, by Mussorgsky and Chummy MacGregor. This argues a restless musical curiosity, a quality that all too many jazzmen lose when youth has passed but that Evans, like Davis, retained nearly all his artistic life. And this never resulted in a directionless eclecticism. An advantage of being self-instructed was that he was as untroubled by conventions of taste as by academic rules of technical procedure. The point of his treatments of Mussorgsky, Tchaikovsky, and Iradier for Thornhill— and of Falla, Rodrigo, and even Cyril Scott later—was not that they were transcendental instances of the normally trivial practice of jazzing the classics but that they were parts of Evans's ongoing demonstration of the essential oneness of music. Long ahead of anyone else in or out of jazz, he had arrived at what has since been defined as the postmodernist position, seeing all styles as currently valid and interrelated.

Not being anchored in any one branch of musical language and least of all in any one style, Evans, though often described as such, was almost of necessity *not* a composer. Even the few themes always attributed to him were actually by others, an example being "Blues for Pablo," which is based on an idea from Falla's ballet *El sombrero de tres picos* (1919) and a Mexican folk song collected by Carlos Chávez. Evans embodies the paradox of a man with real creative power, of great imaginative resource, who was unable to produce an original theme. He could, as it were, make the sturdiest oak trees tower above us, yet he had to be given an acorn first. Once this had set his imagination going, the invention mysteriously overflowed, and, rather in accord with his postmodernist position, it seemed to matter little whether his "found object" was a beautiful melody or a piece of commonplace figuration. Disconcertingly complete transformations would take place, turning the banal into the magical, uncovering relationships between passages of music that had seemed to be of utterly different character. Processes that may have appeared merely decorative were found to be working at much deeper levels. Russell's concept of the writer as improviser scarcely seems adequate, for Evans here approached a procedure virtually new to jazz, one that is most helpfully described as recomposition.

Recomposition amounts to a piece being deconstructed and its elements reassembled at a higher level of integration so that the whole takes on new and more complex meanings. Evans's chosen folk and popular songs, his jazz and classical themes were handled rather as Stravinsky reshaped Pergolesi in the ballet *Pulcinella* (1919–20). Pergolesi's rather simpleminded pieces are still recognizable, but something fundamental has happened to them: they have been possessed from within. Plainly we are remote from the formulaic application of a mechanical device in the manner of a Glenn Miller, for each Evans recomposition was a special case, evolving its own procedures, following its own laws. This is why, the large quantity of music produced in the Thornhill years notwithstanding, he always worked slowly, and as his processes became more individuated, during the collaborations with Davis and beyond, he tended to need more and more time. He put it in his usual down-to-earth way: "I have more craft and speed than I sometimes want to admit. I want to avoid getting into a rut. I can't keep doing the same thing over and over."[14]

Such an outlook was rare in the dance band business, and according to another of the group's arrangers, Bill Borden, Evans's creativity sapped Thornhill's self-confidence.[15] Probably Evans had done all that he could with the band, and in 1948 he left. But that was the year in which, at Evans's urging, Gerry Mulligan joined. Thornhill continued adding jazz to his band's repertoire via such Mulligan scores as "Elevation," "Jeru," and "Godchild," and we shall meet the last two again soon. Meanwhile "Godchild" had roaring performances from the band, demonstrating that Evans in later years presented a jaundiced view of its activities.[16] Comments such as "the band could put you to sleep" and "the sound hung like a cloud" were quoted widely and have become the established latter-day view of Thornhill's ensemble, to which recordings like the 1948 "Godchild" provide a necessary corrective.[17]

Davis had caught the true drift of events the previous year, however, and decades later made the significant remark on his time with Parker's quintet that he was always "interested in developing the band's sound."[18] This in contrast with its leader, who never saw it as more than a fairly casual framework for improvising. And certainly on the first recording session under Davis's name, for Savoy, the Evans-Thornhill influence went some way to supplant the Parker-bop one, even though Parker took part. The latter's quintet seldom rehearsed, whereas Davis called two full rehearsals prior to his date, and the music placed greater emphasis on ensembles, which he had quite elaborately scored, than on solos. The closely worked textures are reflected at the harmonic level, the twelve-bar theme of "Sippin' at Bell's," for instance, containing eighteen chord changes. This is remote from Davis's later stress on space and uncluttered structures, while Parker being on tenor instead of alto underscored the ensemble's weight. More revealing than specific details, though, was the session's entire climate, this being sufficiently divergent from that of bop to be surprising for August 1947.

This, and soon much else, arose not only from musical considerations but out of a social situation that again had Evans at its center. Or rather the center was his one-room basement apartment on 55th Street. This has been described sufficiently often in the anecdotal literature for it to take on the legendary status required of any place that is to survive in the so-called history of jazz. Evans kept open house, and his room was frequented by the brighter of those who worked in the clubs three blocks south on 52nd Street. A few, such as Parker and Gillespie, had already won lasting fame, and a remarkable number of the rest, among them John Lewis, Mulligan, Russell, Konitz, as well as Davis, would soon do so. In his *Autobiography*, Davis repeats almost word for word Russell's description of this haven, and both in particular speak of Evans being "like a mother hen to all of us."[19] Rejecting swing and its embodiment of the American entertainment industry's corrupt values, each was seeking a personal direction in the new jazz of that time, and Evans, considerably older than them, had already found one, as brilliantly demonstrated in the best of the Thornhill band's repertoire.

Here the point was not so much orchestral virtuosity as a fusion of an original instrumentation with Evans's innovative harmony.[20] This departed considerably from conventional jazz practice in terms of chord construction, voicing, progression, and textural density. And his approach was essentially polyphonic, the simultaneous movement of his lines, besides obviously itself giving rise to harmony, also aiding his discovery of many original textures. Was it now possible to take this further, in a more consistently jazz ambience than would ever be viable for Thornhill's large band? Was it conceivable that Evans's elaborate and subtle harmonizations and unprecedented instrumental mixtures could be reproduced by a smaller ensemble without losing their richness of expression?

The band that evolved out of tireless conversations in that room behind a Chinese laundry had predictable affiliations. When the band came to broadcast from the Royal Roost and record for Capitol, the personnel always included Konitz, Mulligan, and Barber and on occasion Sandy Siegelstein (French horn) and Joe Shulman (bass), all of them members of the Thornhill ensemble. And Davis's playing took on a rather flugelhorn-like tone that resembled the sound of such a lead trumpeter as Thornhill's Louis Mucci. But obviously it went further than that, and although Evans and Mulligan paid generous tribute to Davis for getting the band together, prompting others to compose for it, and organizing rehearsals and even some performances in public, it was they who hammered out a nine-piece instrumentation able to distill the Thornhill sounds and textures. Davis in turn acknowledged Mulligan's crucial insistence on Konitz for the alto chair over his own choice of Sonny Stitt, who, despite the contributions of Lewis, George Wallington, and John Carisi, would have unduly strengthened the group's bop orientation.[21]

For this was a new stylistic development, the first in jazz since bop, and the music was both progressive and backward-looking. Indeed, one of the most celebrated of the studio recordings, "Boplicity," jointly composed by Davis and Evans and scored by the latter, is, with its twisting, turning melodic line clothed in quiet, grave colors, almost a commentary on 1940s bop from the viewpoint of the cool 1950s jazz to come. Rhythmically conservative, the nonet's music lacked the aggressive thrust of bop while offering a more oblique tension, the pleasures of understatement and of an altogether different kind of sophistication. Bop produced excellent themes, yet they occupied little time in most performances in that style, whereas this fresh initiative, while finding plenty of room for solos, always made them parts of a greater whole. This sort of integration, familiar in Morton and Ellington, was new to postwar jazz. Only in this sense can Davis's later claim that the nonet's repertoire was "heavily influenced by

Duke Ellington" be justified.[22] This was, almost uniquely, a jazz movement started by composers (and one recomposer).

The nonet had two separate engagements in August and September 1948 and broadcast in both weeks. Recordings from these only became available during the 1970s, offering previously unheard accounts of "Godchild," "Move," "Darn That Dream," two each of "Budo" and "Moon Dreams," and a couple of items hitherto unknown, "S'il vous plaît" and "Why Do I Love You?" These display new strengths and weaknesses, but it is undeniably instructive to hear these pieces, mostly long familiar from the 1949–50 studio recordings, in a variety of fresh perspectives arising through shifts in recording balance. The broadcasts have a spontaneity sometimes lacking at the Capitol sessions, but, contrary to the assumption of much commentary on jazz, spontaneity is not everything. Piano, bass, and tuba are not much heard from the Royal Roost, and we must assume these performances do not fully represent the composers' and arrangers' intentions. In contrast, the finely nuanced studio "Moon Dreams," for example, gives a more sharply focused idea of Evans's thinking than either of the broadcasts, and more is made of its pointillist ending.

Although the broadcasts show the Roost to have been very noisy sometimes, little is known about the audience for Davis's band, although Count Basie, also playing at the Roost, sat and listened to the band repeatedly, as did Pete Rugolo. The latter offered the recording contract without which this music would now be as indistinct a legend as that of Buddy Bolden's outfit. The group caught by the broadcasts was as originally conceived by Davis, Evans, and Mulligan in 1948, whereas the Capitol sessions of the two following years really were re-creations with different personnel each time. The Capitol sessions are dealt with elsewhere in this volume, but a few points may be added in the light of information that has only emerged recently concerning, for example, the absence of any of Evans's scores from the first session. This, recalled Davis, was "because Pete Rugolo wanted to record the faster and medium-tempo tunes first."[23] In fact "Moon Dreams," as thoroughgoing a transformation of a sentimental ballad as can be found in jazz recordings, had to wait till the final date of March 1950. In this piece, blending of the six horns is weighty yet always supple, and although Davis, Konitz, and Mulligan each take the lead briefly, the ensemble, remote from the virtuoso excursions of bop, is always king. Very subtle chord substitutions are often suggested, it seems, by the essential linearity of Evans's discourse, the number of real parts usually being four or five but occasionally three or six. The effect of unified variety is again achieved mainly through contrapuntal thinking, with the role of each instrument changing quite often. Here, if anywhere, "the sound hangs like a cloud," and to indelible effect.

Given the sustained attention this music received in jazz commentary, it is not surprising that several compositions and arrangements have been misattributed. For instance, the Davis-Evans "Boplicity" was credited both to Lewis and to Mulligan,[24] while "S'il vous plaît," which seems obviously Lewis's work, has been attributed to Davis and to Mulligan. Likewise, the arrangement of Bud Powell's "Budo" (alias "Hallucinations") was credited to Evans, although surely by Lewis. "Deception," from the last session, is the sole nonet piece signed by Davis alone as composer, but it is clearly a reworking of Shearing's "Conception" (recorded by him in 1949). And a Davis sextet in February 1950 broadcast a performance of "Conception" from Birdland in an arrangement by Davis plainly influenced by Evans. A disputed case is "Darn That Dream" featuring Kenny Hagood, whose warbling remained the band's only concession to the facile appeal of popular music. This has always sounded like Evans's work to this writer and was assumed to be such in *Down Beat*'s review of the original issue though long claimed by Mulligan.[25] Again, the other vocal accompaniment, "Why Do I Love You?" is also claimed as Mulligan's but sounds even more like Evans, starting with the introduction. The trumpet lead is over the kind of shifting texture recognizable from his Thornhill work, and a brief yet imaginative transition brings us to Davis's solo. Wooden singing from Hagood focuses attention on a carefully worked accompaniment that flows into one of those developmental passages for full ensemble of exactly the kind Evans wrote for Thornhill. Easily the best part of the performance, this ends with a short reference to Kern's melody.

In 1954 Capitol issued eight of the band's studio performances as a ten-inch LP titled *Birth of the Cool*. This had "Jeru," "Godchild," "Israel," and "Venus de Milo," hitherto available only as 78s, plus "Rouge," "Deception," "Moon Dreams," and "Rocker," which had not been available before. Three other pieces, "Move," "Budo," and "Boplicity," had appeared on various Capitol anthologies, and these eleven items were not put together until *Birth of the Cool* was reissued as a twelve-inch LP some years later. "Darn That Dream" was still missing, and the full dozen titles were united only in 1971 (!) in Holland as an LP called *The Complete Birth of the Cool*. Despite *The Real Birth of the Cool* being rather pointedly used for a fine LP of Thornhill performances (CBS/Sony) and a CD of the Roost broadcasts (Bandstand), Capitol's collective title has been almost unanimously accepted even though it has no justification. Jazz that may be described as cool had been heard from such players as Benny Carter, Lester Young, Teddy Wilson, Frankie Trumbauer, and Arthur Whetsol all the way back to Johnny O'Donnell with the Georgians in the early 1920s. Cool jazz was not introduced by Davis, Evans, or even Thornhill.

Yet the history books have decided that the nonet and with it cool jazz were almost entirely Davis-Evans initiatives. The part of Mulligan—who, by no means incidentally, lived at Gil Evans's place during the crucial period—has been minimized by jazz commentary on the nonet, rather like that of Bill Evans in *Kind of Blue*. But Mulligan's role—with the compositions "Jeru," "Venus de Milo," and "Rocker" and his arrangement of George Wallington's "Godchild," a scaling-down of the score he had written for Thornhill—and his playing were more central than is now admitted. Mulligan was also the only one to take the nonet's initiatives further in the immediate future, with his tentet recordings of "Rocker" and "Ontet" (alias "Godchild") and later with his concert jazz band, which recorded "Israel," etc. This latter ensemble extended the nonet's procedures in a way quite different from that eventually heard when Davis and Evans came together again, yet still viable.

The entire question of our response to the nonet's dozen studio performances was complicated by Mulligan's producing new recordings in 1992. If the recording process is a method for stopping time, a project like this is perhaps a way of starting it again. A few stolid eccentrics have complained that many nuances, and even actual details, are different. Yet how could it be otherwise? The players, including the survivors from the original dates—Lewis, Barber, and Mulligan himself—have inevitably been affected by much of what has happened in jazz during the passing decades. Exact reproductions would be pointless even if they were possible. What matters is that the values and meanings of these compositions and arrangements perfectly well survive all changes of emphasis. Comparisons between the two sets of interpretations are fascinating and can produce a very complex balance of gains and losses, but one clear advance is with "Darn That Dream." Mel Tormé takes Hagood's place and shows incomparably more sensitivity and accomplishment, melting into the score's texture in a way surely closer to the arranger's intentions. A pity Mulligan did not also undertake "S'il vous plaît" and "Why Do I Love You?"

That Davis's playing was stylistically inconsistent in those early days is proved by his work at the Salle Pleyel, Paris, in May 1949, between his second and third Capitol sessions. Recordings issued twenty-eight years later show this to have been aggressively boppish and hence very different not only from what he did with the nonet but also from Tadd Dameron's 1949 Roost broadcasts and studio dates. It could be argued that the nonet provided the most apt setting Davis had found thus far, even that he would not find a better one until he and Evans came together again. The truth is, of course, that like any great artist, Davis had a variety of things to express and hence needed to explore other avenues. But the nonet's music did arise out of the depth of his abilities, made his first independent mark as a trumpeter, stylistic innovator, and bandleader, and was the necessary prelude to the milestone achievements with Evans that lay ahead.

At about this time Davis's and Evans's paths diverged, and the former's exploits are dealt with elsewhere in this volume. Evans sank to obscurity as a freelance arranger in New York, doing work for radio, television, and nightclubs, a little jazz writing for Mulligan and Goodman, isolated pieces on memorable LPs by Teddy Charles and Hal McKusick, and a single date with Parker that was no credit to either musician. The reunion of our two protagonists for a major project had three preliminary moves, one each by Davis and by Evans and one involving both of them. Davis's soloing, with flugelhorn and trumpet, on October 1956 recordings by the ensemble of the Jazz and Classical Music Society in a *Music for Brass* LP placed him with the largest group in which he can have played since his days with Billy Eckstine. This organization was headed by Gunther Schuller (who conducted) and John Lewis, and the pieces on which Davis was heard are Lewis's "Three Little Feelings" and J. J. Johnson's "Poem for Brass." These fine performances are outside the scope of this essay,[26] but they show Davis well able to relate to a big ensemble both emotionally and musically. His playing in Lewis's second movement especially points to what he would soon be doing with Evans.

Some of Evans's writing had lately been for superior vocalists such as Helen Merrill, who went through considerable trouble with her record company to use Evans on an LP she made in June 1956. The results were outstanding, however, and she told many people about Evans, including Davis, saying he really should play some of Evans's music. Later Davis claimed that he and Evans had "seen each other occasionally" during those years,[27] whereas according to Miss Merrill, he said, "Well, yeah, I forgot about Gil; and I think I'll give him a call."[28] We cannot complain about this because the rest of us had likewise forgotten Evans. Or if we remembered him from the Thornhill days, we tended, absurdly, to think of him as a figure of the 1940s. A contributory factor was that the notion of jazz as a young man's music still had some currency, and in 1956 Evans was all of forty-four!

Evans and Davis did come together between the Merrill and *Music for Brass* sessions, and in September the trumpeter's quintet, then probably the most prominent band in jazz, recorded "'Round Midnight" in an Evans arrangement. He gave it a simple, though telling, three-part form with the slow and quiet outer section finding Davis, muted, improvising on Monk's theme with supporting tenor saxophone phrases. The central section is a two-chorus vehicle for Coltrane at twice the tempo, and the ensemble passages are brief yet striking. Having played together for some time, this band's members were thoroughly familiar with one another, and Evans adeptly took advantage of this. Having recorded his reading of Monk's piece for Columbia in September 1956, Davis played it a month later for Prestige. Given Evans's modesty, a rare quality in a sphere where almost everyone has a high opinion of him- or herself, his involvement went unmentioned for several years. Those of us acquainted with his Thornhill work might have suspected something if we had heard the LPs by Helen Merrill (EmArcy), Lucy Reed (Fantasy), and Marcy Lutes (Decca) for which he lately had written, but these issues received no attention and were poorly distributed—none of them appearing in Europe, for instance.

The fact remains that the partnership of Davis and Evans on "'Round Midnight" was an encouraging glimpse of the future, and they evidently started planning their forthcoming collaboration at the time of these Columbia and Prestige sessions. They would have used the Capitol nonet music as a partial starting point, since both sensed there was more to be done in that direction. Then Evans and the other composers had nine players including Davis at their disposal, whereas now he had Davis plus eighteen. The larger instrumentation was a thoughtful extension of the nonet (which had been a condensation of Thornhill's): five trumpets, three trombones, bass trombone, two French horns, tuba, two clarinets doubling flutes, bass clarinet, alto saxophone, bass, drums. This departs further from convention than the nonet, especially regarding Evans's drastic revision of the reed section.

Again, the repertoire only arises partly out of that of the nonet, and the selection of ten pieces ranges as widely as Evans's interest would lead us to expect. Only two items can be taken as in any sense backward glances, "Springsville" by John Carisi (who wrote "Israel" for the nonet) and Delibes's "The Maids of Cadiz," an echo of Evans's classical essays for Thornhill. The LP took its title from Davis's "Miles Ahead," a different work, with Evans now listed as co-composer, from the piece of the same name he first recorded in 1953. Of Evans's own thematic contribution, "Blues for Pablo," more below. Other prominent jazz figures are represented by J. J. Johnson's "Lament" and Brubeck's "The Duke," more conventional material for jazz treatment by Weill's "My Ship" and Troup's "The Meaning of the Blues." "I Don't Wanna Be Kissed" may seem a poor ending, but 1957 was a year for lame finales: consider the "Circle of Fourths" close to Ellington's *Such Sweet Thunder*. Serious triviality enters only with "New Rhumba," the one piece that compels strenuous objection, although this is not the place to discuss Ahmad Jamal's deplorable influence on Davis.[29]

The seeming randomness of this selection may even have been deliberate, seeking to prove that Evans's processes of recomposition could transform *any* musical material, from the best to the most abysmal, and discover productive relationships between these extremes. As we pass through his work chronologically, a drive toward the integration of all elements was for a long time apparent, taking further the parallel with Ellington's finest work that emerged in the Thornhill days (until derailed by Evans's involvement with rock). Hence, it is not always easy in *Miles Ahead* to decide where one piece ends and another begins. Speaking of great improvisers of earlier generations, Evans said, "They never could think of the kind of settings they really needed,"[30] but he and his soloist were determined that it should now be different, and each piece is a miniature concerto for Davis. Beyond that, this was an unusually large design for jazz in the 1950s, and the ten pieces fused into a continuous aural panorama whose expressive resonance gained with each addition.

Although Evans was to go further, his scores for *Miles Ahead* embody the late ripening of his powers, and in elaboration and diversity of resource, they surpass anything previously attempted in big band jazz. The unorthodox instrumentation is handled with a freedom and plasticity surpassed only in a few nonjazz composers such as Messiaen, Boulez, Stockhausen, and Babbitt. With Evans, as with Ellington at his best—and with precious few others in jazz—one feels that the music and orchestration were conceived together. In any given chord, sensitive consideration is given to what is the best instrument to sound each constituent note. The weight of that instrument is calculated in relation both to the others used and to the effect the chord is meant to have. All this is allied to a continuing flow of invention. One might have thought that few instrumental combinations remained to be discovered, but Evans, building on his achievement with Thornhill, hit upon endless mixtures that were, at least, extremely unfamiliar.

From amid so much teeming detail, one can only comment at random, though it should be noticed, for example, in "My Ship," how thoroughgoing his reharmonizations sometimes are, not least with regard to harmonic rhythm. In "Blues for Pablo," observe that besides the conflict between the two themes, a milder conflict develops between symmetry and asymmetry via Evans's occasional departures from the four-bar phrase. Another aspect is the highly irregular way that, as in other Evans scores, dominant colors change. Nothing could be further from the predictable shifts of texture and color—dependent on the obvious subdivisions of the blues and the thirty-two-bar song forms—of conventional big band jazz. Another conflict in "Blues for Pablo" is between bass plus drums and the double-time of the orchestra. Indeed the use of bass clarinet, tuba, and string bass is crucial because the bass line, which Evans normally makes very flexible, always has an important role in his music, and it became ever more part of the overall musical fabric. In fact the hilarious accusations of a supposed lack of rhythmic life launched when *Miles Ahead* first appeared were offered by people deaf to the bass line's rhythmic independence, to its developing in highly unpredictable ways, often dialoguing with the melody, sometimes antiphonally.

Davis would soon give a comparable emphasis to the bass in his combo music, but meanwhile it needs to be said that the orchestra's role in his collaborations with Evans obviously should not be considered in isolation. "Blues for Pablo" was transposed up a minor third from its initial recording by Hal McKusick, and while this no doubt was done to take advantage of the upper register of instruments available on the later occasion, it adds to the intensity of the solo flugelhorn passages. A brilliant aspect of Evans's achievement here is that while giving full rein to his own gifts, he wrote settings that were almost eerily precise extensions of the soloist's lyricism. Although Davis's playing is sometimes sharply exposed, as in "The Maids of Cadiz," while in other passages he leads the ensemble, as in "The Duke," his lines are best heard as the most prominent thread in the tonal fabric. Responding to the orchestra's commentary, his sound is full, warm, and of the most varied nuance. But more central is the inner correspondence between the two guiding spirits of this life-enhancing music, the whole being suffused with an alchemy arising out of one of the great partnerships of jazz. "If you're ever depressed, Miles, just listen to 'Springsville,' " said Evans on telephoning Davis at three o'clock one morning, and this is good advice for the rest of us, too.[31]

Yet nothing is perfect. Evans's scores, for this or for any other of his undertakings, have never been available, and so no finally authoritative assessment is possible on the quality of the performances they received. But there are questions to be asked about the textural balance at some points in *Miles Ahead*, about how well some of the musicians understood what they were playing—one of the flutists especially—about the drummer (Art Taylor), and about how much rehearsal there was.[32] Yet the commercial and even artistic success of *Miles Ahead* put Evans on the map, and he was able to make some records of his own at last. They are beyond the scope of this essay, but two from the years 1958–59 should be mentioned in passing, not least because we can regard them, rather than anything he did with Davis, as giving the fullest expression to his powers.

The first was titled *New Bottle, Old Wine* on the sleeve and *Old Bottle, New Wine* on the label. This latter was correct, of course, because the bottles were indeed familiar, ranging from Morton's "King Porter Stomp" to Parker's "Bird Feathers," yet Evans gave them almost disquietingly new contents. The main soloist was Cannonball Adderley, a Parker disciple playing at his best, and these performances offer a potent hint of what might have happened had Evans and Parker recorded together as they—at different times—wanted to. *Great Jazz Standards* ranges even more widely through jazz history, and the execution of Evans's scores on both records appears superlative. There is no sign of the problems that had affected *Miles Ahead* and that would loom considerably larger in his next project with Davis.

Although it proved highly advantageous to Evans and Davis, *Porgy and Bess*, unlike *Miles Ahead*, was not entirely their idea. It began as simply one of many LPs of music from Gershwin's opera that were the record industry's response to what for the period was an unusual amount of public relations activity surrounding the release of Samuel Goldwyn's film. The difference was that the Davis-Evans recording proved far superior to the rest.

As before *Miles Ahead*, there were preliminaries, most especially a session in which Davis took part a month before the *Porgy and Bess* dates began in July 1958, this being with the French composer and arranger Michel Legrand, who was then visiting New York. It reminds us of something forgotten by those puritanical enthusiasts for hard bop who condemned the Capitol nonet and Davis's partnership with Evans, considering that he should have played only with small groups. This was his abiding interest in big bands of which the Evans sessions were only one expression. Witness the large ensemble, reportedly of eighteen pieces, that he co-led with Dameron after returning from Paris in 1949 but that never got past the rehearsal stage. In later years, too, there were several reports of plans, always abortive, of forming a regular big band with Evans. Although the Legrand date is outside this essay's scope, it is interesting to compare Davis's playing in Evans's 1956 arrangement of "'Round Midnight" for the quintet with the Legrand version, where he uses some of the same phrases but to rather different effect. As in his work for the Jazz and Classical Music Society and with Evans, Davis again shows himself well able to adjust and respond to a large nonstandard ensemble, and his playing on Lewis's "Django" with Legrand confirms this.

Gershwin's best music is in *Porgy and Bess*, and Evans needed to make fewer local changes than when tackling lesser material. Reportedly the players at the sessions exclaimed over harmonies—for example, in "My Man's Gone Now"—that were Gershwin's rather than by Evans. Yet always there are exceptions, and the score's most famous number, "Summertime," is turned from a dreamy lullaby into something oblique, nearly laconic, almost stoical. And this piece is a reminder that some of Evans's reharmonizations are highly effective simplifications. As Davis said: "There is a long space where we don't change the chord at all. It just doesn't have to be cluttered up."[33] Most of the other set pieces are here (not all), but Davis and Evans take them in a different sequence. There should be no objection to this, for Gershwin's own orchestral *Catfish Row* suite does not follow the dramatic order, and this happened with concert abstracts from other operas, for instance, Berg's *Lulu* suite.

Such new sequences are seldom arbitrary, however, and the chosen segments of Gershwin's score are here reorchestrated by Evans and improvised on by Davis in such probing ways that new musical and dramatic relationships, meanings, and tensions emerge. Cross-references between "Gone" and "There's a Boat That's Leaving Soon for New York" or between "I Loves You, Porgy" and "Bess, You Is My Woman Now" are merely external signs of a reordering that has taken place at a much deeper level. From "My Man's Gone Now" to "There's a Boat," the emotional range is wide, and in "Prayer"—which has no proper harmonic movement at all—Davis sounds like a preacher with a highly responsive congregation.[34]

Perhaps the full implications can only be grasped by those who are thoroughly acquainted with Gershwin's original. Possibly the ideal experience, undergone several times by this writer, is to hear *Porgy and Bess* in the opera house then go home and listen to Davis's and Evans's enlighteningly different view of the music.

Porgy and Bess remained their most ambitious undertaking. The attempting of such heights exacts a price, and comparison with the sole plausible rival is instructive. This is Bill Potts's *The Jazz Soul of Porgy and Bess*. Such ought to have been the title of the Davis-Evans record, yet Potts offers the virtual reverse image of what they did. He responded to Gershwin's almost Schubertian outpouring of melody with primary colors, huge energy; and whereas Evans's acutely sensitive, tirelessly inventive scores were performed disappointingly, Potts's penny plain thoughts were played superbly. Such is the reward of presenting a straight-ahead jazz blow on some excellent tunes rather than a poetic commentary on an opera. The former was handled with ferocious efficiency, whereas the latter courted many problems. This identification of extremes should imply no simple situation, however, as is hinted by the magnificent performances Evans obtained on *Old Bottle, New Wine*, etc.

Although the brass bites harder than on *Miles Ahead*, there is no question that the *Porgy and Bess* scores were often less than adequately delivered. An inside view was given in a letter to this writer by one of the musicians who took part in these sessions:

> The crux of the matter is that Gil, on both sets of dates, did not rehearse carefully enough, as is already evident on *Miles Ahead*. I believe this is mostly the result of the unfortunate conditions under which American recording is done. It is too costly for any project of more than average difficulty to be done well, unless the music in question is rehearsed before the date (which is illegal according to union rules) or has been previously performed.

> Under these, to say the least, less than ideal circumstances, both Miles and Gil have a too relaxed attitude about accomplishing the tasks they set themselves. In pieces which are scored as sensitively and as intricately as Gil's, it's a shame to let the performances cancel out half of their effectiveness. Many details of scoring simply could not be—or at least were not—touched upon in the sessions I was on. Some things were left undone which *I* would not have let go.

> But, as I've indicated, the blame lies more with the conditions than the people. And I suppose one could say that it's remarkable that both LPs are

as good as they are. If Gil were a better conductor, it would help: he sometimes confused the players. On the other hand, he's quite patient— perhaps too much so for his own good—and very pleasant to work for. Whatever excellence these recordings possess I would attribute (aside from Gil's own magnificent scores, of course) primarily to the supreme abilities of the leading players, like Ernie Royal, Bill Barber, and the very fine reedmen (on all manner of flutes and bass clarinets), and in general the respect which all of us, despite what I've said above, have for Gil Evans.

Further points are that Gil is more apt to check the tempo with Miles than vice versa! And Miles in listening to the playbacks is almost exclusively concerned with eliminating takes with trumpet wrong notes and is very self-conscious about this in front of other musicians—understandably, I think.[35]

Twenty years later Evans confirmed some of this in typically laconic fashion: "One more session would have cleared up most of the clinkers. Looking back on it, I'm outraged at myself for not sticking up for my rights."[36] Given the power and beauty of his *Porgy and Bess* recomposi- tions, it is confusing to think that what we have may be no more than a smudged glimpse of Evans's real intentions. Ideally what ought to happen with such ventures is what sometimes happens when a major symphony orchestra is about to record a large classical work. Namely, they give several public performances of it in rapid succession and only then go into the recording studio. But it is impossible to imagine such circumstances occurring with a big jazz piece. The only way that we might ever discover what else lies beneath the surface of Evans's imperfectly interpreted writings would be if his scores were recovered and played by a thoroughly rehearsed jazz repertoire ensemble. And that again seems most unlikely. Davis and Evans did eventually give a concert, but it was long after these recordings appeared. Meanwhile, they did better on their final major project.

Once again there were some prefatory moves, notably a television appearance in April 1959 on which Davis played "So What" with his quintet and, with an Evans orchestra whose personnel had at least some links with that heard on the record, three sections of *Miles Ahead*. These were "The Duke," "Blues for Pablo," and "New Rhumba." Obvious losses result from these being torn out of context, but the comparisons are sometimes reveal- ing. The television performances are more decisive, occasionally with better separation between individual lines of the textures. They are the only evidence available thus far that obliquely supports what is said in the letter quoted above. The 1957 recordings *do* lack some focus, and there are hints in the television versions that it might well have been possible to interpret the *Miles Ahead* scores differently, let alone the *Porgy and Bess* ones.

Also noteworthy is how well the music of quintet and orchestra accorded on this occasion. This casts doubt on the claim that with Davis's combo work "a very different aesthetic was involved" from that of the larger group.[37]

As with *Porgy and Bess*, the impulse for the last great Davis-Evans achievement was not theirs. Davis attributed it to Joe Mondragon, who drew his attention to *Concierto de Aranjuez*.[38] This guitar concerto, written in 1939 by the prolific yet obscure Valencian composer Joaquín Rodrigo, proved to be the jewel in the crown of *Sketches of Spain*, although it was at first misjudged, not least by this writer. This is not surprising, since Evans turned the slow movement of this work into something disconcertingly at variance with the composer's initial patently lightweight intentions—somber, almost majestic, and a thoroughgoing instance of the Davis-Evans alchemy.

Concierto de Aranjuez was recorded in November 1959, and three days of recording were needed to produce the version of *Concierto* eventually issued. We can presumably conclude that the results are much closer to Evans's orchestral intentions than on *Miles Ahead* and especially *Porgy and Bess*. Nat Hentoff, not a musician, was at one of the dates and said Evans insisted "on hearing exactly what he [had] written."[39] The problems were partly a matter of shifting textures, although Davis provided, despite the elaboration of Evans's writing, the main line of continuity. He did not attend the first date, although he was present at the next two. According to Teo Macero, most of what appeared on the LP came from the final date. The trumpeter referred to tape splicings here as well as on *Porgy and Bess*,[40] and *Concierto* was apparently put together from two or three different takes—a common procedure with classical recordings, of course.

Several pieces were needed to companion this Rodrigo transformation, and these take further the tendencies first made apparent in Evans's music with "La paloma." But they were specifically a result of his recent study of flamenco, in which he later said he had soaked himself, allowing it to take possession of him.[41] Davis relates to these, as to the Rodrigo, remarkably well for one so insular. Not so much to "Will o' the Wisp" from Falla's ballet *El amor brujo* (1915), but to "Solea" and "Saeta," the distinctly flamenco items. He presumably would have accounted for this with something on the lines of "Spain's close to Africa."

Percussion is more prominent than usual in Evans's music, and two rhythms, one flamenco and one jazz, alternate in "Solea" and symbolize the forces shaping *Sketches of Spain*. "Solea" derives from the Andalusian version of a Spanish word, *soledad*, meaning solitude, and this kind of flamenco has been defined as "a plaintive song of sorrow and loneliness."[42] In "Saeta" Davis starts with flamenco and moves toward blues rather than jazz; the music somehow becomes a Spanish blues. This is a jazz impression of the Good Friday procession in Seville also portrayed in the *Fête-Dieu à Seville* movement of Albéniz's great *Iberia* piano cycle. The procession halts at a balcony where a flamenco singer addresses the image of Christ, and whereas in Andalusia the singer expresses communal grief and remorse, Davis is more subjective, personal.[43] He is very exposed here and improvises with a passion that at least equals the most affecting passages in *Porgy and Bess* or in any of his other records.

Evans on his own took the matter of Spain further, particularly in a record with Kenny Burrell titled *Guitar Forms* and above all in "Lotus Land," a piano miniature by the English composer Cyril Scott that is transmuted into an Iberian dream for guitar and jazz orchestra. Lotus Land, indeed, but not Davis. It was as if he had given too much raw emotion for one who liked to think of himself, or who liked others to believe him, very cool. He said: "I didn't have *nothing* inside me. I was drained of all emotion."[44] And it may be no coincidence that he was not seen in any recording studio for a full year after recording "Solea" and "Saeta."

Although they could not be aware of the fact, Davis's and Evans's main achievements now lay behind them, and they offered what in retrospect seems like a postscript. In May 1961 they gave a concert, and while those present insist this was a memorable occasion, its preservation on disc makes it seem like a badly botched affair. In truth it was the first step downhill. It might have been hoped that they would present the complete music of *Miles Ahead*, *Porgy and Bess*, or *Sketches of Spain*, or perhaps two of them, but instead they played little more than bits and pieces of the first and last with Davis's quintet filling in the rest of the time. An LP titled *Miles Davis at Carnegie Hall* had Evans's orchestra in "The Meaning of the Blues," "Lament," and the inevitable "New Rhumba." The orchestra played an introduction and final cadence to the quintet's "So What" and an effective background for Davis on "Spring Is Here." This was the only new orchestral material, although again quintet and orchestra chimed well together. In 1987 came *Miles Davis: More from the Legendary Carnegie*

Hall Concert, which added *Concierto de Aranjuez,* now pointlessly divided into two parts, plus more quintet pieces. It still is instructive to compare these new accounts of *Miles Ahead* excerpts with the 1957 originals, this suggesting further thoughts on how the scores might have been interpreted. Always, it seems, Evans was searching, reaching for something more than what he had in his head, let alone what he had put on paper.

That this search might occasionally reach a dead end was shown by what happened next. Before the Carnegie Hall concert, Davis had said: "Gil and I are interested in doing an African ballet album. I think that will be the next direction."[45] But this was only the first of a series of projects that got no further than the talking, and the same fate would best have served *Quiet Nights.* If this record is the great disappointment of the Davis-Evans canon, it is because compromises were involved of a sort that one then would have believed foreign to both Evans and Davis, although, in view of their later separate involvements with rock, that was naive. The bossa nova was a hugely popular fad of the sort that periodically afflicts popular music, and insofar as jazz could be made out of it, this was best done by such players as Stan Getz. Ironically, the clueless and anonymous liner notes to *Quiet Nights* open by quoting Delacroix's "talent does what it wants to do," since Davis later said: "I didn't really feel nothing about the music we did on this album. I knew I wasn't into what we were doing like I had been in the past."[46] The assertion in the liner notes that this was the first bossa nova record made in the United States was patently false, as was the claim that it was "three years in the making," for it was patched together from various sessions in 1962.

Typical was "Song No. 2," which has an undistinguished ten-bar phrase played and repeated by the orchestra and heard once from Davis; a harp cadenza follows, and that is all. This suggests the music's general air of helplessness and also signals a slackening of creative tension after the indisputable artistic and eventual commercial success of their previous collaborations. It may seem curious that Evans in particular, after the trouble he had taken with *Sketches of Spain,* was so offhand, but clearly his heart was no more in *Quiet Nights* than was Davis's, and they abandoned it before completion. No matter how furious this might have made Davis, Columbia cannot be blamed for issuing what they had gotten so as to recover the cost of expensive sessions, and Evans virtually acknowledged this.[47]

In the midst of the *Quiet Nights* dates came the danger sign of a pair of faintly absurd Davis combo sessions devoted to pieces by Bob Dorough, a singer of almost spectacular unsuitability for any band of the trumpeter's.

He is heard on "Blue Xmas" and "Nothing Like You." Evans is alleged to have scored the instrumental "Devil May Care," although it cannot have cost him much effort. Nor could the bossa nova arrangements he scribbled in 1965 for Astrud Gilberto, these sounding like the work of an ordinary commercial arranger making a bad job of imitating Gil Evans.

In 1966 Evans put together what on paper looked like an excellent band with Johnny Coles, Billy Harper, Howard Johnson, Elvin Jones, and others to play the Monterey Jazz Festival. They fulfilled a few other engagements, but after that the music was not heard of again, except that in October 1966 Davis recorded what may have been a scaling-down of Evans's arrangement of "Freedom Jazz Dance." In September 1963 Davis and Evans devoted two weeks to concentrated work on music for Peter Barnes's comedy *The Time of the Barracudas*, and although union complications prevented its use in the theater, they did record it, in Hollywood.[48] According to Davis a full orchestra was employed,[49] but it seems they actually had the intriguing mixture of four woodwinds, three French horns, bass trombone, harp, the Hancock-Carter-Williams rhythm section, and Davis himself. Fragments of this score were elsewhere recorded by Evans on his own, including "Flute Song," "Hotel Me," and "Barracudas," retitled "General Assembly"; and he later made other recordings of these, for example, of "Hotel Me" with the all-British group with which he toured the United Kingdom in 1983. Another piece from their *Time of the Barracudas* score, "Petits Machins" (alias "Little Stuff"), was recorded by Davis's quintet in 1968 on his *Filles de Kilimanjaro* LP, although neither he nor Columbia showed any inclination to acknowledge Evans's part in it, and the information only came out by chance years later. Again Evans's modesty had done him no good, though he recorded this piece himself in 1974 on the Atlantic *Svengali* LP, duly crediting Davis as co-composer.

Further echoes of their partnership surfaced elsewhere, not least the note-for-note appearance of "Solea" in Jerry Fielding's score for Clint Eastwood's film *The Gauntlet*.[50] Further items lived on in the repertoire of the bands Evans led in later years, for example, "Summertime" in the *Svengali* collection, "Gone" and again "Summertime" on Poljazz's curiously titled *Synthetic Evans* of 1976, and a huge expansion of the "Here Come de Honey Man" interlude from *Porgy and Bess* recorded in Milan during 1986. Davis again started playing "My Man's Gone Now" twenty-three years after first recording it, perhaps as a tribute to the pianist Bill Evans, although Davis of course never said so. A recording seems to fix a piece for all time, yet these new interpretations, very different from the originals, show how deceptive that can be, how a piece might continue growing across the decades.

Probably as a result of the widespread adverse comment on *Quiet Nights*, Columbia never issued the original *Time of the Barracudas* recording, although it is highly spoken of by those few who have heard the tape. For Davis and Evans this can only have added to the frustration experienced over *Quiet Nights*, and they would only work together occasionally now, and inconclusively. It is a melancholy business to pick up such bits and pieces as remained. Surely *Quiet Nights* should be regarded as an emblematic failure, signaling the partnership's effective end. They had explored their joint potentialities to brilliant purpose, creating three bodies of work that will receive attention for as long as anyone cares to listen to jazz. Although historians will always speak of these records together as a major contribution to this music, each has a character of its own, undertakes and succeeds in markedly different things. Yet their vein of expression still was limited because, despite the wildly exaggerated claims made for it in recent years, especially in the land of its birth, jazz remains a minor art. To have expected Davis and Evans to have gone on together for the rest of their days would have been foolish.

They remained in touch and periodically there was talk, by them and by others, of one big project or another. Even before the *Filles de Kilimanjaro* incident, there was a rumor of Davis leading a relatively large band (perhaps twelve pieces) with scores by Evans,[51] but nothing came of it, which is perhaps as well. Nothing can be said about the music recorded by Davis with a full Evans orchestra in February 1968, although presumably some of it was heard again at their second and last concert, given in Berkeley in April. This concert went unrecorded. Evans was the arranger of "You and I," a single track on a dreadful 1975 Island LP by one Betty Mabry concerning which Davis was referred to as "director." This marks the partnership's lowest point, although what followed was trivia, too. Evans again scored the theme statement of "Star on Cicely," a 1982 concoction for which Davis receives dubious credit as composer though it is reputedly derived from a phrase by Mike Stern. Similar circumstances prevailed for "It Gets Better," which uses a snippet by the saxophonist Bill Evans, and for "That's Right" on the 1983 *Decoy* LP, jointly put together by John Scofield and Davis, arranged by Evans and Davis. And on that unappetizing note a once genuinely creative partnership fizzled out.

Notes

1. Miles Davis, with Quincy Troupe, *Miles: The Autobiography* (New York: Simon and Schuster, 1989), 104.

2. One might have thought the authorship settled definitively by Jack Chambers in *Milestones I: The Music and Times of Miles Davis to 1960* (Toronto: University of Toronto Press, 1983), 61. But "Donna Lee" continues to be credited to Parker. See, for example, Gunther Schuller, *The Swing Era: The Development of Jazz, 1930–45* (New York: Oxford University Press, 1989), 755 n. 15; or David Rosenthal, *Hard Bop: Jazz and Black Music, 1955–1965* (New York: Oxford University Press, 1992), 12–13.

3. Compare bars 1–4 and 17–20 of "Donna Lee" with the pickup and bars 1–3 of Navarro's "Ice Freezes Red" solo. Davis is explicit about his admiration for Navarro in his *Autobiography* (p. 45). For a full account of other issues raised by this unusual theme, see Douglass Parker, " 'Donna Lee' and the Ironies of Bebop," in *The Bebop Revolution in Words and Music*, ed. Dave Oliphant (Austin, Tex.: Harry Ransom Humanities Research Center, 1994), 161–201.

4. The information in this paragraph is chiefly from an interview Evans gave Charles Fox on BBC Radio 3, August 28, 1978. This is further quoted below, and much (but not all) of what was said in this conversation confirms an interview Evans had given Richard Williams a few months before, published as "Sketches of Gil," *Melody Maker*, March 4, 1978, 38–39.

5. Evans, BBC Radio 3 interview. Note that this contradicts Davis's obviously thoughtless claim in his *Autobiography* (p. 119) that Thornhill had gotten everything "from Duke Ellington and Fletcher Henderson."

6. Quoted in Ian Crosbie's liner notes for Thornhill's 1948 transcription performances, Hep CD 17, original source unattributed.

7. Evans, BBC Radio 3 interview.

8. Indeed it is remarkable that surprise should ever have been expressed over the high regard in which performing musicians held Evans. See, for example, Chambers, *Milestones I*, 94.

9. Quoted in Crosbie's liner notes for Hep CD 17, original source unattributed.

10. Steve Lacy, "Introducing Steve Lacy," *Jazz Review*, September 1959, 25.

11. George Russell, liner notes for *Jazz Workshop*, RCA-Victor LPM2534. Further remarks by Russell on the ways a jazz composer can influence an improviser, highly relevant to Evans and his partnership with Davis, appear in his essay "Where Do We Go from Here?" in *The Jazz Word*, ed. Dom Cerulli, Burt Korall, and Mort Nasatir (New York: Ballantine Books, 1960), 233–39.

12. It is noteworthy how seldom Davis undertook real bop themes, especially Parker's, once the 1940s were behind him. Among the few instances are the disappointing 1955 "Ah-Leu-Cha" and the even more offhand 1958 Newport version.

13. Evans, BBC Radio 3 interview.

14. Quoted in Nat Hentoff, "The Birth of the Cool," *Down Beat*, May 16, 1957, 16.

15. See Chambers, *Milestones I*, 98.

16. For example, the October 1948 radio transcription on Hep CD 17.

17. Comments quoted in Hentoff, "The Birth of the Cool," *Down Beat*, May 2, 1957, 15–16.

18. Davis, *Autobiography*,104.

19. Quoted in Chambers, *Milestones I*, 92–93.

20. For a study of this large subject, see Robin Dewhurst, "A Study of the Jazz Composition and Orchestration Techniques Adopted by Gil Evans" (master's thesis, De Montfort University, Leicester, 1994).

21. Davis, *Autobiography*, 116.

22. Ibid., 119, and legend to plates 30–34.

23. Ibid., 118.

24. Alun Morgan and Raymond Horricks, *Modern Jazz: A Survey of Developments since 1939* (London: Gollancz, 1956), 106, credited "Boplicity" to Lewis; Leonard Feather, *The Encyclopedia of Jazz* (London: Arthur Barker, 1956), 234, credited the work to Mulligan.

25. Brian Priestley has pointed out that in his quartet performance of "Darn That Dream" recorded in November 1954, Mulligan plays the introduction to the Capitol version note for note on the piano (private communication, October 13, 1992). This is highly suggestive, of course, though not quite conclusive, remembering what a tightly knit group of musicians the members of the nonet were.

26. See Chambers, *Milestones I*, 242–44; and Max Harrison, *A Jazz Retrospect* (London: Quartet Books, 1991), 69–72.

27. Davis, *Autobiography*, 215.

28. Quoted in Chambers, *Milestones I*, 241.

29. However, Tommy Flanagan's dismissal of *Miles Ahead* as "almost a copy of what Ahmad recorded with a trio" (quoted in Chambers, *Milestones I*, 261) deserves to stand as probably the most inane comment anyone has made on any jazz record.

30. "Sketches of Gil," 39.

31. Davis, *Autobiography*, 122.

32. Art Taylor was a good man for blowing dates on Prestige, Riverside, etc., but the incident he relates in Bonnie L. Johnson, "Words and Music by Arthur Taylor," in *Annual Review of Jazz Studies 6, 1993*, ed. Edward Berger et al. (Metuchen, N.J.: Scarecrow Press, 1993), 260–61, strikes this writer as implausible. According to this, his drum part was spread out over three music stands, and he could not read it. Davis came over, knocked the stands down, and said, "I just want you to play what you feel." Whether the then-fastidious Davis would have come out with so resounding a cliché is doubtful, and there is no mention of this incident either in his *Autobiography* or in any traceable Evans interview. But on pages

216–17 of the *Autobiography*, Davis does mention having problems with Taylor in other contexts, and Taylor appeared on no other Davis-Evans sessions.

33. Nat Hentoff, "An Afternoon with Miles Davis," *Jazz Review*, December 1958, 11.

34. Louis Armstrong told Evans that he had bought the *Porgy and Bess* LP and that "Miles Davis sounds like Buddy Bolden on it." See Evans, BBC Radio 3 interview.

35. Letter to author, October 8, 1958.

36. "Sketches of Gil," 39.

37. Ian Carr, *Miles Davis* (London: Granada Publishing, 1982), 105.

38. Davis, *Autobiography*, 241.

39. Quoted in Jack Chambers, *Milestones II: The Music and Times of Miles Davis since 1960* (Toronto: University of Toronto Press, 1985), 8.

40. Davis, *Autobiography*, 252.

41. Evans, BBC Radio 3 interview.

42. Gilbert Chase, *The Music of Spain*, 2d rev. ed. (New York: Dover Publications, 1959), 226.

43. For a brief yet vivid description of this occasion, see ibid., 156–57. Chase describes the *saeta* as "a semi-improvisational manifestation of popular religious feeling."

44. Davis, *Autobiography*, 244.

45. *Down Beat*, October 27, 1960, 57.

46. Davis, *Autobiography*, 259.

47. Leonard Feather, "The Modulated World of Gil Evans," *Down Beat*, February 23, 1967, 16.

48. *Down Beat*, November 7, 1963, 12; December 5, 1963, 14; and December 19, 1963, 17.

49. Davis, *Autobiography*, 265.

50. "Sketches of Gil," 39.

51. Feather, "Modulated World of Gil Evans," 16.

Marc Crawford

Miles and Gil:
Portrait of a Friendship

Originally published in Down Beat, *February 16, 1961, 18–19. Reprinted by permission of Maher Publications and the author.*

At the time he wrote this article, Marc Crawford (1929–96) was one of only a handful of black journalists who were writing about jazz. Crawford, though, included jazz as part of a broader journalistic career. He had been a foreign correspondent for *Jet* magazine and a staff writer for *Ebony;* for the latter, Crawford had done a memorable interview, "Miles Davis: Evil Genius of Jazz."

Crawford clearly had gained Davis's confidence and friendship; in fact, on Davis's advice Crawford had left *Ebony* to pursue a freelance career. He was therefore the ideal candidate to write an article for *Down Beat* documenting Davis's close friendship with Gil Evans.

In later years Crawford held a teaching position at New York University, at the same time maintaining his lifelong interest in jazz. While preparing these notes, I was saddened to learn that he had just died after a prolonged battle with cancer.—Ed.

In the southside Chicago home of his in-laws slumped a bathrobed, slipper-shod Miles Dewey Davis III with a bottle of Dutch beer on the table and Ravel's Piano Concerto in G Major coming from the stereo.

The dishes from the breakfast Miles had prepared (eggs and hamburger and tomatoes, garnished with salts of garlic and celery) rode at anchor in the kitchen sink, and almost forgotten was Miles's earlier refusal on the telephone to talk about his relationship with "Gil." At that time he had growled: "I don't like discussing Gil. I got too much respect for him to do that. It's almost like asking a man to discuss his wife."

But now Miles was relaxed, and pianist Arturo Benedetti Michelangeli was sending him into several shades of ecstasy.

"Listen to those trills!" Miles ordered. The sound of them was sustained as though they had been made by an electrified instrument, and Miles sat there, his first and second finger aflutter, demonstrating how the effect was created. "You know," he volunteered, "Gil thinks like that."

The "Gil" of whom he spoke was, of course, Jeff-tall Gil Evans, who, with Mutt-short Miles, forms one of the most creative and productive friendships in jazz. Miles appeared lost in thought about the forty-eight-year-old Toronto-born Evans, who wrote the arrangements for the celebrated Davis albums *Miles Ahead, Porgy and Bess,* and *Sketches of Spain.* Suddenly he picked up the telephone and long-distanced Evans in New York. Miles asked him to catch the next jet flight for Chicago so he could hear Miles and his group at the Cloister and "just hang out." Evans had said he would, and Miles settled back to await his arrival.

"Gil is my idea of a man," Miles said. "Say you had a friend who was half man and half donkey, and suppose he even wore a straw hat and you said, 'Gil, meet George.' Gil would get up and shake his hand and never care what George looked like.

"You ask Gil a question—you get a straight answer. Like in New York, somebody asked him what he thought of Ornette Coleman's tonal organization, and Gil told him: 'That's Ornette's business. If it isn't good, he'll take care of it.' "

Now Miles got up to flip the record to the Rachmaninoff Concerto no. 4 side. He stabbed the air with a flurry of vicious right and left hooks aimed at a hapless imaginary opponent. He had not been able that day to work out at Coulon's Gym, as is his Chicago custom, and he digressed to say he wished he had. Then he returned to his main subject: "Rachmaninoff and Ravel were way-out—like Gil is way-out. You know, my ambition has always been to write like Gil. I'd give my right arm to do it—no, my left one, because I'd have to write the notes down."

Words spilled freely from Miles now, which is rare, but then he was talking about what, to him, is a rare human being. "I first met Gil when I was with Bird, and he was asking for a release on my tune 'Donna Lee.' He wanted to make an arrangement for a government electrical transcription of it. I told him he could have it and asked him to teach me some chords and let me study some of the scores he was doing for Claude Thornhill.

"He really flipped me on the arrangement of 'Robbins' Nest' he did for Claude. See," said Miles, placing his left hand on the table that suddenly in his mind's eye had become a piano, "Gil had this cluster of chords and superimposed another cluster over it," Miles demonstrated, covering the left hand with his right so that the fingers of the hand above fitted between those on the bottom. "Now the chord ends," Miles explained, suddenly taking his right hand off the piano, "and now these three notes of the remaining cluster are gone," he went on, removing the thumb, first and second fingers of the left hand. "The overtone of the remaining two produced a note way up there." Miles swore, pointing at the other end of the piano. "I was puzzled. I had studied the score for days trying to find the note I heard. But it didn't even exist—at least, on paper it didn't. That's Gil for you.

"We've been friends since that first meeting. I got stranded once in St. Louis, and he sent me $75. I bet he's forgotten it." The expression on Miles's face was fine—warm and rare. All the sneer was gone. Not once had he walked off the bandstand, this Miles Davis in bathrobe and house slippers, alone in the big house with his music. "He's my favorite arranger, yet he's never really made money out of the business."

Miles had finished his own bottle of beer and was taking back half of the bottle he had provided his visitor. "You know, in New York we go over to each other's house, but we don't drop our problems on each other. When Gil is writing, he might spend three days on ten bars of music. He'll lock himself up in a room of his house, put a 'do not disturb' sign on the door, and not even his wife, Lillian, can come in. It's torture for her when he's writing. It's like he's out to lunch. Sometimes he'll get in there and play the piano for twelve hours. He's not only a composer and a hell of an orchestrator, he just knows instruments and what you can get out of them. He and Duke Ellington are the same way. They can use four instruments when others need eight.

"Listen to what Rachmaninoff is saying," Miles commanded suddenly, turning his attention again to the stereo. "Gil once said he would like to go to Africa and teach music just so he could hear all those African rhythms."

Now Miles was addressing himself to what Gil calls "a merchandising problem," which he claims has "nothing to do with music at all." Said Miles: "People always want to categorize music—jazz, classical. Put labels on it. But Gil says all music comes from the people, and the people are folk. Therefore, all music is folk.

"I used to write and send Gil my scores for evaluation. Gil used to say they were good but cluttered up with too many notes. I used to think you had to use a lot of notes and stuff to be writing. Now I've learned enough about writing *not* to write. I just let Gil write. I give him an outline of what I want, and he finishes it. I can even call him on the phone and just tell him what I got in mind, and when I see the score, it is exactly what I wanted. Nobody but Gil could think for me that way. He just has a gift of being able to put instruments together. Some people have it, some don't, Gil has it.

"He is as well versed on music in general as Leonard Bernstein. And what the classical guys don't know is what Gil knows. They don't know folks. Gil is always listening to Gypsy, South American, and African things. Everytime he comes to my house, he's got some new record for me.

"Hey!" Miles laughed, "you know what Gil will do sometimes? You'll be playing one of his arrangements in 4/4 time, and, all of a sudden, you'll come upon a bar of 3/2. That Gil is something."

Since early morning and continuing through a pot of neckbones and pinto beans he had cooked himself, Miles talked about Gil. The streetlights along Michigan Avenue had been burning for hours when the phone rang. "That was Gil," Miles said, hanging up. Evans's jet flight had just arrived at Chicago's O'Hare field, and he was now en route through town. Less than an hour later, the doorbell rang and silver-maned Gil Evans filled up the door with his six-feet-plus. "Hi, Miles," Gil said. "Hi," Miles said casually. It was as if Evans had been there all day—or at least, had gone out five minutes before to get a pack of cigarettes. Then they sat down and watched TV, with nothing more to say. "Look," Miles would mutter, pointing to the action on TV. "Uh-huh," Gil would answer. But that was all the conversation that passed between them.

The incomplete utterances explained something Miles had said earlier. "Sometimes when I'm playing, I start a phrase and never complete it because it isn't necessary. I have communicated the idea. Let's suppose somebody tells you something that bugs you and then asks your opinion about it. You might just say 'Aw!' and from the way you have said it, they get the message that you don't dig it." And in quite another vein, here was the scholarly, soft-spoken Evans and the sometimes volatile and always hard-spoken Miles Davis achieving absolute communication with the sparest of sounds.

Next day they watched football games on TV, ate well, smoked, drank, talked, joked, and listened to music from other lands, joined by their wives, as in a family visit.

The day before, Gil had told me that he felt Miles was a "first-rate musician." "But," Gil said now, "that is what I felt yesterday. Today I feel he is a genuine artist, and there are very few of them in the world today. I also think he's a pretty fine specimen of the human animal in most things he does. Today I admire his approach to life."

On only one thing does Evans seem to have his mind thoroughly fixed: "I only work for Miles and myself." He said he could not do anything he did not want to do, yet insisted he was a "commercial arranger," but only in the sense "that what I write is popular." And while Evans admitted that each year his income seems to wind up some $500 under what his needs require, he rejects Miles's contention that he is just now receiving the acclaim his talents have long deserved. "I haven't been around music for twenty years just waiting to be discovered," Evans said, "nor am I a recent discovery. I am just now able to do the things I couldn't do before. My product just wasn't ready."

And, of course, Gil—christened Ian Ernest Gilmore Green by his Australian parents—is no novice to the musical world. He led his own band in Stockton, California, from 1933 to 1938. Skinnay Ennis later took it over, but Gil stayed on as arranger until 1941. Then he became musical architect for the Claude Thornhill band, remaining with it until 1948.

Evans is a symphony of contradictions. Despite his vast knowledge of instruments, he never played one professionally until he took up the piano seriously in 1952. In recent years he has been writing big-band arrangements—with no standing big band at his disposal.

In October, however, he resolved some of this contradiction with the formation of his own twelve-piece orchestra. "I need a band as a workshop," he said. "In the past, I didn't get to be around a band but once a year, like when Miles and I are doing something. Before, I had to hear music in my imagination." Evans's band recently recorded its first LP, titled *Out of the Cool*, for the Impulse label. It was released late in January.

The gangling Evans, who strikes you as a cross between Gary Cooper and Henry Fonda, likes to talk philosophy, poetry, travel, politics—but rarely does so with Miles. Yet he insists, "We think alike." Their communication is at the music level. "We are complementary in that we are opposites," Evans said. "My inclination is just less extroverted than his. We both like the same kind of music."

Modern music's Mutt and Jeff, however, rarely sit down and say "let's do this type of LP" and then plan around their decision. For an example of how they work, take *Sketches of Spain*, of which Evans says: "We were just ready for flamenco music and fell into it. We don't have anything specifically planned at present, but we will be doing some more things."

The compatibility of these two diverse personalities was first evidenced in the late 1940s, when Evans helped Miles and Gerry Mulligan set up their historic nine-piece band. Ever since then, they have shared a common wish: to go on growing musically together.

All the evidence indicates that they will.

Don Heckman

Miles Davis Times Three:
The Evolution of a Jazz Artist

Originally published in Down Beat, *August 30, 1962, 16–19. Reprinted by permission of Maher Publications and the author.*

There is general agreement that Miles Davis has been one of the most influential of jazz trumpeters; his impact as a stylist has extended to players of other instruments as well. Seldom, however, has the Davis style been as carefully examined as in this article by Don Heckman.

Active since the late 1950s as a saxophonist, composer, journalist, and record producer, Heckman has written for *Jazz Review, Down Beat, American Record Guide, Stereo Review*, the *Village Voice*, the *New York Times*, and most recently the *Los Angeles Times*. In the 1960s Heckman wrote for *Down Beat* valuable analyses of the work of Coleman Hawkins and Lester Young, Charlie Parker, Davis, and Ornette Coleman. (His Hawkins/Young article is reprinted in this volume's series companion, *A Lester Young Reader*.) Heckman combines meticulous prose with transcriptions of seven Davis solos dating from 1947 through 1961. The transcriptions are all in concert keys, that is, where they sound on the piano, untransposed for trumpet. I've kept Heckman's concluding discography just as he wrote it; the recordings have since appeared in other formats and repackagings.—Ed.

Ernest Hemingway once said that what an artist knows he need not write about. Like an iceberg, only a small portion of what he has to say is visible while the balance rests beneath the surface to provide an unshakable foundation. There is, of course, no special virtue in economy for its own sake. Rudimentary as Hemingway's style may seem, it has never been successfully duplicated or imitated. The unwritten part of his work is filled with accumulated experience and richly gifted imagination, making it possible for him to state only the important facts, those that have universal meaning.

While making specific analogies between the arts is never without peril, the elements of this principle seem to be reflected in the playing of Miles Davis. Like Hemingway, Davis is wry, epigrammatic, witty; he minces neither words nor phrases, seldom plays notes that are unnecessary. And like Hemingway, he employs a mythic imagery that reaches down into the collective unconscious of contemporary society.

This is both a strength and a weakness. Davis's music, like Hemingway's writing was for his time, is so precisely right for ours, so reflective of the lonely nihilism that courses through so many lives that it may some day fade, like a spent flower.

Intangible as all of this may seem, it is an important part of the Davis gestalt—a part that cannot be notated or accurately described but that nonetheless has its importance.

Jazz is a music that requires first of all a personality. Technical considerations are meaningless without an appreciation of the importance of the individual player. It is this very subjectivity that gives the music its originality. This is not to say that jazz cannot be notated. More accurately, certain *elements* of the jazz creative act cannot be notated. It would take a system of unbelievable complexity to depict accurately the fine rhythmic nuances, the variegated attack devices, and the endless array of dynamic shadings that a soloist of Davis's stature employs in the construction of a solo. Even if this were possible, the transcription would still lack an explanation of the catalytic relationship between soloist and rhythm section—the shifting and alternating of accent and emphasis that is ever new, always different from the previous time, making each performance definitive. But no matter how inadequate, a notated example of the work of an important jazzman has much to offer: in combination with the actual recording, it furnishes a meaningful insight into the method and techniques by which an artist fashions his work.

One of the persistent myths about Davis concerns his ability to play the horn. Musicians have said, "Miles is a great jazzman, but he just doesn't know how to play the trumpet." Recorded evidence, however, indicates that this conclusion, though fairly widespread, is quite mistaken.

Davis does play his share of clams, a high percentage having appeared in his work with Charlie Parker. This is hardly surprising when one considers that Davis was still a teenager when he made his first recordings with a man who was, for musicians at least, one of the giants.

Close listening indicates that his mistakes often stemmed as much from uncertainty over his choice of notes as from any special technical failings. In an often tortuous attempt to find a personal voice, his ideas would come pouring forth too fast for his fingers. Without a model to fall back upon, a player with original ideas is forced to develop his own methods and procedures.

Too often, as with Thelonious Monk and Ornette Coleman, these new procedures, although perfectly suited to the artist's individual needs, suggest to the listening audience ineptness and even lack of talent. Despite its difficulties, Davis chose the rough road of artistic innovation. It is nothing short of amazing that he did not fall completely under the then-dominant spell of the Dizzy Gillespie style. There is little in the early Davis recordings to indicate that he ever chose to be anything except his own man.

The division of an artist's work into periods results in a haphazard categorization at best. Too often the chronicler is faced with a work that doesn't compartmentalize into a neat sequence of "early," "middle," and "late." Yet the temptation remains and in one sense can be justified by the fact that such a categorization, if not applied inflexibly, can be a genuine help toward proper appreciation of the artist's total work. Rather than attempt in this article to formalize areas that are at best vaguely defined, I have delineated "aspects," or different phases of what is a singularly complex musical personality, for this purpose.

Davis's first recording period is almost completely circumscribed by an association with Parker. From his first record date (1945) to the Metronome All-Star date (1949), Davis made few recordings other than those with Parker. Having completed this association, Davis returned to his mentor only twice—once in a 1951 session that introduced "Au Privave," "She Rote," "K.C. Blues," and "Star Eyes" and again in a date for Prestige in 1953.

That this period of Davis's creative life should have been dominated by Parker is not surprising, since Davis obviously reflected and complemented Parker's music to perfection. In this sense the relationship was valuable for both. Recordings such as "Now's the Time," "Chasin' the Bird," "Dexterity," and "Embraceable You," for example, are classics not only of the decade but of the history of jazz.

Davis did not stand still during this period. His hesitant, but nonetheless startling, chorus on "Now's the Time" is a distant cry from the thoroughly professional craftsmanship of "Bird Feathers," "Bongo Bop," and "Ah-Leu-Cha," the last recorded in late 1948. A comparison of the work at the opposite ends of this period shows that a major artist had developed in the interim, with an improvement apparent in almost every session. The five 1947 dates, in particular, show an almost unbelievable development in style, technique, and maturity.

Even during this early stage, Davis's outlook encompassed wide areas, ranging from the lonely introspectiveness of "Out of Nowhere" and "Don't Blame Me" to the Niagara-like stream of notes on up-tempo numbers such as "The Hymn" and "Bird Gets the Worm."

An especially interesting recording from June 1947, and one that includes many of the characteristics of his work at that time, is "Cheryl," in which he plays three excellent blues choruses, as transcribed in example 1. The unique Davis tone is evident from the beginning. Then in the fourth bar he plays one of the most typical devices (and one that was eventually discarded)—a substituted chromatic chord change in place of the normal blues modulation to the IV chord. Although one note is missed and played as an F♮, it was almost certainly intended to be a D♯ (in parentheses), thereby preserving the natural sequential progression of the melody.

Interestingly, the first two choruses of "Cheryl" are remarkably similar in phrasing and shape. Both use on-the-beat figures based on a minor third in the first two bars. Bars 3 and 4 of chorus 2 are a further development of bars 3 and 4 of chorus 1 and use an identical descending chromatic chord sequence. Again, bars 5 and 6 of chorus 2 are a freer-swinging development of bars 5 and 6 of chorus 1. Bar 7 is almost identical in both choruses. Bars 8 and 9 in chorus 2 are a simplification, both rhythmically and melodically, of the harmonically derived melody in bars 8 and 9 of chorus 1. Bars 10 and 11, while not necessarily related in the first two choruses, both end on the third beat of the eleventh bar, allowing an open space at the end of the chorus.

The third chorus is the most interesting, since—with the exception of the last four bars, which are typical of the way Davis often ended his choruses, almost rushing the beat with long curlicues of altered chords—it is not as harmonically bound as the first choruses.

EXAMPLE 1

In this last chorus Davis uses the chord changes to further his own expression rather than respond—as in the first two choruses—with ideas that, although interesting, satisfy more a musical idea than a musical expression.

The first five bars in particular are excellent, leading with clear, direct certainty to the brief turn on E♭ in bar 5. Once again a typical Davis pattern is included, one that appears constantly in his solos from this period and that has been widely imitated by trumpet players ever since. It is basically a rhythmic figure ♫♫ with a heavy upbeat accent, and Davis characteristically uses it in a manner similar to the last two beats of bar 3 and the second and third beats of bar 4 of chorus 3. Davis's rhythmic playing is rather conservative in this solo. At this time he generally played fairly close to the beat, depending upon simple eighth-note accents for rhythmic contrast and drive.

The 1949–50 Capitol dates with Gerry Mulligan and Gil Evans were, symbolically, Davis's liberation from the status of sideman and the first expression of musical ideas that extended beyond the vistas of his own playing abilities.

He has spoken of the difficulties of adjusting to playing both an ensemble lead and a solo voice and having to switch abruptly from a written to an improvised passage. But his difficulties are not especially apparent in the recordings, for he succeeds not only in making the transition but also in finding a relevant relationship between his solo and the cushion of composed sound that envelops it. Undoubtedly the experience of making this adjustment had some effect upon his growing feeling for the proper use of space.

John Carisi's "Israel," one of the finest compositions recorded at the session, includes an exceptionally concise and well-thought-out solo by Davis (see ex. 2). Its most striking feature is that it fits so well with what is happening in the accompaniment. Davis consistently (especially in bars 3, 5, 6, 7, 8, and 10 of chorus 2) opens up with phrases to let the ensemble ring through. The second chorus starts with a beautifully declamatory statement that paraphrases the main theme and ends with just the right amount of space before Davis's reentry with the ensemble. Once again he projects a strong phrase relationship between the two choruses; bar 9 is almost identical both times, and bars 10 and 11 of chorus 2 are very similar to the same bars in chorus 1. It is also interesting to note the sureness of Davis's playing throughout this date. Despite the demands made upon him as leader, trumpet soloist, and lead trumpet, he is stronger and more controlled than ever before.

The second phase of Davis's playing is not so clear-cut or easy to identify as the first. It extends generally from the 1949–50 Capitol recordings to the establishment in 1955 of a quintet that included John Coltrane, Red Garland, Paul Chambers, and Philly Joe Jones. It is a period of rich artistic growth in which Davis molded the experience from his years with Parker into an altogether original playing style.

Perhaps its most readily identifiable feature is his rejection of harmonic limitations. He became a completely melodic player, disregarding chordal restrictions in favor of long, clean-flowing lines much the way Lester Young did. Davis, however, relied less on short, rifflike patterns and

EXAMPLE 2

nore on extended statements. By the time of the late 1954 date with Thelonious Monk and Milt Jackson, Davis was a masterful player, with every element—swing, economy of statement, melodic variation, soloistic development—under control. He also began in this period to experiment with sound. In his earlier playing, tonal expression had been limited to playing with or without a mute. At this time he began an exploration, still uncompleted, of the varieties of sound possible from a trumpet—and, later, a flugelhorn.

Fairly representative of the early stages of this period is a recording made in his next-to-last date with Parker entitled "K.C. Blues" (see ex. 3). (Examples are confined as much as possible to blues choruses in the hope that this will give an accurate picture of Davis's development through a basic and easily understandable jazz form.) The difference between this chorus and the chorus on "Cheryl" is rather interesting, not in what is played but in the manner employed. The use of time is completely different; instead of remaining close to the basic pulse by playing a regular pattern of eighth notes, Davis uses a heavy staccato to emphasize a lag-behind rhythmic feeling not unlike the postwar playing of Lester Young. As a result, this example is less accurately notated than the first two, for so many of the notes are attacked somewhere between the beats.

EXAMPLE 3

The emphasis upon melodic development is noticeable in bars 1, 2, and 3 of the first chorus. Bar 3 is a partial displacement, partial repetition of the phrase Davis uses to open the chorus. The second chorus has no direct connection to the first; Davis is instead concerned with a further development of his opening phrase, which he repeats on the third beat of bar 3 and alters slightly to make the chord change. Only in bar 9 of chorus 2 does he refer back to chorus 1 with a phrase that is quite similar (except a third higher) to the phrase used in the same bar of chorus 1.

The lack of chromatic substitutions is obvious; Davis no longer is interested in harmony for its own sake. His solo is a highly distilled version of what is basically a rather complicated musical thought. But since he uses only notes that are important to the thought, it becomes direct and to the point.

Davis's work in this period also reflects an interest in pop ballads such as "My Old Flame," "It Never Entered My Mind," "You Don't Know What Love Is," and "Easy Living." All of these, of course, emphasize the particular sort of romantic urgency expressed so well by the Davis tone. In the date made with Monk and Milt Jackson, we are given the opportunity of examining two takes of "The Man I Love." Since these give such an excellent insight into the development of an improvised solo, following is a transcription of the first sixteen bars of both versions (see ex. 4).

EXAMPLE 4
a. Take no. 1

b. Take no. 2

The first eight bars of both are similar, although take no. 2 has a stronger rhythmic emphasis and relies less on sequential repetitions. The second eight bars of take no. 1 are concerned almost completely with a variation consisting of open fourths and fifths. The second eight bars of take no. 2 are more interesting. Davis departs from the tonic and fifth and builds a series of brilliant calls using the flat fifth, ninth, and major seventh and culminating in the crisp B♭ in bar 10. The next phrase is a long swooping figure that descends to the very bottom of the horn, and finally, near the end of the phrase, he refers once again, in somewhat altered form, to his initial motif.

Davis's assertion that Monk's comping is of negligible value is somewhat curious. ("I love the way Monk plays and writes, but I can't stand him behind me. He doesn't give you any support."—*Jazz Review*, December 1958.)

When Monk lays out ("Swing Spring," for example), Davis's playing occasionally seems unsteady and lacks the strong assertiveness of his excellent choruses on "Bemsha Swing." It's easy to second guess, of course, but it's likely that Monk's contribution played a significant role in the success of Davis's other solos.

At the time of the session, Davis was deeply involved in a style that emphasized the subtleties of implication and suggestion. Such an approach to improvisation depends upon the taste and timing of the piano player and, in fact, of the whole rhythm section. While this section does not have the sinuosity of the later Garland-Jones-Chambers trinity, it has other advantages. Instead of resting upon an enveloping cushion of sound and rhythm that permits him to understate, sometimes to the point of sparseness, Davis is obligated by the irregularity and unexpectedness of Monk's accents to stretch out more, to find some coherent balance between the sounds and the silences of his solos.

In late 1955 Davis made his first recordings with the group that became a classic in modern jazz (Coltrane, Garland, Chambers, and Jones). This was the beginning of the phase of his career that continues into the present.

As a leader, Davis was confronted with more complex problems. Whether or not this affected his playing is questionable. Many of the quintet recordings in the last six years have had a similarity in approach and programming.

On the other hand, Davis has shown, through his association with Gil Evans and in his own experiments with the use of scales for improvisations (well documented on the Columbia album *Kind of Blue*), that he is far from being a mossbacked conservative. His solo on "Saeta" from the *Sketches of Spain* album is not really very different from the point of view and instrumental technique found in the music of Ornette Coleman. It is not surprising that the playing on "The Man I Love" should have evolved into the playing on *Sketches of Spain* or that the scalar line "Swing Spring" should have led to "So What," "Blue in Green," and "All Blues."

What is surprising is that there has been such a notable disparity between his recorded work and his club and concert playing. This difference is apparent in a comparison of any recent studio work with the location recording *Miles Davis in Person—Friday and Saturday Nights at the Blackhawk.* The Davis on these recordings is so much livelier, so much more prone to take chances than the Davis on the studio recordings that he sounds at times like two different players.

EXAMPLE 5

a. 1954 VERSION

b. 1961 version

A brief example from *Friday and Saturday Nights at the Blackhawk* helps to highlight this but only partially indicates the fiery, driving quality of the playing. Since he has recorded "Walkin'" before, in early 1954, the first two choruses of both the 1954 and 1961 versions have been transcribed in example 5.

The 1954 version is considerably slower and deceptively simple in structure. Its most important asset is a consistent, rocking rhythm.

Solos such as this—outlining the bare skeleton of the blues—were copied extensively in the late 1950s by many other, lesser musicians who mistook Davis's refinement of the technique for the whole thing. They failed to understand that Davis plays this way only in terms of specific accompanying rhythmic factors and that the musical facts that Davis *suggests* are easily as important as those he *states*.

The 1961 version is executed at a rapid clip, making the stream of eighth notes in bars 17–20 especially impressive. Since the transcription only includes the first part of a long solo, it fails to include the subsequent development of some of the motives. Bar 2 of the second chorus, for example, is a favorite Davis phrase, which he develops at some length later in the solo. While not necessarily the best solo from this two-record set, it is a good example of the kind of brilliant improvisation Davis displays in his live appearances.

As he has matured artistically, the range of his interests has correspondingly broadened, resulting in some outstanding successes and a few disappointments. Hemingway was often plagued in later years by critics who said he should be writing another *The Sun Also Rises* instead of *The Old Man and the Sea*. It would be just as foolish to criticize Davis because he no longer plays the way he did in 1954. A young, still productive artist, Miles Davis will have much more to say.

Discography

Solo examples cited in this article were transcribed from the following twelve-inch LP recordings:

"Cheryl," Savoy 12001.
"Israel," Capitol 762.
"K.C. Blues," Verve 8010.
"The Man I Love" (both takes), Prestige 7150.
"Walkin'" (1954 version), Prestige 7076; (1961 version), Columbia 1669.

The selections mentioned in the course of the article may be found on the following albums:

"Ah-Leu-Cha," Savoy 12000.
"All Blues," Columbia 1355.
"Au Privave," Verve 8010.
"Bemsha Swing," Prestige 7150.
"Bird Feathers," Baronet 107
"Bird Gets the Worm," Savoy 12000, 12009, 12014.
"Blue in Green," Columbia 1355.
"Bongo Bop," Baronet 107.
"Chasin' the Bird," Savoy 12000, 12001, 12014 (alternate takes).
"Dexterity," Baronet 107.
"Don't Blame Me," Baronet 107.
"Easy Living," Fantasy 6001.
"Embraceable You," Roost 2210.
"The Hymn," Baronet 107.
"It Never Entered My Mind," Blue Note 1502.
"My Old Flame," Prestige 7013.
"Now's the Time," Savoy 12001.
"Out of Nowhere," Baronet 107.
"She Rote," Verve 8010.
"So What," Columbia 1355.
"Star Eyes," Verve 8010.
"Swing Spring," Prestige 7150.
"You Don't Know What Love Is," Prestige 7076.

Leonard Feather

The Blindfold Tests

Originally published in Down Beat, *September 21, 1955, 33–34; August 7, 1958, 29; June 18, 1964, 31; June 13, 1968, 34; and June 27, 1968, 33. Reprinted by permission of Maher Publications and Mrs. Leonard Feather.*

In a career that lasted a half century, Leonard Feather (1914–94) became, along with John Hammond, the best-known of all jazz critics; he probably was the most prolific, too. In addition to writing hundreds of album liner notes and newspaper columns, Feather authored several editions of the indispensable *Encyclopedia of Jazz* as well as *Inside Bebop, Laughter from the Hip* (with Jack Tracy), *The Book of Jazz, From Satchmo to Miles, The Jazz Years: Earwitness to an Era,* and others. He also was active as a publicist, record producer, composer, and consultant.

Feather also conceived one of the mainstays of the jazz vernacular, "The Blindfold Test." First appearing in *Metronome* in the late 1940s and later in *Down Beat,* blindfold tests consist of reactions by prominent jazz figures to a series of recordings, about which the blindfoldees are told nothing. The responses are often revealing and much-quoted, none more so than the series of tests conducted between 1955 and 1968 with Miles Davis.

In the 1960s tests Davis frequently used his famous colorful language in responding to the recordings. In the original *Down Beat* printings, these expletives were deleted, but I have restored them here in the interest of authenticity.—Ed.

For a long time, Miles Davis and I had been trying to get together for a blindfold session. I was determined that when the interview did take place, it would be something out of the ordinary run of blindfold tests; and that's just the way it turned out.

Every record selected was one that featured at least two trumpet players. As you will see, this selection of material did not faze Miles.

Miles was given no information whatever, either before or during the test, about the records played for him.

The Records

1. Clifford Brown, "Falling in Love with Love" (Prestige). Brown, Art Farmer, trumpets; Bengt Hallberg, piano.

That was Arthur Farmer and Brownie blowing trumpet. The arrangement was pretty good; I think they played it too fast, though. They missed the content of the tune.

The piano player gasses me—I don't know his name, I've been trying to find out his name. He's from Sweden. . . . I think he made those records with Stan, like "Dear Old Stockholm." I never heard anybody play in a high register like that. So clean, and he swings and plays his own things; but they had the piano up too loud in the ensembles. If there's anything that drags me, it's when they put the piano up too loud in the control room.

Aside from the trumpets, I didn't care for the other soloists at all . . . also I think that Arthur should improve his tone and that Clifford should swing more. Four stars, though.

2. Roy Eldridge and Dizzy Gillespie, "Algo Bueno" (Clef). Eldridge, Gillespie, trumpets; Oscar Peterson, piano; Herb Ellis, guitar; Louie Bellson, drums.

That was Diz and Roy. Sounded like Oscar Peterson on piano. Guitar messed it all up—and the brushes. And one of the four bars that Dizzy played wasn't too good. One of the fours that Roy played wasn't too good. They're two of my favorite trumpet players; I love Roy, and you know I love Diz.

I don't know why they recorded together . . . sounded like something of Norman Granz's . . . one of his get-togethers. It's nice to listen to for a while, but Oscar messes it up with that Nat Cole style; and that kind of rhythm section, with brushes.

It's not that kind of song. You can't play that kind of song like that, with those chords. There's another way to swing on that. It could have been much better. I'd give it three stars on account of Diz's and Roy's horns.

3. Buck Clayton and Ruby Braff, "Love Is Just Around the Corner" (Vanguard). Clayton, trumpet; Braff, cornet; Benny Morton, trombone; Steve Jordan, guitar; Aaron Bell, bass.

Sounded like Buck Clayton; the other sounded like Charlie Shavers. I don't know who was on trombone; sounded like Jack Teagarden. I don't know about that rhythm section.

Maybe they want to play like that, huh? But the bass and guitar—they always seem to clash when they play 1-3-5 chords that don't vary. You know—C, C, G, G, IV, IV, V, V, like that—seems to be some clash in there. When they play straight 4/4, I like it. I did think the guitar was too loud. Two stars.

4. Don Elliott, Rusty Dedrick, "Gargantuan Chant" (Riverside). Dick Hyman, composer, arranger, piano; Dedrick, first trumpet solo; Elliott, second trumpet solo; Mundell Lowe, guitar.

Sounds kind of fine. Sounds like Howard McGhee and Ray Nance, but I don't know who it is. The arrangement was pretty nice, but not the inter-pretation. Piano, whoever he is, is crazy. That's about all I can say about it. Two stars. Guitar was nice. I preferred the last trumpet solo to the earlier one for that kind of thing.

5. Metronome All-Stars, "Look Out" (Victor). Sy Oliver, composer and arranger; Tiny Grimes, guitar; Flip Phillips, Georgie Auld, tenor saxophones; Buddy DeFranco, clarinet; Harry Edison, Cootie Williams, Rex Stewart, trumpets; Teddy Wilson, piano.

Gee, that sure sounded like an all-star record! Sounded like Teddy Wilson. I think I heard Harry Edison, Georgie Auld, Cootie Williams, Al Killian. Guitar player was nice. I don't know who that was. Sure was a funny arrangement.

I don't know who could have done that arrangement . . . pretty nice record, though. It kinda swings. I couldn't tell the clarinet player; I can't tell anybody but Benny Goodman and Artie Shaw and Buddy DeFranco. It was sort of a short solo. . . . Give it four stars. I liked that.

6. Charlie Barnet, "Terry Tune" (Columbia). Clark Terry, Jimmy Nottingham, trumpets.

That was Clark Terry and somebody; I don't know who the other trumpet was. Sounded a little like Willie Cook. I don't recognize that band. I know Duke didn't write these arrangements. . . . For a moment it sounded like Maynard; but I guess Maynard would be doing more acrobatics. He always does.

I like Terry. . . . I met him in St. Louis when I was about thirteen and playing in a school band. He was playing like Buck Clayton then—but fast, just the way he is now. So I started trying to play like Terry; I idolized him. He's a very original trumpet player; but I don't like to hear him strong-arming the horn just to try to be exciting.

He's much better when he plays soft, when he sounds like Buck. I like him when he plays *down,* instead up, always upward, phrases. . . . I don't like that arrangement, though. I know it must be Terry's tune, 'cause it sounds like him. I'd rate it three stars on account of Terry. I don't know who that other trumpet player would be.

7. Bobby Byrne–Kai Winding, "Hot and Cool Blues" (*Dixieland vs. Birdland,* MGM). Byrne, Winding, trombones; Eddie Shu, Mike Baker, clarinets; Howard McGhee, Yank Lawson, trumpets; John Lewis, Kenny Clarke, Percy Heath, rhythm.

Jeez! That was Howard McGhee, and Percy, wasn't it? Kai Winding. Howard played nice. I liked the contrast idea . . . but I just don't know what to say about that record; there's too big a switch when they go from that riff into the sudden Dixieland. . . . I like good Dixieland, you know. . . . I like Sidney Bechet. . . . Kai and Howard swing. I'd give the record a couple stars on account of Kai and Howard.

8. Louis Armstrong, "Ain't Misbehavin'" (Victor). Bobby Hackett, Armstrong, trumpets; Jack Teagarden, trombone.

I like Louis! Anything he does is all right. I don't know about his *statements,* though. . . . I could do without them. That's Bobby Hackett, too; I always did like Bobby Hackett—anything by him. Jack Teagarden's on trombone. I'd give it five stars.

9. Duke Ellington, "Stormy Weather" (Capitol). Harry Carney, baritone saxophone; Willie Cook, Ray Nance, Cat Anderson, trumpets; Billy Strayhorn, arranger.

Oh, God! You can give that twenty-five stars! I *love* Duke. That sounded like Billy Strayhorn's arrangement; it's warmer than Duke usually writes. Must be Billy Strayhorn.

That band kills me. I think all the musicians should get together one certain day and get down on their knees and thank Duke. Especially Mingus, who always idolized Duke and wanted to play with him; and why he didn't mention it in his blindfold test, I don't know. Yes, everybody should bow to Duke and Strayhorn—and Charlie Parker and Diz. . . . Cat Anderson sounds good on that; Ray ALWAYS sounds good.

The beginning soloist sounded real good, too. That's Harry Carney, too, in there; if he wasn't in Duke's band, the band wouldn't be Duke. . . . They take in all schools of jazz. . . . Give this all the stars you can.

—September 21, 1955

The last time Miles Davis took the blindfold test, in the issue dated September 21, 1955, the feature bore the headline "Miles and Miles of Trumpet Players." Each of the nine records played for Davis featured at least two trumpet soloists.

This time, by way of contrast, I avoided this emphasis; in fact, a couple of the records played had no trumpet at all, and others used the horn only as a secondary instrument.

However, just for laughs, I retained one record out of the previous test, the Elliott-Dedrick "Gargantuan Chant." In 1955 Davis thought it sounded like Howard McGhee and Ray Nance, said the arrangement was nice but not the interpretation, considered the piano great and liked the guitar, and rated the record two stars.

Davis won't know until he reads this that he was played the same record twice, three years apart. Now, as then, he was given no information about the records played.

The Records

1. John Lewis, "Warmeland (Dear Old Stockholm)" (Atlantic).

I'll give it ten stars. . . . On top of that, John loves Sweden, you know. I like John . . . his interpretation of a song is too much. Last night, Lennie

Hayton played something for me from this same album, and like Lena Horne says, "All I do is sing the song like the man wrote it." That's how John plays the piano. I don't go for guitar at all, and John complemented him there. . . . All the stars are for John.

2. Tiny Grimes and Coleman Hawkins, "A Smooth One" (Prestige). Musa Kaleem, flute.

"A Smooth One." We used to play that in St. Louis. I don't know who that flute player was, but if he was up to the Apollo Theater when Puerto Rico was living, he would have blown the horn on that whole record. The guitar player was terrible. . . . I really can't say anything about it. Give it half a star just because Coleman Hawkins is on it.

3. Buddy Collette, "Cycle" (Contemporary). Collette, arranger, tenor saxophone; Gerald Wilson, trumpet; Red Callender, bass.

You know what that sounds like to me? It sounds like Gigi Gryce arrangements with Oscar Pettiford, but I don't know—all those white tenor players sound alike to me . . . unless it's Zoot Sims or Stan Getz. It must have been Ray Copeland on trumpet. . . . I don't know for sure, but I don't like that type of still trumpet playing.

That's a very old kind of modern arrangement—like an old modern picture with skeletons. I'd rate it two stars.

4. Sonny Rollins with Thelonious Monk, "The Way You Look Tonight" (Prestige). Tommy Potter, bass; Arthur Taylor, drums.

I know that's Sonny Rollins, but I don't see how a record company can record something like that. You know the way Monk plays—he never gives any support to a rhythm section. When I had him on my date, I had him lay out until the ensemble. I like to hear him play, but I can't stand him in a rhythm section unless it's one of his own songs.

I can't understand a record like this. I don't know who the drummer and bass player are. Is that "The Way You Look Tonight"? That's what I used to play behind Bird, only we used to play it twice as fast, I'll give this $2^1/_2$ on account of Sonny.

5. Eddie Condon, "Eddie and the Milkman" (MGM). Rex Stewart, cornet.

It's Don Elliott. . . . No, I don't know who that was on trumpet. In fact, Leonard, I don't know anything about that at all. It has a nice beat, but it sounded like Don Elliott to me, imitating somebody, but I know it wasn't him.

I like the piece, but you know Don is always "da, da, da, da, *da.*" I know it isn't him because he doesn't have that much feeling. I'll give this four.

6. Don Elliott and Rusty Dedrick, "Gargantuan Chant" (Riverside). Mundell Lowe, guitar; Dick Hyman, piano.

I don't know who that was, Leonard. Sounds good in spots, but I don't like that kind of trumpet playing. The guitar sounds good in spots, and the piano player sounds good. It's a good little number except for that interlude and that tired way of playing trumpet. I'll give that three stars. Who were those two trumpet players?

7. John Lewis and Sacha Distel, "Dear Old Stockholm" (Atlantic). Lewis, piano; Distel, guitar; Barney Wilen, tenor saxophone; Percy Heath, bass; Kenny Clarke, drums.

I like the tune. I'll give it four stars, especially for the rhythm section. I think it was John Lewis and Kenny Clarke, but I'm not sure. Whoever they were they were very sympathetic and very swinging.

I know the two other fellows—I like them very much. I think I can speak better about the guitar than the saxophonist—Sacha Distel is the guitarist, and I believe if he continues to develop, he will be very good. . . . I don't think he has too individual a voice yet. I'll give this four stars for the swinging rhythm section.

8. Bobby Hackett, "Albatross" (Capitol). Dick Cary, E-flat horn; Ernie Caceres, baritone.

I'll give it five stars. . . . I like that. The trombone player knocked me out. Who was that playing baritone?. . . That trombone player gassed me. The trumpet? It sounded better than Ruby Braff. I don't understand Ruby at all. In that style I like Red Allen, Louis, and Bobby Hackett plays nice, but I can't tell anybody else.

9. Shorty Rogers, "I'm Glad I'm Not Young Anymore" (Victor). Bill Holman, tenor saxophone.

I know it's a West Coast record. Right? Shorty playing trumpet and I've never heard James Clay, but I guess it must be him. I don't know anything about that. I'll give it two stars.

—August 7, 1958

Miles Davis is unusually selective in his listening habits. This attitude should not be interpreted as reflecting any general misanthropy. He was in a perfectly good mood on the day of the interview reproduced below; it just happened that the records selected did not, for the most part, make much of an impression.

Clark Terry, for example, is an old friend and idol of Davis's from St. Louis, and the Duke Ellington Orchestra has always been on Davis's preferred list.

Davis does not have an automatic tendency to want to put everything down, as an inspection of his earlier blindfold tests will confirm (*Down Beat*, September 21, 1955, and August 7, 1958).

The Cecil Taylor item was played as an afterthought, because we were discussing artists who have impressed critics, and I said I'd like to play an example. Aside from this, Davis was given no information about the records played.

The Records

1. Les McCann and the Jazz Crusaders, "All Blues" (Pacific Jazz). Wayne Henderson, trombone; Wilton Felder, tenor saxophone; Joe Sample, piano; McCann, electric piano; Miles Davis, composer.

What's that supposed to be? That ain't nothin'. They don't know what to do with it—you either play it bluesy or you play on the scale. You don't just play flat notes. I didn't write it to play flat notes on—you know, like minor thirds. Either you play a whole chord against it, or else . . . but don't try to play it like you'd play, ah, "Walkin' the Dog." You know what I mean?

That trombone player—trombone ain't supposed to sound like that. This is 1964, not 1924. Maybe if the piano player had played it by himself, something would have happened.

Rate it? How can I rate that?

2. Clark Terry, "Cielito Lindo" (*3 in Jazz*, RCA Victor). Terry, trumpet; Hank Jones, piano; Kenny Burrell, guitar.

Clark Terry, right? You know, I've always liked Clark. But this is a sad record. Why do they make records like that? With the guitar in the way, and that sad shit piano player. He didn't do nothing for the rhythm section—didn't you hear it get jumbled up? All they needed was a bass and Terry.

That's what's fucked up music, you know. Record companies. They make too many sad records, man.

3. Rod Levitt, "Ah! Spain" (*Dynamic Sound Patterns*, **Riverside**). **Levitt, trombone, composer; John Beal, bass.**

There was a nice idea, but they didn't do nothing with it. The bass player was a motherfucker though.

What are they trying to do, copy Gil? It doesn't have the Spanish feeling—doesn't move. They move up in triads, but there's all those chords missing—and I never heard any Spanish thing where they had a figure that went

That's some old shit, man. Sounds like Steve Allen's TV band. Give it some stars just for the bass player.

4. Duke Ellington, "Caravan" (*Money Jungle*, **United Artists**). **Ellington, piano; Charles Mingus, bass; Max Roach, drums.**

What am I supposed to say to that? That's ridiculous. You see the way they can fuck up music? It's a mismatch. They don't complement each other. Max and Mingus can play together, by themselves. Mingus is a hell of a bass player, and Max is a hell of a drummer. But Duke can't play with them, and they can't play with Duke.

Now, how are you going to give a thing like that some stars? Record companies should be kicked in the ass. Somebody should take a picket sign and picket the record company.

5. Sonny Rollins, "You Are My Lucky Star" (*3 in Jazz*, **RCA Victor**). **Don Cherry, trumpet; Rollins, tenor saxophone; Henry Grimes, bass; Billy Higgins, drums.**

Now, why did they have to end it like that? Don Cherry I like, and Sonny I like, and the true idea is nice. The rhythm is nice. I didn't care too much for the bass player's solo. Five stars is real good? It's just good, no more. Give it three.

6. Stan Getz and João Gilberto, "Desafinado" (*Getz-Gilberto*, **Verve**). **Getz, tenor saxophone; Gilberto, vocal.**

Gilberto and Stan Getz made an album together? Stan plays good on that. I like Gilberto; I'm not particularly crazy about just *anybody's* bossa nova. I like the samba. And I like Stan, because he has so much patience, the way he plays those melodies—other people can't get nothing out of a song, but he can. Which takes a lot of imagination, that he has, that so many other people don't have.

As for Gilberto, he could read a newspaper and sound good! I'll give that one five stars.

7. Eric Dolphy, "Mary Ann" (*Far Cry*, New Jazz). Booker Little, trumpet; Dolphy, composer, alto saxophone; Jaki Byard, piano.

That's got to be Eric Dolphy—nobody else could sound that bad! The next time I see him I'm going to step on his foot. You print that. I think he's ridiculous. He's a sad shit.

FEATHER: *Down Beat* won't print those words.

DAVIS: Just put he's a sad shhhhhhh, that's all! The composition is sad. The piano player fucks it up, getting in the way so that you can't hear how things are supposed to be accented.

It's a sad record, and it's the record company's fault again. I didn't like the trumpet player's tone, and he don't do nothing. The running is all right if you're going to play that way, like Freddie Hubbard or Lee Morgan; but you've got to inject something, and you've got to have the rhythm section along; you just can't keep on playing all eighth notes.

The piano player's sad. You have to *think* when you play; you have to help each other—you just can't play for yourself. You've got to play with whomever you're playing. If I'm playing Basie, I'm going to try to help what he's doing—that particular feeling.

8. Cecil Taylor, "Lena" (*Live at the Café Montmartre*, Fantasy). Jimmy Lyons, alto saxophone; Taylor, piano.

Take it off! That's some sad shit, man. In the first place, I hear some Charlie Parker clichés. . . . They don't even fit. Is that what the critics are digging? Them critics better stop having coffee. If there ain't nothing to listen to, they might as well admit it. Just to take something like that and say it's great, because there ain't nothing to listen to, that's like going out and getting a prostitute.

FEATHER: This man said he was influenced by Duke Ellington.

DAVIS: I don't give a fuck! It must be Cecil Taylor. Right? I don't care who he's inspired by. That shit ain't nothing. In the first place he don't have the—you know, the way you touch a piano. He doesn't have the touch that would make the sound of whatever he thinks of come off.

I can tell he's influenced by Duke, but to put the loud pedal on the piano and make a run is very old-fashioned to me. And when the alto player sits up there and plays without no tone. . . . That's the reasons I don't buy any records.

—June 18, 1964

Four years ago, the last time Miles Davis was blindfold-tested, I remarked that he was "unusually selective in his listening habits." The only record that drew a favorable reaction was one by Stan Getz and João Gilberto, which brought a five-star rave. Everything else was put down in varying degrees: Les McCann, Rod Levitt, Sonny Rollins, Eric Dolphy, Cecil Taylor; even his early favorite Clark Terry and his idol Duke Ellington.

Looking back at earlier interviews with Miles, I am reminded that he was not always such a tough sale. In his first test (September 21, 1955), he gave four stars to Clifford Brown, four to a Metronome All-Stars track, and five to a record featuring Louis Armstrong, Bobby Hackett, and Jack Teagarden. Ellington elicited a twenty-five-star rating—or at least, the wish that there were such a rating. (He now abstains from using the rating system.)

Recently, visiting Miles in his Hollywood hotel suite, I found strewn around the room records or tape cartridges by James Brown, Dionne Warwick, Tony Bennett, the Byrds, Aretha Franklin, and the Fifth Dimension. Not a single jazz instrumental. More about this in the next installment. Meanwhile, here is the first half of a two-part test.

The Records

1. Freddie Hubbard, "On the Que-Tee" (*Backlash*, **Atlantic**). **Hubbard, trumpet, composer.**

I don't dig that kind of shit, man, just a straight thirty-two bars, I mean whatever it is. The time they were playing was too tight, you know. It's formal, man, and scales and all that. . . . No kind of sound, straight sound— no imagination. They shouldn't even put that out.

Freddie's a great trumpet player, but if he had some kind of other direction to go . . . if you place a guy in a spot where he has to do something else, other than what he can do, so he can do *that*. He's got to have something that challenges his imagination, far above what he thinks he's going to play, and what it might lead into, then above *that*, so he won't be fighting when things change.

That's what I tell all my musicians; I tell them be ready to play what you know and play above what you know. Anything might happen above what you've been used to playing—you're ready to get into that, and above that, and take that out.

But this sounds like just a lead sheet.

FEATHER: Do you think he's capable of more than that?

DAVIS: Yes, if he's directed, because he must have other imagination, other than this. I wouldn't even put that shit on a record.

2. Thad Jones and Mel Lewis, "Bachafillen" (*Live at the Village Vanguard*, **Solid State**). **Jones, flugelhorn; Garnett Brown, trombone, composer; Joe Farrell, tenor saxophone; Roland Hanna, piano; Richard Davis, bass; Lewis, drums.**

It's got to be Thad's big band. . . . I don't understand why guys have to push themselves and say "wow! wee!" and all that during an arrangement to make somebody think it's more than what it is, when it ain't nothing. I like the way Thad writes, but I also like the way he plays when he writes. I like when he plays his tunes, without all that stuff—no solos, you know. It's nothing to play off of.

FEATHER: There was a long tenor solo on that.

DAVIS: Yes, but it was nothing; they didn't need that, and the trombone player should be shot.

FEATHER: Well, who do you think wrote that?

DAVIS: I don't really know, but I don't like those kind of arrangements. You don't write arrangements like that for white guys . . . (*humming*). That ain't nothing.

In the first place, a band with that instrumentation fucks up an arrangement—the saxophones particularly. They could play other instruments, but you only get one sound like that. On that arrangement, the only one that rates is the piano player. He's something else. And Richard Davis. The drummer just plays straight, no shading. I couldn't stand a band like that for myself. It makes me feel like I'm broke and wearing a slip that doesn't belong to me, and my hair's combed the wrong way; it makes me feel funny, even as a listener.

Those guys don't have a musical mind—just playing what's written. They don't know what the notes mean.

FEATHER: Have you heard that band much in person?

DAVIS: Yes, I've heard them, but I don't like them. I like Thad's arrangements, but I don't like the guys pushing the arrangements, and shouting, because there's nothing happening. It would be better if they recorded the shouts at the end—or at least shout in tune!

3. Archie Shepp, "The Funeral" (*Archie Shepp in Europe*, **Delmark, recorded 1963**). **Don Cherry, cornet; John Tchicai, alto saxophone; Shepp, tenor saxophone.**

You're putting me on with that! . . . I know who it is—Ornette, fucking up the trumpet and the alto. I don't understand that jive at all. The guy has nice rhythm on saxophone.

People are so gullible—they go for that—they go for something they don't know about.

FEATHER: Why do you think they go for it?

DAVIS: Because they feel it's not hip *not* to go for it. But if something sounds terrible, man, a person should have enough respect for his own mind to say it doesn't sound good. It doesn't to me, and I'm not going to listen to it. No matter how long you listen to it, it doesn't sound any good.

Anyone can tell that guy's not a trumpet player—it's just notes that come out, and every note he plays, he looks serious about it, and people will go for it—especially white people. They go for anything. They want to be hipper than any other race, and they go for anything ridiculous like that.

FEATHER: Actually, you got that one wrong—it wasn't Ornette. It was an Archie Shepp date with John Tchicai on alto and Don Cherry on trumpet.

DAVIS: Well, whoever it is, it sounds the same—Ornette sounds the same way. That's where Archie and them got that shit from; there sure ain't nothing there.

4. Fifth Dimension, "Prologue, the Magic Garden" (*The Magic Garden*, **Soul City**). **Jim Webb, composer, arranger.**

That record is planned, you know. It's like when I do things, it's planned and you lead into other things. It makes sense. It has different sounds in the voicing, and they're using the stereo—they can sure use stereo today, coming out from different sides and different people making statements and things like that. That's the way you should record!

Yeah, that's a nice record; it sounds nice. I liked the composition and the arrangement. It's Jim Webb and the Fifth Dimension. It could be a little smoother—they push it too hard for the singers. You don't have to push that hard. When you push, you get a raggedy edge, and an edge gives another vibration.

I liked the instrumental introduction too. We did things like that on *Porgy and Bess*—just played parts of things.

I told Diahann Carroll about an idea I had for her to record, based on things like that. There are certain tunes—parts of tunes—that you like, and you have to go through all that other shit to get to that part—but she can just sing that part. She could sing it in any kind of musical form—eighteenth century, today's beat, and she can say the statement over and make the background change the mood and change the time. They could also use her as an instrument; instead of the strings under her, she could be *in* the strings, and have her coming out from each side of the stereo. She told me to set it up for her, and I was trying to do it for her.

Jimmy Webb would be great for her. I think Wayne could do it for her, too; but I told her to get a guy like Mel to put the story together.

FEATHER: Which Mel?

DAVIS: Mel Tormé. And you could have the music in between, to change the mood to whatever mood she wanted to sing in. She was interested and insisted that I produce it, but I don't want to get involved in that end of it.

—June 13, 1968

As I pointed out in the first part of this test [June 13, 1968], Miles Davis's hotel room was cluttered with pop vocal records. Why? There are several explanations, but the simplest and most logical, it seems to me, is that when you have reached the aesthetic mountaintop, there is no place to look but down.

Instead of judging other artists in terms of their own ideas and ideals, Miles looks for every other trumpet player, every other combo leader, to achieve what he has achieved.

Clearly this must lead to disappointment, for not every pianist today can be a Herbie Hancock, not every drummer a Tony Williams, or every saxophonist-composer a Wayne Shorter. Finding nothing that measures up to the standards he has set and met, Miles turns to other idioms. He relies on pop music for entertainment and classical music for serious listening.

There is nothing unprecedented about this. Walking into Charlie Parker's apartment, you were more likely to find him listening to Bartók than to some contemporary saxophonist. Similarly, there was nothing Art Tatum could learn from other pianists.

The taped interview was slightly censored; otherwise it represents Davis's precise comments on the records, about which he was given no information.

The Records

1. The Electric Flag, "Over-Lovin' You" (*A Long Time Comin'*, **Columbia). Barry Goldberg, Mike Bloomfield, composers.**

Who was that? Leave that record here, it's a nice record. I like guys that get into what they're supposed to be singing, and the guys that play behind it really get into what *they're* doing—when the mood changes they go right in it. It makes the record smooth; makes it mean something.

It's a pleasure to get a record like that, because you know they're serious no matter what they do. . . . I liked the rhythm on that. I mean, if you're going to do something like that, man, you've got to *do* it. You know what I mean? If you're going to play like that, play like that—*good*—but don't jive around.

I like to cop myself—I don't like to miss. I like to get into the meat of things, and sometimes it don't happen and sometimes it does; when it does, it feels great, and it makes up for the times when it doesn't. But if you know it's going to happen one night, it keeps you going.

2. Sun Ra, "Brainville" (*Sun Song*, **Delmark, recorded in 1956). Dave Young, trumpet; Sun Ra, composer.**

That's gotta come from Europe. We wouldn't play no shit like that. It's so sad. It sounds funny to me. Sounds like a 1935 arrangement by Raymond Scott. They must be joking—the Florida A. & M. band sounds better than that. They should record them, rather than that shit. They've got more spirit than that. That ain't nothing.

Why put that on record? What does that do? You mean there's somebody around here that feels like that? Even the white people don't feel that sad.

FEATHER: Do you think that's a white group?

DAVIS: The trumpet player didn't sound white. . . . I don't know, man. You know, there's a little thing that trumpet players play to make a jazz sound, that if you don't have your own sound, you can hear an adopted jazz sound, which is a drag, especially in the mute. I mean you can tell when a guy's got his own thing.

People should have good friends to tell them, "Man, that ain't it, so don't play trumpet," you know what I mean? Or, "Don't play drums, 'cause you don't have anything." I'd rather have that said to me than to go on playing trumpet when it doesn't sound like I want it to sound. I know he doesn't want it to sound like that, so he should work at it, or play another instrument—a lower instrument.

When an arrangement's tight like that, you have to play every chord, because the background parts when they record, like they play them single, instead of making it smooth—and it's hard to play like that. You have to play each chord, then play the other chords or you never connect anything, and in between it's just blank.

To me it's just like canned music. Even canned music sounds good sometimes, but not shit like this.

3. Don Ellis, "Alone" (*Electric Bath*, Columbia). Ellis, trumpet; Hank Levy, composer.

Who's that supposed to be? It's too straight, man. You know, you'd be surprised, this trumpet player probably can play, he sounds all right, but with a strong rhythm like that—if you have a straight rhythm like that, the band has to play against the rhythm, because the rhythm is never gonna change, and that's very hard to do. The best way to do that is for the rhythm to play real soft.

You don't need a trumpet in something like that. It was just one of those major, minor, major. . . .

It's a kind of mood tune. I would play it slower and have the band way down, so they could have got some kind of feeling into it. You could tell they don't feel like playing this. Somebody was impressed with 5/4 time, but what difference does that make? What's so great about a whole number in 5/4? In our group we change the beat around and do all kind of things with time, but not just to say, "Look at me, I'm playing 5/4!" There's nothing there, but I guess the critics will have something to write about.

FEATHER: It was Don Ellis. Have you ever heard him?

DAVIS: Yeah, I heard him. He's no soloist. I mean, he's a nice guy and all that, but to me he's just another white trumpet player. He can't play in a chord, can't play with any feeling; that's the reason I guess they use all that time shit.

Anybody can make a record and try to do something new to sell; but to me a record is more than something new, and I don't care how much it sells. You have to capture some feeling—you can't just play like a fucking machine. You can't even turn on with any kind of dope and get any feeling to play if you don't have it in your heart. No matter what you do, it won't make you play any better. You are what you are, no matter what you do. I can be loud and no good, soft and no good, in 7/8 and no good. You can be black and no good, white and no good. . . . A guy like Bobby Hackett plays what he plays with feeling, and you can put him into any kind of thing and he'll do it.

4. Al Hirt, "Goin' to Chicago Blues" (*Live at Carnegie Hall*, RCA). **Hirt, trumpet.**

It's Al Hirt. I think he's a very good trumpet player. For anyone that feels that way, I guess he hits them. He's a good trumpet player, but that's some corny-ass shit he plays here.

They want him to be fat and white and funny and talented, but he ain't. They want something that looks good on television; fat, with a beard, and jovial and jolly. He's like a white Uncle Tom. And he's a nice guy; it's a drag. You know, white folks made Negroes tom a long time ago by giving them money. To do this in front of some white people, to pay you to have that kind of personality, like him, it's tomming. I can't see why a guy like Al Hirt . . . I guess if he was thin he wouldn't do it.

Harry James is a good trumpet player, and he never did tom or no shit like that. Harry had some feeling.

For a guy to shake his unattractive body and think somebody thinks it's funny—it ain't funny, it's disgusting. He can't entertain me like that; he can entertain some corny ofays, but all the colored folks I know would say, "Oh, fuck! I don't want to hear that!"

—June 27, 1968

Howard Brofsky

Miles Davis and "My Funny Valentine": The Evolution of a Solo

Originally published in Black Music Research Journal *3 (1983): 23–44.*
Reprinted by permission of the Center for Black Music Research and the author.

In a sense, Howard Brofsky's analysis and comparison of three Miles Davis recorded solos on "My Funny Valentine" pick up where Don Heckman's article left off. The three versions were recorded in 1956, 1958, and 1964, and the comparisons are, to say the least, enlightening. As with Heckman's transcriptions, all musical examples are in concert key. Brofsky, a musicologist, is professor emeritus of music at the City University of New York/Queens College.

Some words are in order about the account Brofsky quotes concerning Davis allegedly sitting in with the Max Roach/Clifford Brown quintet in Detroit. Although this colorful story has cropped up in several varying accounts—including one in Davis's autobiography—it makes no historical sense. We know that Davis spent several months in Detroit in late 1953 and early 1954, returning to New York in February. (Davis resumed his recording activities in New York on March 6 with a date for Blue Note.) The Roach/Brown group did not even exist during that entire period; it was formed in Los Angeles shortly thereafter.—Ed.

Between 1950 and 1953 Miles Davis, then in his mid-twenties, was at or near the top of the readers' polls in both *Down Beat* and *Metronome* magazines. But in December 1953 Davis was ousted from this position by the young white trumpeter Chet Baker, whose recording of "My Funny Valentine" with Gerry Mulligan in September 1952 was a "smash hit." The *Metronome Yearbook 1954* (p. 21) named Baker one of four "Musicians of the Year" and his "My Funny Valentine" one of the "Jazz Records of the Year." *Down Beat* (December 24, 1954, 7) listed Baker as one of five "Jazz Personalities of the Year" and the "Critics' New Star of 1953." One might ask how much attention should be paid to readers' polls in popular magazines or even to the editorial opinions of these magazines, except perhaps from the sociological point of view. After all, in the 1952 *Down Beat* readers' poll (December 31, 1952, 8), Miles Davis was in second place *after* Maynard Ferguson!—and, of the above-mentioned five "Jazz Personalities of the Year," four were white.

Some critics did acknowledge Miles Davis's influence on Chet Baker. For example, Barry Ulanov wrote of Baker's "Miles Davisish sound" (*Metronome*, January 1953, 26) and of his "style owing much to Miles" (*Metronome*, April 1953, 25). At the same time, the critics were captivated by Baker: the English pianist Dill Jones called him "one of the greatest white players ever" (*Melody Maker*, May 30, 1953, 4); the English critic Alun Morgan wrote of him as "one of the most poetic, most lyrical and accomplished soloists in jazz today" (*Jazz Journal*, February 1954, 7); and the American Charles Emge described Baker's "My Funny Valentine" as "the song that has become associated with Chet much like Bunny Berigan's 'I Can't Get Started,' an identification that will undoubtedly last throughout Chet's playing career" (*Down Beat*, August 12, 1953, 16).

Ulanov reviewed Baker's recording (*Metronome*, April 1953, 25): "'Valentine' hasn't received such lovely treatment as Chet Baker's trumpet accords it here . . . an effect little short of surpassing beauty." A month later in reviewing two recent Miles Davis recordings (Blue Note LP 5013 and Prestige LP 140), Ulanov referred to Davis's "eggshell trumpet" and "inadequate technical management of his horn," and wrote that "Miles is feeble again" (*Metronome*, May 1953, 24).

These were the years of Davis's heroin addiction (Baker's as well). Leonard Feather wrote that "his [Davis's] career has been at a virtual standstill since 1950" (*Melody Maker*, February 23, 1952, 4),[1] and now the young white trumpeter from California ("today the liveliest center of developing jazz," according to *Time*, February 1, 1954), with the "Miles Davisish sound," had replaced Davis in the polls as best trumpeter.

Chet Baker was featured in *Harper's Bazaar* (June 1954, 72, with a large picture) and *Time* (February 1, 1954, 38), and he appeared on the cover of the French *Jazz Magazine* (July/August 1955). In a full-page ad by the Martin Band Instrument Company, a comic-strip biography of Chet Baker exemplified "Successful Careers in Music," referring to his "My Funny Valentine" as "on its way toward becoming a jazz classic" (*Metronome*, November 1954, 9). And in an article on jazz trumpeters (*Metronome*, July 1956, 22), Don Ferrara (a jazz trumpeter himself) wrote: "Baker's whole expressions, because it is [*sic*] easier to understand, has more general appeal than Miles'. . . . Melodically, Chet has explored even more than Miles." The predominantly white press, inadvertently or not, preferred a white trumpeter on the pedestal rather than a black one. How did Miles Davis feel about all this? What did he think? "It [discrimination he suffered in high school music contests] made me so mad I made up my mind to outdo anybody white on my horn. If I hadn't met that prejudice, I probably wouldn't have had as much drive in my work" (*Playboy*, September 1962, 60).

On October 26, 1956, Davis went into the studio and recorded Baker's hit, "My Funny Valentine," and over the next nine years, he played it frequently in public. Davis, by sheer artistry, took the song away from Baker and with it created several fine performances, and at least one masterpiece.[2]

Richard Rodgers and Lorenz Hart wrote "My Funny Valentine" in 1937 for the show *Babes in Arms*, and it is one of the finest American popular songs. It has the characteristic AABA structure of the genre, but Rodgers extends the thirty-two measures to thirty-six by the addition of a four-measure tag at the end. Also distinguishing the song is the ambiguity of key and mode; while it is predominantly in C minor, the bridge is in the relative major, Eb, and the tag brings the song to a conclusion in Eb major. Of further interest are the sources of melodic unity in the song (for example, the manipulation of the motive ♩ ♩ ♩ |♩. ♪♩) and the gentle but imposing melodic curve, which reaches a pitch climax in measures 31 and 32 with the held Eb (see Appendix A).

One could easily devote an entire paper to the relationship between a jazz improvisation and the original melody on which it is based. How much of the original—melody, rhythm, harmony, form, or even text—does the improviser retain? Or, to put it differently, what are the relationships between theme and variations? In the three versions of "My Funny Valentine" under discussion here,[3] the perceptive listener usually remains aware of the original tune, although the last version takes you the greatest distance from it, the farthest "out."

October 26, 1956 (studio, Prestige LP 7094, 24001)
   Miles Davis, trumpet
   Red Garland, piano
   Paul Chambers, bass
   Philly Joe Jones, drums

July 28, 1958 (live, Columbia C 32470)
   Miles Davis, trumpet
   Bill Evans, piano
   Paul Chambers, bass
   Jimmy Cobb, drums

February 12, 1964 (live, Columbia PC 9106[4])
   Miles Davis, trumpet
   George Coleman, tenor saxophone
   Herbie Hancock, piano
   Ron Carter, bass
   Tony Williams, drums

   By 1964 Davis's "My Funny Valentine" had evolved into a great solo, one that pushes the original tune to its limits and has a vast emotional and musical range. In an excellent book on Davis, Ian Carr notes of this performance that Davis "had taken the technical and emotional exploration of standard song structures as far as was possible before they disintegrated completely and metamorphosed into something else." He observes also that compared with the 1956 version (he doesn't discuss the 1958 one), "the emotional range is very much greater" (Carr 1982, 139).
   Obviously, Davis responds differently to the three highly distinctive and superlative rhythm sections, and this is an important factor in the differences between one performance and another. Furthermore, the overall structure changes significantly, from only two and one-half choruses in 1956, three in 1958, to six choruses in 1964. Tempo does not play a

significant role, except that the 1958 version is quite a bit slower than the others:

1956 ♩ = ca. 67
1958 ♩ = ca. 46
1964 ♩ = ca. 60

    I don't know to what extent Davis played the song in public before first recording it in 1956, but Hentoff (1962, 162) quotes him as follows: "I played 'My Funny Valentine' for a long time—and didn't like it—and all of a sudden it meant something." About when was that, one might ask—and what part did Baker's success with the song play, if any? Cole (1974, 55–56) has the following anecdotal account:

> It seems more than just an accident of history that Miles should dramatically walk into Baker's [not Chet] Keyboard Lounge in Detroit with the Max Roach/Clifford Brown quintet performing and begin playing "My Funny Valentine." This was early in 1954, and Miles was playing single with a local rhythm section at the Bluebird Bar, not far from Baker's. Drugs had now taken their toll and pushed him near the point of no return. That night, he suddenly walked into the lounge where his competitor group was playing, interrupted the band with his own rendition of his favorite ballad, and walked out.[5]

    Chet Baker, in his recording, played the song with his broad, open tone and little vibrato. Davis, in his first recording, immediately distinguishes himself playing with a Harmon mute into the microphone, an effect he used frequently at that time. He further asserts his individuality very early on by a striking harmonic substitution: instead of the traditional chromatic descending bass line in the first four measures (as in the original, ex. 1a, and in Baker's recording), Davis substitutes an Ab-seventh (augmented eleventh) chord against the D in the melody in measure 2 (ex. 1b).

EXAMPLE 1

    a.

b.

The piece opens with a piano introduction, and here Red Garland quotes a melody played by Nat "King" Cole at the end of his "The Man I Love," recorded some twelve years earlier (see ex. 2). (Garland also uses this theme to close the piece.)

EXAMPLE 2

Then Davis, toward the end of his solo, pays tribute to his early mentor, quoting from the last eight measures of Charlie Parker's solo on "Sepian Bounce" with the Jay McShann Orchestra in 1942 (see ex. 3)[6] (The "III/19" in ex. 3 means the third chorus, m. 19; see the complete transcription in Appendix B.)

EXAMPLE 3

III/19

In a sense these quotations illustrate the oral tradition: they show an implicit historical understanding, as the jazz musicians pay homage to their predecessors.

After the piano introduction, Davis's statement of the melody is fairly straightforward in the first eight measures—as straightforward as Davis ever can be; that is, he stays fairly close to the original tune, though of course playing it with great subtlety of timbre and rhythm. Comparing these first eight measures with the original (see ex. 4), we can see some of this, although even in a statement as relatively simple as this, the notational system is inadequate to the task.[7] Note, for example, how Davis begins each of the three phrases (2 + 2 + 4 measures) far into the measure (cer-

EXAMPLE 4

tainly an illustration of the concept "laid back"); how he compresses the second phrase (literally repeated in the original); and how effectively he adds only one note—the E♭ in measure 6.

In the second A section, Davis leaves the original far behind at first, then returns to it in the latter part. The bridge and final A section deviate significantly from the original in the following noteworthy details: the pitch climax at measure 25 (independent of the melodic curve of the original) and the outlining of the augmented fourth with its "bluesy" effect (ex. 5); the repositioning and diminution of a phrase from the bridge of the original at the end of his solo (ex. 6); the general avoidance of the tonic; and, finally, how Davis blurs the structural outlines by carrying his solo two measures over into the next chorus.

EXAMPLE 5

EXAMPLE 6

from

After a full chorus by the piano, Davis returns with the bridge, seemingly catching Paul Chambers, the bassist, unaware, because Chambers goes back to the C minor of the opening rather than the E♭ major of the bridge. Davis calls the listener back by his reentry with the original melody, except for the final note of the phrase, which he characteristically deflects (see ex. 7). Then follows the quote from Charlie Parker (ex. 3 above) and, a few measures later, a most telling silence in conjunction with a tension-building C pedal in the bass (III/25–27). Finally, Davis plays a brief cadenza, the most chromatic passage of the piece and one with the highest note (Db).

EXAMPLE 7

This 1956 version is the shortest of the three, in some ways the simplest, and what one might describe, with reference to the classical compositional process, as a "sketch" for the 1964 version, the last one.

On July 28, 1958, the Miles Davis Sextet played a special performance, along with the Duke Ellington Orchestra, at the Plaza Hotel in New York, sponsored by Columbia Records. Columbia recorded the session but did not issue it until some fifteen years later. One of the four selections was "My Funny Valentine," featuring Davis alone with the rhythm section. Bill Evans presents a rather dreamy introduction that sets not only the mood but also the very slow tempo (or did Davis set it?). After Davis's first chorus, Evans takes the second, and then, differing from the 1956 version, Chambers takes a sixteen-measure solo (A + A) and Davis returns for the bridge and final A.

The accompaniment to Davis's first chorus features a much more active bass part in the context of the very slow tempo. Thus, compared with the earlier recording, we can see how, in a span of less than two years, the rhythm section moves more into the foreground, assuming a less subordinate role. The bass is no longer confined to merely "walking," instead creating a more complex accompaniment with a less explicit pulse.

Davis, again playing with a Harmon mute, begins his solo similarly to the earlier version: a literal statement of the first four measures of the melody, though again very compressed and "laid back." In measure 5 a new figure appears (see ex. 8), one that recurs, though varied, at the analogous place in the second A (m. 13) and reappears in the 1964 performance.

EXAMPLE 8

In the first four measures of the second A section, Davis emphasizes the eleventh and ninth against the C-minor harmony and then returns to the original tune (see ex. 9).

EXAMPLE 9

As in the earlier version, the beginning of the bridge calls forth a descending phrase, one that moves effectively in contrary motion to the original tune (see ex. 10).

EXAMPLE 10

Now Davis ends the bridge more subtly, with a phrase that carries over into the first measure of the final A section. At this point Davis, as in 1956, plays a figure with the pitch climax on the high C, followed by the Gb (cf. ex. 5). Then an interesting rhythmic intensification (ex. 11) occurs at the point of melodic climax in the original tune (mm. 31–32), contrary in effect to the held note in the 1956 performance. Davis ends his solo this time three measures into the next chorus but with a figure very close to that of the 1956 version (see ex. 12).

EXAMPLE 11

EXAMPLE 12

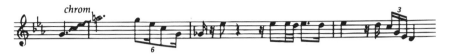

We next hear wonderful solos by Evans (the recorded piano sound is not what it should be) and Chambers; then a drum roll prepares the listener (and the rest of the band) for Davis's return at the bridge. His first phrase has the same melodic curve, bounded by the same pitches, as when he first played the bridge in this performance. But he extends the phrase by one measure with the interesting interpolation of a figure from measures 10–12 (cf. exx. 9, 10, and 13).

EXAMPLE 13

Davis emphasizes the augmented fourth once again at the beginning of the final A section, as he had done in the first chorus as well as in the first chorus of the earlier version (cf. ex. 5). He then intensifies the ending compared with the 1956 version by a rapid run up to the high D♭ in measure 32, and then descends in preparation for another sweep up to the high D♭ in the cadenza. From this high point, Davis descends all the way to the bottom of the range of the instrument and even tries at the very end to go below the lowest note down to the E♭. Along the way, over the V chord, Davis repeats a large segment from the 1956 cadenza.

While there are many points of similarity between this 1958 performance and the one from 1956, the later version is generally looser, with Davis going further "out" ("We play 'My Funny Valentine' like with a scale all the way through," Davis said [Hentoff 1962, 167]), playing in a somewhat more florid style and with more facility. Perhaps Evans's chord voicings and general style had some effect; "Cannonball" Adderley, with the band at this time, said that "when he started to use Bill Evans, Miles changed his style from very hard to a softer approach" (James 1961, 71).

The six-year gap between this performance at the Plaza and the Lincoln Center concert in 1964 is reflected in the tremendous differences between these two versions. It would be interesting if we had a "My Funny Valentine" midway between these two, possibly with Wynton Kelly at the piano in 1960 or 1961. In 1964, apart from the fact that everyone "stretches out" more, so that there are now six complete choruses (two by Davis, two by the tenor saxophonist George Coleman, one and one-half by the pianist Herbie Hancock, and the final half chorus by Davis), the trumpeter thoroughly explores the original song, and his solo has an emotional intensity that, to my mind, makes it a masterpiece.

It must be noted that Davis has here a younger, more modern rhythm section, and in the case of Hancock and Carter, conservatory-trained musicians with a wide knowledge of contemporary harmony. Thus, the rhythm and harmonies are much more complex, even to the point of being difficult to follow on first or second hearing. But we still hear relationships to the original tune and to earlier versions and can see how this solo has evolved—how Davis, in a kind of compositional process, keeps some ideas, discards others, and thus refines and develops his finest version.

Without giving a blow-by-blow description of the complex events in this piece, I will cite some of the more interesting aspects, pointing out relationships with the two other versions. For one thing, Davis's trumpet playing here is extraordinary and ought to have dispelled continuing criticism of his "limited technique." Apart from his exploitation of a three-octave range, Davis, who plays without mute in this version, creates an unusual variety of timbres. Making instruments talk is, of course, a part of jazz tradition and goes back to its roots. But Davis makes the trumpet cry and shout and moan with overpowering effect.

After the free piano introduction, Davis enters with the first four measures of the original melody, again very "laid back" as in the other versions. This time, however, the bass does not enter until measure 9, so we have a very fluid, undefined pulse in the first A section. In measure 5 Davis expands the pitch range with a partial restatement of the figure from 1958 (cf. ex. 8). With the entrance of the bass playing a G-to-C pedal in the second A section, Davis's Ab and Db create a striking dissonance, after which he returns to the original tune (see ex. 14).

A prominent motive in this performance goes back to 1958. It is in fact a Davis cliché during this period, for we hear it as well on *Miles Davis in Person—Friday and Saturday Nights at the Blackhawk* (1961) or *Quiet Nights* (1962). (See ex. 15.)

The change into double-time for the second chorus begins subtly in the four-measure tag at the end of the first chorus, thus blurring the articulation. (We are reminded of how Davis also disguises the structural outlines by carrying his improvisations over into the following chorus.) The rhythmic excitement generated by the rhythm section here is matched by

EXAMPLE 14

EXAMPLE 15

EXAMPLE 16

Davis's feral playing, as in the many different sounds he makes (half-valves, smears, etc.) or in a run such as that shown in example 16.

EXAMPLE 16

As in the earlier pieces (cf. ex. 5), the C and Gb appear at analogous points, where the Gb-seventh has been substituted (I/26, II/2, II/10). An interesting anticipation of the tune, and then its statement in the right place, occurs at the end of the second A section (see ex. 17).

EXAMPLE 17

The rhythm section provides further evidence of the broad emotional range here when it changes into a "Latin" style in the bridge of Davis's second chorus—an effect that would have been incongruous in the earlier versions but seems right here.[8] Then for the first time, coincident with the pitch climax of the original melody, Davis goes into the extreme upper register (F and G above high C), and then rapidly drops down through three octaves. He then continues over into the next chorus with the same sixth of the C-minor chord, the A, as he did in both earlier versions (cf. ex. 12).

Endings are, of course, crucial, and Davis's mastery shows itself here as well. He returns at the bridge in the middle of Hancock's second chorus, with references to the original melody. Then the figure that goes back to 1958 (cf. ex. 8), and which marks the initial unfolding of the solo, is now recalled and quickly abandoned (VI/29). Finally, we have no cadenza this time—the piece has been sufficiently long (more than fourteen minutes) and certainly rich enough; instead Davis plays a subtly arpeggiated tonic triad above the cadential chords of the last four measures.

In studying these three versions of the same song, I first thought that there was an analogue here to the classical composer's workshop: sketches, material discarded, modified, or refined; polishing; and finally the completed piece, the fruit of a great deal of labor. (Schuller 1968, x, writes that "jazz improvisation constitutes 'work in progress.' ") While successive performances allow the improviser the opportunity to do all of this, if we view it only in this way, we apply a European standard to this improvised music which really seems inappropriate. (Is the last version always the best? What about the chance element—the spontaneous event—in improvisation? Not to mention that the soloist is not alone but is subject to influence and inspiration from the rest of the group.) From this perspective the 1956 and 1958 versions are then only "sketches," and we might not appreciate their unique qualities. On the other hand, there is, among these three versions, a kind of progression from improvisation to composition, from unique moments in the earlier pieces to the global conception of the 1964 performance.

In studying these pieces, I listened to them countless times and applied the tools of traditional analysis to the transcriptions. The music continues to surprise, delight, and move me, and this is surely the test of great art.

Notes

This paper was read at the National Conference on Black Music Research at Fisk University, Nashville, Tennessee, in March 1982. I want to thank Joan Stiles, a student in my doctoral seminar in 1980, for allowing me to work with and modify her transcriptions of Davis's solos. The part of the transcription of the 1964 solo in brackets is from Kerschbaumer 1978, here transposed to concert pitch.

1. With the critic's characteristic hyperbole, Feather is describing a period of only two years, during which Davis recorded four of the *Birth of the Cool* sides (March 1950) and did the January 1951 session with Charlie Parker ("Au Privave," etc.) and the Prestige *Conception* album (October 1951).

2. I must note that I personally like Baker's playing and feel he has an original, sensitive style. But in the pantheon, Davis, not Baker, joins Armstrong, Young, Parker, and others.

3. These are the only recordings generally available; the Japanese have issued a record of Davis in Tokyo in 1964, and there are other live performances of the tune on tape, although these have not been released.

4. A drastically truncated version, which eliminates the saxophone and piano solos, as well as Davis's half chorus at the end, appears on Columbia PC 9808, as one of the trumpeter's "Greatest Hits."

5. Eric Nisenson gives a more detailed account of this incident, attributing it to "former Detroiter and artist Richard (Prophet) Jennings." In this version Davis walked onstage, interrupted a rapid "Sweet Georgia Brown," and just started to play "My Funny Valentine." This is such unorthodox behavior that, if true, Davis must have been in some kind of intense emotional state at the time (Nisenson 1982, 88–89).

6. Davis: "In high school, we used to buy old jukebox records for a dime apiece. We listened to Jay McShann records like 'Hootie Blues' and 'Swingmatism' to hear Charlie Parker" (Anderson 1958, 58).

7. The reader may wish to compare my transcriptions with those in Carr 1982: 1956 version, pp. 256–57; 1964 version, pp. 260–61. The differences are primarily rhythmic.

8. The rhythm section also does this on "Stella by Starlight," performed at the same concert. This ballad has an overall plan similar to "My Funny Valentine."

References

Anderson, J. L. 1958. "The Musings of Miles." *Saturday Review*, October 11, 41, 58–59.

Carr, Ian. 1982. *Miles Davis: A Biography.* New York: William Morrow.

Cole, Bill. 1974. *Miles Davis: A Musical Biography.* New York: William Morrow.

Down Beat, December 31, 1952; August 12, 1953; December 24, 1954.

Harper's Bazaar, June 1954.

Hentoff, Nat. 1962. "An Afternoon with Miles Davis." *Jazz Review*, December 1958. Reprint, *Jazz Panorama: From the Pages of "The Jazz Review,"* edited by Martin Williams, 161–68. New York: Crowell-Collier Press.

James, Michael. 1961. *Miles Davis.* New York: A. S. Barnes.

Jazz Journal, February 1954.

Jazz Magazine (Paris), July/August 1955.

Kerschbaumer, Franz. 1978. *Miles Davis: Stilkritische Untersuchungen zur musikalischen Entwicklung seines Personalstils.* Beiträge zur Jazzforschung, no. 5. Graz: Akademische Druck-u. Verlagsanstalt.

Melody Maker, February 23, 1952; May 30, 1953.

Metronome, January 1953, April 1953, May 1953, November 1954, July 1956.

Metronome Yearbook 1954.

Nisenson, Eric. 1982. *'Round About Midnight: A Portrait of Miles Davis.* New York: Dial Press.

Playboy, September 1962.

Schuller, Gunther. 1968. *Early Jazz.* New York: Oxford University Press.

Time, February 1, 1954.

Appendix A. "My Funny Valentine." Music by Richard Rodgers, words by Lorenz Hart. Copyright © 1937 by Williamson Music and The Estate of Lorenz Hart in the United States. Copyright Renewed. All Rights on behalf of The Estate of Lorenz Hart administered by WB Music Corp. International Copyright Secured. All Rights Reserved.

Appendix B. Transcription by Joan Stiles and Howard Brofsky.

Harvey Pekar

Miles Davis: 1964–69 Recordings

Originally published in Coda, *May 1976, 8–14. Reprinted by permission of* Coda *and the author.*

When Harvey Pekar wrote this piece, the band now commonly regarded as Miles Davis's "second great quintet" was more than a half decade in the past and little discussed. The 1970s were, for Davis and many other premier jazz musicians, years of jazz-rock fusion. But gradually, more and more of the music that this quintet had recorded was released, and in the 1980s and 1990s, a number of prominent younger musicians became intrigued with the innovations that Davis, Wayne Shorter, Herbie Hancock, Ron Carter, and Tony Williams had pioneered a generation earlier. Today, the Davis quintet of the mid- to late 1960s is revered as one of the finest ensembles in jazz history, and its lessons are still being absorbed.

Pekar was restricted to a discussion of a small number of then-available albums, but his analysis remains sound. This does credit to a veteran critic who has written since 1959 for the *Jazz Review, Down Beat, Jazz Journal, Coda,* and the *Village Voice.* He also is the author of a unique series of comic books known under the collective title *American Splendor.*—Ed.

Perhaps the most unjustifiably neglected group that Miles Davis ever led was the one including Wayne Shorter, Herbie Hancock, Ron Carter, and Tony Williams. The group was formed in 1964 and recorded as an intact unit through 1968. Actually Carter, Hancock, and Williams had been with Miles's previous band. The only personnel change involved the replacement of George Coleman, a fine tenor saxophonist, by Wayne Shorter. (Actually Sam Rivers did play tenor with Miles briefly between Coleman and Shorter.)

After the breakup of his great sextet including Bill Evans, John Coltrane, and Cannonball Adderley, Miles seemed to have reached a plateau in his career. He continued to employ top-notch sidemen, including Hank Mobley and Coleman, and to make excellent albums. On them, however, Miles often seemed content to record standards ("My Funny Valentine," "Stella by Starlight," "Autumn Leaves") and compositions that he'd made famous in the past ("Walkin'," "So What"). His bent for experimentation seems to have temporarily left him. When Shorter joined him, however, Miles embarked on a new era of exploration that rivaled his 1955–59 period: the one that produced *Kind of Blue.*

The achievements of Miles, Shorter, Hancock, Carter, and Williams were not sufficiently appreciated by jazz fans and musicians. Their music was often exquisitely refined and subtle—apparently too subtle for many listeners. In the mid-sixties the more violent music of John Coltrane and the "new thing" musicians such as Ornette Coleman and Albert Ayler was more influential than that of Miles. However, Miles's music continued to evolve, and by 1969 he'd developed a group style, heard on *Bitches Brew,* which was widely acclaimed, attracting pop as well as jazz fans, and which made him once again the most influential of jazz musicians. The characteristics of Miles's albums with Shorter and the evolution of his group concept from 1964 to 1969 will be discussed here.

Miles in Berlin was the first LP that Miles's quintet including Shorter made. Cut in September 1964, it was briefly issued in the 1980s by American Columbia. (The album was originally released on German CBS.)

Miles in Berlin is pretty much in the mold of records Miles had been making in the early sixties with his previous groups. All of the pieces on it had been recorded by Miles before. Although not a revolutionary album, it contains excellent work by him and his sidemen.

Miles was still, in 1964, the best of all jazz trumpeters—inventive, tasteful, technically assured, possessed of a good range and warm tone, capable of bringing all registers of his horn into play effectively, and of improvising lyrically or heatedly as the occasion demanded.

Wayne Shorter is one of the great Coltrane-influenced tenor saxophonists. By 1964 Shorter had already established himself as an original stylist. Coltrane's influence was still discernible in his work, but Shorter's tone was broader, softer, and less dark than Trane's. Shorter's rhythm conception was unique: he could swing powerfully but sometimes chose not to; instead he used long tones and rests to half-time and float over the rhythm section. In this respect his work was reminiscent of that of Lester Young and Sonny Rollins, who also sometimes seemed to be playing slower than the rhythm sections that accompanied them. Melodically and harmonically Shorter's work was also fresh: his choice of notes was often unusual, and he seldom used clichés. He constructed his solos imaginatively, varying the length of his phrases unpredictably.

Herbie Hancock ranks among the best pianists to come to the fore since 1955. His style has been drawn from several sources. Around 1961–62 his work sometimes had an earthy quality that could be attributed to the influence of Wynton Kelly. However, his light touch and graceful articulation were reminiscent of Hank Jones and Tommy Flanagan. By 1964 Hancock had obviously been influenced by Bill Evans and possibly McCoy Tyner. In addition to this, Hancock had picked up some devices from classical music, as his brilliant work on Williams's Blue Note LP *Spring* illustrates. He blended his influences beautifully. From 1963 on, he was as versatile, tasteful, and consistently excellent as any pianist in jazz.

At eighteen Tony Williams was one of the most technically accomplished, creative drummers in jazz. He had extraordinary independence of hands and feet and could play with great speed. His work was crisp and precise. He was capable of driving soloists with considerable authority but could also play sensitively. An imaginative rhythm section drummer, he was known for turning the time around (in a positive sense) quite frequently.

Although not an outstanding soloist, Ron Carter is a great rhythm section bassist. His time and intonation are excellent, and his walking is very alive and springy.

Not only were Hancock, Williams, and Carter excellent individually, they had uncanny rapport in the rhythm section. They functioned with considerable independence and freedom within the section yet complemented each other beautifully. The smoothness with which they executed spontaneous tempo changes was marvelous. They were a powerful as well as intelligent rhythm section. Williams and Carter pushed the beat aggressively, emphasizing its leading edge to a greater extent than bassists and drummers had done previously.

The amazing skill and sensitivity of the Hancock-Williams-Carter rhythm section are demonstrated on "Milestones," the opening track on *Miles in Berlin.* The solo work by Miles, Shorter, and Hancock is fine, but perhaps even more interesting is the playing of the rhythm section and its interaction with the soloists. There are all sorts of interesting things happening on "Milestones," including tempo changes, quasi tempo changes (during which the tempo remains constant but the soloist and rhythm section appear to be playing at different rates of speed), and even a meter change during Shorter's solo.

Throughout *Miles in Berlin* the variety of figures employed by the rhythm section is astonishing, as is the section's ability to hold together while playing against one another. They employ actual and quasi tempo changes on "Walkin'" as well as "Milestones."

Hancock's great ability as a rhythm section member is sometimes not appreciated. Sometimes he is primarily concerned with booting Davis and Shorter, but often he goes beyond that to not only provide effects that stimulate and complement them but add to the interest of the performance in general.

Miles's playing on this LP is quite good, although the breakneck pace of "Milestones" and "Walkin'" seems to hamper him a bit. He generally plays more inventively and constructs better solos at more comfortable tempos. As for the development of his solo style—essentially it did not change much between 1961 and 1964, nor would it for several years to come. He evolved much more as a group leader during 1964–68 than as a soloist.

Shorter, a fine technician, plays confidently and securely even at extremely rapid tempos. All of his spots on this LP are idea-rich. His harmonic and rhythmic daring on "Milestones" and "So What" is particularly worthy of note.

Hancock solos in a consistently relaxed manner no matter how fast he's playing. He turns in marvelously clean single-note line playing, employing the upper register quite a bit. He half-times very effectively at times, varying the rate of speed of his playing more than Miles and Shorter. Hancock uses contrasts very well—contrasts of sparsely and many-noted phrases, contrasts of registers, contrasts of single-note lines and chords, and contrasts of volume, textures, and note densities. The importance of contrast in his soloing as well as its delicacy and smoothness are reminiscent of the playing of Ahmad Jamal.

A final word about the solos on *Miles in Berlin:* two of the pieces on the album, "Milestones" and "So What," have been called "modal" compositions. Whether they actually are modal in the strict sense is debatable. However, they do have simple, uncluttered harmonic foundations that are supposed to afford the soloists a greater opportunity to develop their melodic ideas than did the complicated chord patterns often employed by the boppers and postboppers. However, Miles, Shorter, and Hancock add chords to the harmonic foundations of "Milestones" and "So What" when they improvise; consequently their solos have the twists and turns and complexity of those played by the boppers and postboppers on tightly packed chord progressions. This and the fact that "Milestones" and "So What" are taken at breakneck tempos ironically make them sound much like the wild bebop performances of the 1940s that Miles at one time expressed distaste for.

In January 1965 Miles, Shorter, Hancock, Carter, and Williams made their first studio LP, *E.S.P.*, for Columbia. This record was a great breakthrough for Miles. It contained seven titles, all originals. This was the first time Miles had recorded an album containing so much new material in years. Moreover, the style of music he presented was unique; it began a new phase in his evolution as a group leader.

Many of the compositions that Miles and his group recorded on *E.S.P.* and several albums that followed it are very spare. They are simple in structure and sparse melodically, containing relatively few notes, and are opened up by rests. Sustained notes are employed in some of them, sometimes along with rests, to help create a "spacey," airy, otherworldly quality. These spare, spacey melodies forecast a similar category of composition that Weather Report would sometimes use.

"E.S.P.," the title track, is a sixteen-bar up-tempo tune by Shorter and Miles that has a sparsely noted melody but is based on rather frequently occurring chord changes. The theme is interesting for several reasons including the fact that fourths are employed in it. Partly due to the influence of John Coltrane and, later, Chick Corea, fourths were used during the late sixties and seventies much more frequently than before.

There are superb swinging solos by Miles, Shorter, and Hancock here, backed by impeccable rhythm section work.

"Eighty-one" is a blues by Miles and Carter that begins with two choruses of ensemble work. Each chorus contains a different theme. Rests and long tones are employed on "Eighty-one" to create the kind of airy effects referred to above. In the rhythm section Williams and Carter do some busy rhythm-and-blues-influenced playing, and Hancock employs block chords. These effects, when combined, account for a rich, complex rhythm section sound. During the last two choruses of Miles's and Shorter's solos, Williams and Carter revert to more traditional smoothly swinging rhythm section playing, with Carter walking. This creates contrast and releases the tension they've built with their busier work.

Miles has a nicely put together spot on "Eighty-one," but it is Shorter's solo, a model of lucid construction and melodic inventiveness, that steals the show. Back in 1965 Shorter was an underrated soloist, thought by some to be just another better than average postbop player, but he was already a brilliant musician.

"Little One," by Herbie Hancock, is a waltz that opens and closes with out-of-tempo sections during which Miles and Shorter engage in a lovely, apparently written, dialogue. The unhurried lyricism of the solos here is reminiscent of the playing of Miles's *Kind of Blue* LP. Here and on other tracks on this record Shorter's tone is very attractive; it's fairly soft and broad, but the tenor saxophonist uses very little vibrato.

"R. J." is a rhythmically unusual twenty-one-bar theme by Carter. The solos on it are taken at a swinging up-tempo. Miles has a well-paced, swinging spot here. Shorter's solo contains swinging and nonswinging phrases.

"Agitation," by Miles, opens with a long drum solo after which the theme, an eight-bar motif separated by rhythm interludes, is stated by muted trumpet. During Miles's spot here there's a beautifully set up tempo change. Shorter improvises magnificently, employing both restraint and forcefulness. His pure attractive tone is again notable. Hancock turns in a gem of a solo, then stops short. Between the end of his spot and the closing theme statement, nothing can be heard but Carter's pedal tones.

"Iris," by Shorter, and "Mood," by Carter, are slow waltzes. There's heartfelt playing on these tracks. Miles and Shorter improvise lovely, song-like lines. Hancock's soloing is economical but romantic. His chordal work stands out on both tracks. There's some nice duet work by Miles and Shorter on "Mood," with Miles improvising over Shorter's repeated figures.

The group's next LP, *Miles Smiles*, was cut in 1966. The intelligence and sensitivity that went into the making of *E.S.P.* are also apparent in the playing and writing on this LP. It opens with "Orbits," a Shorter composition. The introduction has a boppish stop-and-start quality and builds beautifully into the main theme. At one point during the introduction while the horns are playing, the rhythm section lays out completely for a moment. Then Williams enters with a roll that accompanies Miles and Shorter as they state the theme's main motif. Miles's quintet LPs with Shorter are loaded with hip, subtle effects like this.

"Orbits" cooks like crazy, partly due to the great, swinging work of Williams. He's all over the place but doesn't get in the way. Hancock takes an excellent solo here during which he employs the lower register extensively. His forcefulness, rhythmic ideas, and use of long lines remind me of Bill Evans's work in 1956 and 1957. Hancock does not comp for himself or anyone else on "Orbits." The horn players improvise well here; Miles takes a punching, compact solo, Shorter plays thoughtfully.

"Circle" is a waltz by Davis containing fine solos and sensitive rhythm section playing. Williams turns in very good brush work here.

"Footprints," by Shorter, is a $6/4$ blues. However, there is some use of $4/4$ as well as $6/4$ meter during the improvised section of "Footprints." This track has marvelous, varied work by the rhythm section, one of the very greatest in jazz history. I can enjoy myself just by listening to them play and forgetting about the solos. This is not meant to slight Miles and Shorter, however, as they play with passion and intelligence here. Hancock's chorded solo is economical and fairly percussive and dissonant.

The up-tempo "Dolores," by Shorter, has a brief theme that is not always stated in its entirety at the beginning and end of the track. Williams and Carter play short duets between theme statements.

The theme has chord changes, but the solos on it are not based on them. By 1966, of course, this was not an unusual occurrence. To my knowledge the first jazz recordings containing improvisation not based on a preset harmonic foundation were Lennie Tristano's "Intuition" and "Digression," cut in 1949. Shelly Manne's "Abstract No. 1," made in 1954 with Shorty Rogers and Jimmy Giuffre, did not have preset changes. Of course, Ornette Coleman, who came to the fore in 1958, deserves credit for popularizing among jazz musicians the concept of "free" improvisation— improvisation that is not based on preset changes. However, Miles's quintet sounded like no other group when they eschewed preset changes. Their work on "Dolores" differs from that of the free jazzmen in several respects. For one thing, they swing as much on "Dolores" as they do on most other pieces. Many free jazzmen of the mid-sixties didn't even try to swing. Also, the great knowledge of chord changes that Miles, Shorter, and Hancock had acquired in the past is in evidence on "Dolores." Although they don't use preset changes, they do seem to improvise changes as they play, basing their solos on them. Miles, Shorter, and Hancock had much greater harmonic sophistication than most free jazzmen. Because Miles and his sidemen usually swung no matter what kind of composition they played, and because Miles, Shorter, and Hancock improvised changes even when they were not preset, the solos on "Dolores," which are not based on a predetermined harmonic foundation, sound much like solos on 1965–66 Davis LPs that are based on changes. Miles, Shorter, and Hancock construct their spots with great intelligence and in such a way as to reflect the general characteristics of the theme. Shorter, as a matter of fact, quotes from the theme. Again Hancock does not comp for himself or the horn players on this track. He probably wants to keep out of their way. Carter does a brilliant job of adjusting to the soloists.

The last two selections on *Miles Smiles* were composed by nonmembers of Davis's band. Eddie Harris wrote "Freedom Jazz Dance," a piece that is notable for its abundance of fourths. Harris originally recorded it as a ten-bar piece. On Miles's LP, "Freedom Jazz Dance" has been opened up by rests and expanded to a sixteen-bar piece.

Williams turns in some unusual work on "Freedom Jazz Dance," stating four beats per bar by closing his hi-hat cymbals on each beat. Jimmy Cobb had played four quarter notes per bar on the ride cymbal, and now Williams was doing it on the hi-hat. By keeping time with the hi-hat, Williams's hands were left free to maintain a running dialogue with the soloists.

Partly due to the evenness of Williams's timekeeping, the theme statements and solos on "Freedom Jazz Dance" have a straight up-and-down feeling rather than a leaning-into-the-beat quality. This is one time Davis's group does not emphasize swinging; as a matter of fact Eddie Harris's performance of "Freedom Jazz Dance" swings more, I think, than Miles's. This is not to say that Harris's performance is superior, however, as the solos on Miles's version are well thought out and very substantive.

The LP's final selection, Jimmy Heath's "Ginger Bread Boy," has a sixteen-bar theme that, depending on one's definition, could be called a blues. "Ginger Bread Boy" is a composition after Miles's own heart because it contains so much space. On Heath's Riverside version the openings in the theme are filled with a Kenny Burrell guitar figure; on Miles's performance there are fills by Tony Williams. Miles, Shorter, and

Hancock solo buoyantly here, playing with continuity and imagination. Once again Hancock does not comp for himself or for the horn solos.

In May 1967 Miles cut the tracks included on the *Sorcerer* LP. It opens with Shorter's "Prince of Darkness," an infectious sixteen-bar tune. Miles takes a fine, straight-ahead swinging solo. Shorter's Coltranish spot is broken up into a mosaic of short phrases. There's all sorts of rhythmic variety in Hancock's single-note lines. He comps on this track, but very sparingly and discreetly. In fact he doesn't play at all during Shorter's solo.

"Pee Wee" is a waltz by Williams that contains a lovely Shorter solo. Note how well he employs variation in tone color and texture, register and volume. He uses multinote phrases but plays them unusually quietly. His work is very controlled here. Hancock's pretty solo is Bill Evans–influenced. However, his playing is texturally leaner, less lush than Evans's work often is on slow-tempo compositions. Miles does not play on "Pee Wee."

The *misterioso*, rather Spanish-sounding "Masqualero" is one of Shorter's finest, most intriguing compositions. Although only twenty-two bars long and based on a spare harmonic foundation, it contains a surprising amount of melodic and rhythmic substance and variety. The rhythm section work deserves plenty of attention here. Carter's active, moving bass lines give "Masqualero" a good deal of lift. Williams's work is generally busy but varies quite a bit in volume.

Miles's solo here is passionate; Shorter's relaxed and thoughtful. Hancock turns in a graceful gem of a spot; particularly notable is his use of rippling two-handed runs.

Hancock's rather boppish "The Sorcerer" features a chase by Miles and Shorter. Most of the time they trade eights, but a few of the phrases they play are not eight bars long. (You could take nothing for granted about this band.) Hancock plays with excellent continuity in the course of taking one of the hardest swinging solos he's ever recorded.

"Limbo," by Shorter, contains excellent but very different solos by Miles, Shorter, and Hancock. Miles swings infectiously during his spot, but Shorter plays a controlled, very fragmented solo during which he does not attempt to swing much. Hancock takes a pretty free-tempo solo during which there is fascinating interplay between him, Carter, and Williams.

Shorter's "Vonetta" is a melancholy selection that contains a Miles solo full of unusual intervals but still warm and songlike. Shorter projects a feeling of tenderness and pain. He again uses contrasts in register and texture effectively.

The last selection on this LP, "Nothing Like You," was cut in 1962. A discussion of it is not relevant here.

Miles's *Nefertiti* LP was cut in June 1967. The title track, "Nefertiti," by Shorter, is sixteen bars long. For some reason there are no solos on it except for a brief Carter spot. Instead, the horns repeat the theme over and over throughout the length of the track. Frankly, I would have preferred to hear Miles, Shorter, and Hancock solo here, but still "Nefertiti" is an important selection. Its unhurried, languorous, almost hypnotic quality, caused partly by the use of rests and long tones, forecast a style of composition later employed not only by Shorter but by Joe Zawinul.

"Fall," a graceful sixteen-bar composition with a gentle rising and falling quality, contains plenty of solo work, but it is still one of the most tightly arranged pieces a Davis combo has ever recorded. Each of the soloists is alternately absorbed by and emerges from ensemble passages. They receive backing by one or, in the case of Hancock, both of the horn players. The background effects have been worked out; they are repeated over and over again and are not improvised.

"Fall" is one of the easiest to enjoy of Davis's combo performances. The arrangement, with its recurring effects, makes it relatively easy for neophyte listeners to follow. And one doesn't have to be a veteran jazz fan to enjoy the serenity and melodic beauty of the solo work.

During Hancock's solo Williams does some fine work, employing his foot to play a triplet beat in the hi-hat and using his sticks to play counter-rhythms. Interestingly, he does not induce Hancock to "get hot." The pianist's solo is quite calm, contrasting interestingly with the aggressive drum accompaniment.

"Hand Jive," by Williams, is an eighteen-bar tune containing several bars of silence. The solos on it are fine. Miles, Shorter, and Hancock are supremely inventive and pace themselves beautifully.

"Madness," by Hancock, has some interesting rhythmic contrasts in its theme. Again the solos are superbly constructed. Shorter improvises in a very restrained manner, even by his standards. I don't think "relaxed" is quite the correct word to describe his work, however. There's a great deal of intellectual intensity in his playing, even at its most restrained, and it is always apparent. Lester Young's playing sometimes has a lazy, loose quality when he improvises in a laid-back way, but even when Shorter employs his floating style, he often seems to me to be thinking furiously. He's a very calculating player.

During the beginning of Hancock's solo, Carter and Williams accompany him with very economical work and do not state a beat. Eventually, however, the bassist and drummer get into stating the beat and swinging behind Hancock. It's very interesting to follow the evolution of their work behind Herbie here.

"Riot," also by Hancock, is an exciting piece that finds the pianist in the front line during the theme statement. The solos by Miles and Hancock are among the highlights of this rather brief track. Hancock comps strongly and sometimes dissonantly for the horn players and himself.

"Pinocchio," by Shorter, has an eighteen-bar theme that ascends and descends rapidly several times. Miles and Shorter play fine, economical solos on this track. They don't use a lot of notes, but the ones that they do employ make a lot of sense. Hancock turns in a gracefully swinging spot here.

Miles in the Sky was recorded in 1968, with "Paraphernalia" being cut in January and the other tracks in May of that year. This LP is a very important record in Davis's evolution as a trendsetting leader. There are hints of his style of the seventies here.

"Stuff" illustrates this point. Written by Miles, it contains phrases that are almost, but not quite, funky clichés. They appear to be stock phrases, but closer listening indicates that they're fresher than they seem. The theme is played in a deliberately wooden manner by Miles and Shorter; they almost seem to be parodying it.

Hancock plays electric piano on this track, one of the earliest times he'd done so with Miles. It was Miles's idea, not Hancock's, to use the instrument. It is interesting to speculate about where he got the idea and why he decided to employ the electric instrument. Ray Charles had been playing electric piano since the fifties and was a good jazz soloist on it. Sun Ra, of course, had been using a variety of electric keyboard instruments for years before *Miles in the Sky* was cut. Joe Zawinul, with whom Miles had a close association, used an electric piano on Cannonball Adderley's "Mercy, Mercy, Mercy." Back in the late sixties there was a general interest in electronic instruments budding among rock and jazz musicians. Don Ellis and Eddie Harris were among the jazzmen to experiment with them. Maybe Miles's use of electric piano was due to this general interest in the air, rather than to the inspiration of a single musician.

Carter and Williams use rhythm-and-blues devices in the rhythm section on "Stuff."

Miles and Shorter take hot, aggressive solos here. Shorter's playing is reminiscent of his work with Art Blakey in 1962. Hancock's spot contains a nice mixture of earthiness and impressionism.

On "Paraphernalia," a spare Shorter composition, guitarist George Benson is added to Miles's group. His chordal figures and comping give this piece a distinctive feature. He and Hancock manage to stay out of each other's way in the rhythm section. Miles, Shorter, and Hancock vary the note density of their solos here quite a bit; they use rests creatively and contrast sparsely with many-noted phrases well. Benson contributes a restrained, thoughtful solo.

"Black Comedy" is a slight, attractive Williams composition. The solos on it are excellent, but perhaps even more of interest is the work of the rhythm section, which is quite active and imaginative and vies with the soloists for the listener's attention. On "Black Comedy" the rhythm section is less in the background, far closer to the front line, than it had been on earlier Davis performances.

The rhythm section also stars on Miles's "Country Son," a long, constantly changing track that contains tempo changes and out-of-tempo playing. The mood and intensity of the improvisation vary tremendously throughout the course of the piece, and it is a great tribute to the soloists and rhythm section members that they play so inventively and react so well with each other on it.

On *Miles in the Sky* there is evidence that Miles is aware of developments going on in rock and in rhythm and blues and is attempting to incorporate some of them into his music. The rhythm section work, as mentioned above, is rhythm-and-blues-influenced on "Stuff." Rock musicians as well as jazzmen were experimenting with electronic instruments around the time *Miles in the Sky* was cut. They may have helped create the climate that caused Miles to use a couple of these instruments, an electric piano on "Stuff" and an electric guitar on "Paraphernalia," on the album.

Also notable is that the general character of Miles's music seems to change beginning with *Miles in the Sky*. On it he and his sidemen generally play more aggressively and are less interested in improvising lyrically.

Miles's interest in rhythm and blues and electronic instruments is also in evidence on his next LP, *Filles de Kilimanjaro*, cut in June and September 1968. (On two tracks here, "Frelon Brun" and "Mademoiselle Mabry," Hancock and Carter are replaced by Chick Corea and Dave Holland, both outstanding musicians.) Its opening track, Davis's "Frelon Brun," opens with rhythm-and-blues-like work by Williams. Williams is all over the place in playing with the soloists; it's almost as if he's playing alongside of rather than accompanying them. Corea's comping is strong and rather dissonant here. Driven by Williams and Corea, Miles and Shorter take forceful solos.

In general, "Frelon Brun" gives evidence of the new "hot" approach that Miles was evolving.

However, this does not mean that Miles had totally abandoned lyricism. His "Tout de suite" is a pretty composition. The improvised section of this track, though, is hotter than the theme. The tempo changes to a rather quick tempo (it slows down near the end of Hancock's solo), and Miles, Shorter, and Hancock, on electric piano, play with intensity. Shorter's method of playing forcefully but employing short phrases reminds me of the work of John Gilmore around 1960 and Coltrane's Gilmore-influenced playing of 1961.

The rhythm section accompaniment of the soloists on "Tout de suite" is very unusual. Williams keeps a steady chick-chick-chick-chick sound going on his hi-hat, but Carter does not keep time here; instead he punctuates irregularly. His and Hancock's jabbing work as accompanists have a pointillistic quality.

The title selection, "Filles de Kilimanjaro," is a delightful, gentle tune by Davis that sounds somewhat like a Latin American folk tune. The solos vary quite a bit here. Miles turns in a pretty, economical spot. Shorter plays a lot of notes but, as on "Pee Wee," plays them quietly. Hancock, on electric piano, usually plays simply and lyrically, although he does employ a few runs. Carter deserves a great deal of credit on this track. His buoyant, dancing work adds a great deal of infectiousness to "Filles."

"Petits Machins" is an exciting up-tempo piece by Miles and Gil Evans. The theme is simple; its main motif consists of a three-note figure that is stated, repeated, and followed by four ascending chords by Hancock. Miles is in top-notch form on this track. His solo is impassioned, meaty, and excellently put together; his climaxes are very well set up. Shorter varies the intensity of his work superbly, sometimes playing forcefully, sometimes laying back. Hancock, on electric piano, is very inspired; he plays with good continuity, improvising some long, idea-rich lines.

There's outstanding rhythm section work on "Petits Machins" that is sometimes almost as much in the foreground as the soloists.

Miles is credited with writing all of the selections on this album. The final one, "Mademoiselle Mabry," is unlike anything I've heard him record, before or since. It's a ruminative piece that mixes impressionistic and gospel influences. Williams and Holland play discreetly as Corea conducts a dialogue with Davis and Shorter as they solo. Both hornmen play well, although Miles's solo has an earthier, more down-home flavor and more in common with the composition than Shorter's. Corea, on electric piano, turns in a pensive Bill Evans-influenced solo.

On *In a Silent Way*, recorded in February 1969, Miles demonstrates that he has developed a new group conception. His personnel is radically different from before. He employs a large rhythm section, including Hancock and Corea on electric piano; Joe Zawinul, electric piano and organ; John McLaughlin, guitar; Holland, bass; and Williams, drums. Shorter, on soprano saxophone, and Miles are the horn players.

Miles's "SHHH/Peaceful," which takes up one side of the LP, has Williams playing quietly and deliberately repetitiously throughout. Similarly, Holland plays a two-note figure throughout the performance. The keyboard players and McLaughlin improvise simultaneously through-out the track by themselves or in support of Miles and Shorter. Sometimes McLaughlin will emerge as a lead voice or soloist.

The music here is static harmonically. It depends for interest on the inventiveness of the soloists and the contrapuntal and textural blend that the players can create while improvising simultaneously.

I find "SHHH/Peaceful" to be a good, though rather monotonous, performance. Miles plays warmly. Shorter displays a pure, unique soprano saxophone tone; he uses almost no vibrato and produces an English horn-like sound.

The keyboard players and McLaughlin play tastefully; they have good rapport and sometimes create pretty, shimmering effects.

The second side of this LP consists of "In a Silent Way/It's About That Time." The side opens and closes with a statement of Zawinul's "In a Silent Way." The theme is stated first by McLaughlin, then by Shorter, then by Shorter and Miles together. Between the opening and closing portions of the second side, during which Zawinul's composition is played, there is a long improvised section. Again Williams's work is deliberately repetitious, and the solos are based on a harmonically static foundation. Miles and Shorter play well, although I've heard them play better in other contexts. The function of the keyboard players and McLaughlin is similar on this side to their role on "SHHH/Peaceful." McLaughlin is more prominent, on both sides of this record, as a soloist or lead voice than the keyboard players.

Bitches Brew, cut in August 1969, is generally considered to be one of Miles's most important albums. It is supposed to have initiated a new phase in his career. This is to some extent true, but many of the new musi-cal characteristics supposedly heard for the first time on *Bitches Brew* were present in some of his earlier albums, especially on *In a Silent Way*.

Improvisation not based on conventional preset chord changes occurs on the *Bitches Brew* album, but this can be said about the improvisation on the *In a Silent Way* LP or, for that matter, about the solos on "Dolores." There is collective improvisation on *Bitches Brew*, but there was collective improvisation on *In a Silent Way*, too. There is rock- and rhythm-and-blues-influenced rhythm section work on *Bitches Brew*, but this had occurred on earlier Miles tracks, including "Eighty-one" and "Stuff." Electronic instruments are used on *Bitches Brew*, but Miles had used them before, beginning with "Stuff." In fact, he'd used a few men playing electronic instruments simultaneously on *In a Silent Way*. Pointillistic effects are employed by the rhythm section on *Bitches Brew*, but they had been used earlier on "Tout de suite."

Actually, a good case could be made for *In a Silent Way* being just as innovative an album as *Bitches Brew*. However, I think *Bitches Brew* is a better, more interesting album for these reasons: there are more and a greater variety of instrumentalists on *Bitches Brew* than on *In a Silent Way*, and the music on *Bitches Brew* is better organized and more powerful and varied than on *In a Silent Way*.

Although the personnel varies somewhat from track to track, Miles has used about a dozen men per track on *Bitches Brew*, including two bassists (rock musician Harvey Brooks appears on Fender electric bass), four drummers or percussionists, several electric keyboard players, guitarist McLaughlin, Shorter on soprano, and Bennie Maupin on bass clarinet. Miles plays trumpet, which he sometimes uses with electronic attachments. This was not unprecedented; Don Ellis had done it previously.

Simultaneous improvisation intended to produce varied tone colors and textures is an important feature of both *In a Silent Way* and *Bitches Brew*. On *Bitches Brew*, though, Miles has added enough men to produce a greater, richer variety of tone colors and textures than on the *In a Silent Way* LP. However, he has not added so many that the improvisation becomes cluttered. Use of the bass clarinet is important because it gives *Bitches Brew* a low voice that was not present on *In a Silent Way*. The rhythm section work on *In a Silent Way* is subdued and monotonous; on *Bitches Brew* it is much more varied and colorful.

The selections on *Bitches Brew*, a two LP set, are lengthy. "Bitches Brew," the title track, lasts 27:00; "Pharaoh's Dance," 20:07; "Spanish Key," 17:30; "Miles Runs the Voodoo Down," 14:03; "Sanctuary," 10:54; and the short one, "John McLaughlin," 4:33. Shorter wrote "Sanctuary," and Zawinul composed "Pharaoh's Dance." The other compositions are credited to Miles. There are real compositions on this album, incidentally;

the music is not all improvised. Some phrases, figures, and effects have been worked out in advance. This is obvious on "Sanctuary," "Pharaoh's Dance," and the title selection.

Much of the improvisation on the *Bitches Brew* album, as on the *In a Silent Way* LP, is based on one chord for long periods of time. This can make for monotonous music, and, in fact, I do find *In a Silent Way* a little boring. But the music on *Bitches Brew* is much more varied and better organized than on *In a Silent Way*. I don't know how much preplanning went into the creation of *Bitches Brew*, to what extent the selections on it had been arranged prior to being cut. But there is organization on them, whether it is prearranged, spontaneous, or both. A great deal of the music on "Pharaoh's Dance," "Bitches Brew," "Spanish Key," "Miles Runs the Voodoo Down," and "John McLaughlin" sounds completely improvised, but it is paced, controlled improvisation. Instruments are added to and dropped from the ensemble passages. Sometimes there is a clear-cut distinction between the soloist, playing in the front line, and the rhythm section accompanying him. On other occasions there may be just a lead instrumental voice, around which other musicians improvise, or collective improvisation in which no voice stands out as a lead. Changes in the textures, colors, and density of the group sound occur frequently, making for consistently interesting listening. In fact, along with some of Sun Ra's work, I find that on *Bitches Brew* Miles has produced some of the best simultaneous free improvisation ever recorded.

Of course, part of the success of *Bitches Brew* should be attributed to Miles's excellent playing. He stands out as a soloist and ensemble leader, playing economically and with feeling and blending his work intelligently with the other musicians' improvisation. Miles uses electronic devices well; I particularly enjoyed his echo effects during the title track, "Bitches Brew."

The other soloists play well. Maupin was not well known in 1969, but his rich-toned bass clarinet playing is certainly a distinctive and enjoyable feature of the album.

"John McLaughlin" is a feature for the guitarist, who weaves in and out of the ensemble, now a lead voice, now a soloist. Miles does not appear on this selection.

Shorter turns in some supple, graceful work. His playing is thoughtful and inventive. Its elegance reminds me of some of Benny Carter's finest playing.

Shorter's composition "Sanctuary" differs in several ways from the other selections on this album. Miles's playing is featured throughout the

track, and there is a clear-cut distinction between him and his accompanists; the line between the soloist and the musicians backing him up is not
indistinct here as it sometimes is on this album. Miles is the soloist, and
the work of the other musicians on "Sanctuary" is subordinate to his.
Throughout the track Miles uses the melodic and harmonic material
contained in Shorter's composition. In fact, it's hard to tell how much of
his work on "Sanctuary" is written and how much improvised. In any
event, "Sanctuary" is the most tightly organized selection on *Bitches Brew*.
Miles's playing on it is outstanding; it sometimes has a pastoral beauty
reminiscent of his work on "Three Little Feelings."

The concepts, techniques, and devices that Miles put together in *In a
Silent Way* and *Bitches Brew* were not all invented by him. However, it is to
his credit as a leader and organizer that he blended them so successfully, as
he had absorbed influences from, among others, Ahmad Jamal and Gil and
Bill Evans in the fifties to create a unique and very influential band style.

The men who influenced Miles and/or were moving in the same
direction that he was in 1969 deserve to be cited. Among them was
Shorter. In August and September 1969, he cut an album entitled *Super
Nova* (Blue Note 84332) with an enlarged rhythm section, including Jack
DeJohnette, drums and thumb piano; Chick Corea, drums and vibes;
McLaughlin and Sonny Sharrock, guitars; Miroslav Vitous, bass; and Airto
Moreira, percussion. Fine simultaneous improvisation occurs here, with
Moreira providing some effects that had seldom, if ever, been heard
before in a recorded jazz context.

Joe Zawinul, who had written "In a Silent Way" and "Pharaoh's
Dance," deserves to be mentioned here. Zawinul later recorded "In a
Silent Way" on an LP entitled *Zawinul* (Atlantic 1572) on which two
electric pianists, two bassists, a flutist, trumpeter, soprano saxophonist,
and drum and percussion section appear. The music on this LP is cerebral
and calm. Sometimes there is a contrast between the laid-back playing of
the horn players, who use sustained tones quite a bit, and the rhythm
section, which sometimes does some busy playing.

In November 1969, a couple of months after *Bitches Brew* was recorded,
Miroslav Vitous made a fine LP, *Mountain in the Clouds* (Atlantic 1622), on
which Hancock, on electric piano; McLaughlin; Jack DeJohnette or Joe
Chambers, drums; and Joe Henderson, tenor saxophone, appeared. These
men do some excellent simultaneous improvisation.

Tony Williams's *Lifetime* album (Polydor 25-3001), cut in May 1969,
is also recommended to listeners interested in the creation of Miles's

Bitches Brew style. Williams's playing is very busy here, and McLaughlin and organist Larry Young sometimes create interesting electronic effects. Considering that only three musicians appear on it, a great variety of tone colors and textures are created on Williams's album.

Gil Evans's recorded work, beginning with his 1970 Ampex LP, has qualities in common with and possibly was influenced by the music on *Bitches Brew*. In any event, beginning with his Ampex LP, Evans's rhythm sections played more aggressively and colorfully than before and were influenced by rock and rhythm-and-blues rhythm sections. Also beginning in 1970, Evans employed electronic effects prominently.

Miles's group style, with its emphasis on electronic effects, simultaneous textural improvisation, and varied—including rock- and rhythm-and-blues-influenced—rhythm section playing, was very influential in the seventies. The music of Weather Report, which originally included Zawinul, Shorter, Vitous, and Moreira, obviously grew from it. So did some of the work done by groups led by Hancock, Corea, and McLaughlin.

Bitches Brew was not only an influential but a popular LP. Not only jazz but rock fans bought it. It established Miles as a pop music star. Before its release Miles's record sales had been slumping. Considering his renewed musical influences and the greater-than-ever popularity that it achieved for him, some people believe that *Bitches Brew* saw Miles rising like a phoenix from the ashes. But, in fact, Miles had been leading extraordinarily creative groups ever since Shorter, Miles's main composer from 1965 to 1968, joined him.

I have detailed the evolution of Miles as a leader from *Miles in Berlin* to *Bitches Brew*, trying to show how he created the group style employed on *Bitches Brew*. But this is not the only reason I wrote this article. I am very concerned with pointing out that *E.S.P., Miles Smiles, Sorcerer, Nefertiti, Miles in the Sky,* and *Filles de Kilimanjaro* are marvelous albums, just as good, if not better, in quality than *Bitches Brew*, and that *In a Silent Way* can be considered as revolutionary an album as *Bitches Brew*. It is not widely appreciated that the groups Miles led including Shorter from 1964 to 1968 were among the best he'd ever had and that they employed a very original style. The problem was that it was a subtle, restrained style that evolved at a time when much contemporary jazz was far more violent. In the mid-sixties the explosive music of John Coltrane and the "free" jazzmen seemed to interest young musicians more than the refined, though still emotional, work of Miles's groups. Miles's rhythm section members were influential as individuals and as a section, but his overall group concept from 1965 to 1968 had too little impact. (I mention 1965 rather than 1964 as a starting point because, although Miles had hired Shorter in 1964 and already had a great band then, he did not record any original material with it until 1965.) There were precedents for Miles's 1965–68 band style, and there were some musicians who recorded LPs containing music similar to or influenced by the material that Miles was recording in that period.

Actually the 1965 style of Davis's band was in the process of being evolved prior to Miles's 1965 recording of the *E.S.P.* album. The 1964 *Miles in Berlin* LP illustrates that Hancock, Carter, and Williams had evolved the rhythm section style and Miles, Shorter, and Hancock the solo styles that they would employ on later Davis LPs beginning with *E.S.P.* A major difference between *Miles in Berlin* and *E.S.P.* is that Miles had recorded all of the compositions on *Miles in Berlin* previously, whereas none of the compositions on *E.S.P.* had been recorded before. However, the fresh compositional styles that Shorter's and Hancock's pieces on *E.S.P.*, *Miles Smiles*, *Sorcerer*, and *Nefertiti* illustrated had been largely developed by them prior to 1965. At the time, and even before, Hancock and Shorter were making such great contributions to Miles's 1965–68 quintet, they were recording albums for Blue Note containing selections similar to the ones they were doing with Miles. Hancock's writing on his *Empyrean Isles* LP (Blue Note 84175), recorded in 1964, illustrates that he had developed a fully evolved compositional style. The music on this LP, on which Freddie Hubbard and, significantly, Carter and Williams appear, forecasts the material that Miles would begin recording in 1965.

Hancock's 1965 *Maiden Voyage* (Blue Note 84195), on which he employed Hubbard, Coleman, Carter, and Williams, and Shorter's *Adam's Apple* (Blue Note 84232), on which Hancock and Joe Chambers play, also reflect the style of Miles's 1965 quintet. When their compositional as well as improvisational contributions are taken into account, Hancock and Shorter can be seen to be among the most valuable, direction-setting sidemen that Miles ever had. It should be pointed out that Shorter contributed much more original material to Miles's LPs than Hancock. Hancock's own LPs contain far more of his outstanding compositions than Miles's records. Shorter's and Hancock's compositional styles were probably influenced by Davis and Coltrane and possibly by McCoy Tyner, incidentally.

Carter and Williams made some fine contributions to the wealth of original compositions that the 1965–68 Miles Davis quintet recorded. Williams and Sam Rivers each were leaders on Blue Note LPs containing music that was similar, in some areas, to the music recorded by Miles's quintets with Shorter, although not quite as similar as the material on the Hancock and Shorter LPs just cited. On those LPs Williams and Rivers employed each other as sidemen. Both men also employed Hancock. Rivers used Hubbard, Carter, and Joe Chambers, and Williams employed Shorter on their Blue Note LPs. Thus it can be seen that there was a small clique of musicians whose mid-1960s recorded work was similar to or influenced by the Miles Davis performances of the same period. Not surprisingly this clique included Davis sidemen and ex-sidemen including Shorter, Hancock, Carter, Williams, Coleman, and Rivers. Since Miles became a leader in the late 1940s, there has been a stimulating interchange of influences between him and his sidemen.

The music of the 1965–68 Davis quintets also marked some of Freddie Hubbard's LPs in the late 1960s and early 1970s, particularly *Red Clay* (CTI 6003), a record on which Hancock, Carter, and Joe Henderson appear. It should be pointed out, however, that the music on Hubbard's records is drawn from a variety of sources in addition to Miles's 1965–68 quintets.

Miles's quintets with Shorter also marked strongly Joe Henderson's outstanding 1969 LP *Power to the People* (Milestone 9024), on which Hancock and Carter appear.

However, considering its original and attractive features, Miles's 1965–68 group style influenced the work of an unfortunately small number of combos. His quintets with Shorter were great and deserve far more attention. I urge Miles's old fans who started losing interest in his LPs after *Kind of Blue* and his new ones, who became acquainted with him through *Bitches Brew,* to listen to the albums from *E.S.P.* to *Filles de Kilimanjaro.* These records, some of Miles's least appreciated, are among his best.

Discography

[All recordings have been issued on CD by Columbia with the exception of *Miles in Berlin.*—Ed.]

Bitches Brew
E.S.P.
Filles de Kilimanjaro
In a Silent Way
Miles in Berlin. Japanese Sony.
Miles in the Sky
Miles Smiles
Nefertiti
Sorcerer

Peter Keepnews

The Lost Quintet

Originally published in The Village Voice Jazz Supplement *("Miles Davis at 60"), August 1986, 22–23. Reprinted by permission of the* Village Voice *and the author.*

The 1969 Davis quintet, the immediate successor to the Shorter-Hancock-Carter-Williams band, fell into a kind of historical black hole. Except for one track ("Sanctuary," on the *Bitches Brew* album), it went unrecorded in a studio setting by Columbia Records, and virtually the only aural documentation we have of the group is a handful of bootleg recordings and private tapes. From these sources we can hear that this quintet—with Shorter, Chick Corea, Dave Holland, and Jack DeJohnette—was indeed extraordinary. It was the equal of its antecedent in terms of innovation and energy, and it was in the unique position of exploring three generations of Davis's repertoire: earlier pieces ("'Round Midnight" and "I Fall in Love Too Easily"), mid-1960s staples ("Masqualero," "Agitation," and "Paraphernalia"), and *Bitches Brew* fare (the eponymous piece and "Miles Runs the Voodoo Down").

In "The Lost Quintet," Peter Keepnews gives us a vivid account of this group and the era of which it was part. Keepnews, son of the noted record producer/author Orrin Keepnews, has an extensive background in jazz journalism: he has written for *Down Beat* and the *Village Voice*, worked as a reporter/critic for the *New York Post*, and served as managing editor of *Jazz*

Magazine. He also was a jazz publicist for Columbia Records in the late 1970s.—Ed.

One of the most serious problems confronted by jazz historians is that, while recordings offer the only tangible evidence we have of the music's development, some of the most important stages in that development were insufficiently recorded. Miles Davis's transitional protofusion period is a case in point. Miles spent a lot of time in the studio in 1969, and he came up with *In a Silent Way* and *Bitches Brew,* the two albums that are widely credited—or blamed—with ushering in the age of jazz-rock fusion. But Miles also spent a lot of time on the road that year, and the music he made with his working band was even more extraordinary than the music on those two remarkable albums.

"The band's music would change every three months," Herbie Hancock, who left Miles by 1969 but continued to participate in his recording sessions, told Bob Blumenthal, "and certain developments were never recorded. Recordings are the landmarks, but they're not the whole trip."

Indeed they're not. I can attest to that, because I spent some very trippy evenings in 1969 transfixed by the music of Miles Davis and the Last Quintet. I call it the Last Quintet because it was the last band Miles ever led that adhered to the standard instrumentation of trumpet, saxophone, piano, bass, and drums; it might also be the *Lost* Quintet, because for some reason it was never recorded.

At least, the Last Quintet (which included Wayne Shorter, the only holdover from the mid-1960s quintet, on tenor and soprano sax; Chick Corea on electric piano; Dave Holland on bass and electric bass; and Jack DeJohnette on drums) never recorded *as a quintet.* They're all on *Bitches Brew,* but so are eight other musicians, and the heavily layered, insistently rocking sound of that album is not the sound of that group. According to Davis's biographer Jack Chambers, "In the studio, [the quintet] always shared the floor with guest players, and Columbia, holding what they considered a superabundance of Davis's studio sessions, felt no need to add to it by recording his concerts."

That's a shame, because whatever the reasons, the studio Miles and the concert Miles were not the same thing in 1969. On the very pretty, very atmospheric *In a Silent Way* and especially on the denser, wilder *Bitches Brew,*

Miles created a distinct and compelling sound. It was not just about layering impressionistic, modal, jazz-oriented solos on top of rock rhythms and funky bass lines; it was also about new and unusual colors and textures—multiple keyboards, multiple percussion, highly distorted electric guitar, the exotic timbres of soprano saxophone and bass clarinet. The music of the Last Quintet was a different story: tougher, leaner, more adventurous.

Chick Corea, speaking as a participant, echoed my feelings as a listener when he told Lee Jeske that the Last Quintet's live work "really should have been gotten on tape, because that's when the band was burning. . . . That quintet developed some really beautiful, improvised stuff." Actually, some of the Last Quintet's performances *were* captured on tape, but not by Columbia. According to Chambers, there are a number of private recordings floating around. But the only studio performances, released as yet, to offer even a hint of what the Last Quintet sounded like are two takes of Joe Zawinul's "Directions," recorded in November 1968, and included on the two-record compilation of the same name released in 1981.

"Directions" was composed by Zawinul, who played a key role in Miles's musical transition (he also wrote "In a Silent Way," and he was the person who turned Miles on to the electric piano). Miles adopted the line as his regular set opener, and when Shorter left the band to form Weather Report with Zawinul, it became that group's regular set closer. Listening to it now brings back vivid memories of seeing the Last Quintet in action, and it evokes, at least partly, the impact of that band.

The most obvious thing about "Directions" is that, while its multiple keyboards and insistent rhythms relate it to the music on *In a Silent Way,* recorded three months later, it packs much more of a punch. Miles's playing in particular has a brusque, staccato quality that stands in stark contrast to his lyrical trumpet work on *Silent Way.* And the rhythm section rocks harder and swings with more abandon, if that's not a contradiction: DeJohnette's drumming is looser and more exciting than the polite tick-tick into which Tony Williams is locked throughout *Silent Way.* (As much as I like that album, I've never understood why the volcanic Tony Williams was reined in so tightly. DeJohnette proved conclusively that a drummer could maintain a rock-steady backbeat without sounding monotonous: for that matter, so did Williams as soon as he left Miles to lead his own band.)

I don't know why the music Miles created in the studio in 1969 was so much more genteel and restrained than the music he created with his working group. Maybe, as so many people have charged, it has to do with compromise and commercialism—although the rich, hypnotic grooves of

In a Silent Way and *Bitches Brew* have never sounded very much like a sell-out to me. I do know that the studio versions of "Directions" have palpable energy and vitality—and that the music of the Last Quintet had even more energy and vitality than these tracks suggest. It was an *intense* band; had it made a record, a good name for it would have been *In a Violent Way*.

The Last Quintet offered fewer readily recognizable points of reference than any previous Miles Davis band, and as such scared off many longtime fans. But it didn't represent a totally radical break with the past. For one thing, as I mentioned, the instrumentation was conventional except for the electricity and the addition of the then-unusual soprano sax. For another, Miles had been dropping hints for a few years on his albums (and, it would later be revealed, at various recording sessions that were not released) that he was looking for a change in the rhythmic and textural makeup of his music: he was experimenting with a modified back-beat at least as far back as the blues "Eighty-one," recorded in 1965, and recording with electric piano as early as 1967. And, of course, he had already gone through so many changes of style and outlook that change was almost expected of him.

Actually, the *really* radical break had come in 1964 and 1965, when Miles slowly but surely began jettisoning not just his familiar repertoire but his entire approach to improvising. Picking up on ideas he had first toyed with in 1959, he plunged headfirst into the modal maelstrom, and he and his sidemen eventually developed an almost telepathic type of improvisation that not only wasn't based on chord structures but sometimes seemed to be based on nothing more than whim. Much of what the Last Quintet was into could be seen as a further exploration along those lines; the main difference was that a funky bass pattern was more likely to provide the foundation for improvisation than a scale or a mode.

Sometimes the Last Quintet took things pretty far out. Few fusion bands ever picked up on its propensity to move the music in a *free* direction. (DeJohnette has described the group as "a lot more avant-garde than people were ready to admit.") The music always came back to that rock-like pulse, but in the interim the rhythms could get to some surprising places. (I remember one gig at the Village Gate where Corea got up from the keyboard in the middle of a solo, walked over to a second set of drums sitting unused on the bandstand, and launched into a very credible percussion dialogue with DeJohnette.)

For all its radicalism, the Last Quintet was still a *jazz* group as most people understood the term in 1969—auxiliary percussion, Motown-rooted electric bass, wah-wah attachments, and a phalanx of screaming guitarists were still around the corner. Yet it was new and different enough to upset people, or excite them. In fact, to some of us it was the band we had been waiting for.

I loved the mix of old and new, electric and acoustic, jazz and rock and funk. I loved that, on top of that churning rhythm section, Miles was still recognizably himself and still playing his ass off—playing, it seemed, with more fire and chops than ever. I even loved the way the band *looked:* the fact that suits and ties were out and a sort of modified psychedelic look was in struck me as being the hippest thing in the world. These days, of course, the pendulum has swung decisively back in the other direction, and it's the hippest thing in the world to wear suits and ties and play like Miles was playing in 1965. But the Last Quintet came along at a very opportune time for a restless, electric music lover like me.

I had grown up listening to jazz and, at nineteen, considered myself a serious fan, but I was finding myself, almost against my will, drawn more and more to rock. I didn't buy the "jazz is dead" line that some people were selling, but I was beginning to feel that it was at the very least moribund. Coltrane was dead; the avant-garde was hard to listen to; major figures like Mingus and Rollins were off the scene entirely; other major figures like Monk and Gillespie seemed to be stuck in a rut. At the same time, groups like the Grateful Dead and Jefferson Airplane were experimenting with long, open-ended improvisation; Frank Zappa was displaying chops, erudition, heavy energy, *and* a sense of humor; Jimi Hendrix was playing dazzling guitar solos that mixed authentic blues sensibility with wild electronic flash. I was impressed and excited by the way rock musicians were borrowing ideas from jazz, and I was at a loss to understand why more jazz musicians weren't borrowing ideas, or at least sounds and rhythms, from rock.

Maybe they thought it was uncool. Maybe they didn't want to be perceived as selling out to "the kids." Maybe they just didn't dig rock. But as soon as Miles gave his imprimatur to a synthesis, it suddenly became okay. To paraphrase a remark Miles himself once made about Monk, he gave the other musicians freedom; if Miles could use funky rhythms and electric instruments and get away with it, so could they.

At first, fusion really did seem like a viable artistic option, and a number of genuinely ambitious fusion groups took shape, many of them Miles Davis spin-offs. Weather Report refined and reshaped some of his ideas about colors, textures, and rhythms; the Tony Williams Lifetime, with John McLaughlin on guitar, effected its fusion from a more overtly rockish direction, with bracing results; McLaughlin's supercharged Mahavishnu Orchestra veered between the visceral and the pompous and was occasionally brilliant.

Miles himself kept getting more electric, more funky, more rhythmic, and more *out,* all at the same time. He was picking up new listeners as fast as he was losing old ones. When he finally did make a live album, at the Fillmore East in June 1970, his audience had ballooned, but the complexion of his band changed, and the special magic of the Last Quintet was gone. The workmanlike Steve Grossman had replaced the always inspired Wayne Shorter, and the addition of Keith Jarrett on organ and Airto Moreira on percussion tended to make the music cluttered and muddy rather than dense and polyrhythmic. But Miles hadn't run out of juice: *A Tribute to Jack Johnson,* recorded earlier in 1970 with a different group, was a convincing amalgam of jazz concepts and funk feeling (bassist Michael Henderson provided most of the latter); the concert material on *Live-Evil,* recorded that December with still another configuration, was short on subtlety but long on impact, ignited by the forceful playing of Miles and saxophonist Gary Bartz and anchored by a rhythm section (Jarrett, McLaughlin, Henderson, DeJohnette, and Moreira) that really rocked.

Still, it wasn't long before fusion had become a dirty word, and it's not hard to see why: countless minimally inventive musicians, clever record producers, and opportunistic salespeople figured out how to reduce it to a formula and turned it almost overnight from an artistic option to a marketing gimmick. Even more dispiriting was the phenomenon of many veteran musicians, who, taking their cue from Miles but misreading his signals (they thought he was only in it for the money and that it really was only a matter of turning on the electricity, adjusting the beat, and changing your clothes), tried to jump on the bandwagon and fell on their faces.

But if fusion turned out to be a cul-de-sac, don't blame Miles. He never said he was starting a movement; he just played. (Besides, after listening to the band Sting took on tour last year—and, for that matter, to Ornette Coleman with Prime Time—I'm not so sure the concept of fusion can be written off entirely.) The bottom line is that the music he played back then holds up pretty well. If those private concert recordings of the Last Quintet are ever issued, the world will know just how good it could get.

Chris Albertson

The Unmasking of Miles Davis

Originally published in Saturday Review, *November 27, 1971, 67–69, 87.*
Reprinted by permission of the author.

This 1971 article/interview found Davis in the midst of newfound jazz/rock celebrity. Although the piece contains no startling revelations, it is intelligently assembled and gives us insights into the trumpeter's view of himself as a black artist in a society then in the throes of tumultuous changes.

Author Chris Albertson is a longtime jazz journalist and critic who has written for the *Saturday Review, Down Beat,* and *Stereo Review.* He also is the author of *Bessie,* an admirable 1972 biography of Bessie Smith.—Ed.

When Miles Davis returns from a tour of Europe and takes his quintet into Philharmonic Hall this week, chances are that a good percentage of his audience will consist of young black people. This is not a writer's prediction based on a typical Miles Davis following—no one has determined just what that might be—but a request Miles made in a phone call from Paris four weeks ago. Jack Whittemore, his agent, was to take half of Miles's fee, spend it on tickets for the concert, and hand the tickets out to young black people who otherwise could not afford to attend. "Miles has never done anything like this before, but nothing he does surprises me," says Whittemore, admitting that he doesn't quite know how to go about distributing more than two thousand dollars worth of free tickets to the right people.

Such unusual gestures are as typical of Miles as they are atypical of most performing artists, and they come as a surprise only to those who know the enigmatic trumpet player from a distance. Since his first appearance on the musical scene some twenty-six years ago, Miles Davis has been the subject of controversy—endearing with his music, offending with his personality. That is to say, his personality as it is most commonly interpreted, for the forbidding mask of hostility that in many minds characterizes Miles is just that: an image fostered by his own deliberate lack of showmanship and sculptured by reporters who have failed to recognize a serious artist at work. We don't, after all, expect Rostropovich or Casadesus to warm up their audiences with small talk, and Miles Davis is as serious about his music as were Brahms and Schubert.

The music performed by Miles Davis today has undeniably evolved from that—labeled "jazz"—which New Orleans pioneers played sixty years ago, but there are other elements contained in it, too, and if Miles's music is jazz, then so is Stravinsky's *Ragtime for Twelve Instruments*. He himself feels that jazz is "a white man's word" that, when applied to his music, is tantamount to calling a black person "nigger." Accordingly, though he still must give performances in noisy, smoke-filled nightclubs, Miles approaches his work with the dignity it deserves.

During club or concert appearances he never addresses his audience or announces his selections, generally wears clothing that reflects future fashion trends (*Gentlemen's Quarterly* named him best-dressed man ten years ago), saunters off the bandstand or to the rear of the stage when not playing, and occasionally turns his back to the audience while focusing attention on his fellow musicians. "I have been with him on several occasions when he left the stage during a performance," says Robert Altschuler, Columbia Records's publicity director. "He either crouches or ambles to the side of the audience, and you realize that he is deeply concentrating on everything that his musicians are playing—he is digging his own band, digging it in a way a Miles Davis fan would. He simply becomes a part of his own audience."

Club owners and concert promoters have been known to go into a rage over Miles's seeming detachment, but conformity is not a part of his vocabulary, and, despite the constant criticism, he has for twenty years remained the dark, brooding, wandering loner who doesn't care whether he is regarded as an eccentric genius or a bellicose bastard as long as people listen to what he has to say through his music.

The son of a well-to-do dental surgeon, Miles Davis has never been poor, but money cannot cure the inherent stigma that society has attached to people of dark skin, and, faced with prejudices that sometimes are so subtle that only their victims can detect them, he has always sought to fight back on his own. "I am not a Black Panther or nothing like that," he explains. "I don't need to be, but I was raised to think like they do and people sometimes think I'm difficult because I always say what's on my mind, and they can't always see what I see."

One thing Miles never fails to see is someone taking advantage of him. "Back in the days when he was only getting a thousand dollars for a concert, Miles was booked into Town Hall," recalls Jack Whittemore. "The tickets were selling very well, so the promoter suggested doing two shows instead of one. As was customary in such cases, Miles was to get half fee, five hundred dollars, for the second concert, but when I approached him with this, he looked puzzled. 'You mean I go on stage,' he said, 'pick up my horn, play a concert, and get a thousand dollars. Then they empty the hall, fill it again, I pick up my horn again, play the same thing, and get only five hundred—I don't understand it.' I told him that this was how it was normally done, but he was not satisfied. Finally he turned to me and said he'd do it for five hundred dollars if they would rope off half the hall and only sell half the tickets. When the promoters heard this, they decided to give him another thousand for the second concert."

If Miles is "difficult," it is because his scrupulous honesty is a trait so rare in the world of show business that few people in that field know how to deal with it. His monumental disdain for the complimentary small talk and instant familiarity that entertainers are exposed to, and his absolute refusal to indulge in such trivia, have earned him the reputation of being unapproachable. "I have found," observes Altschuler, "that when Miles meets someone new—people from the press I've introduced him to—he will check them out first. They don't always know this, but Miles is actually laying down the ground rules for a totally honest exchange of questions and answers, and he will accept his interviewer only if he can be sure that his time is not going to be wasted with inane questions." As one might expect, Miles is reluctant to appear on TV talk shows.

"Dick Cavett and Johnny Carson don't know what to say to anybody black, unless there's some black bitch on the show and she's all over them," he told me while conducting a guided tour of his bizarre but comfortable Upper West Side residence. "It's so awkward for them because they know all the white facial expressions, but they're not hip to black expressions, and—God knows—they're not hip to Chinese expressions. You see, they've seen all the white expressions like fear, sex, revenge, and white actors imitate other white actors when they express emotions, but they don't know how black people react. Dick Cavett is quiet now when a black cat is talking to him, because he doesn't know if the expression on his face means 'I'm going to kick your ass,' or if 'right on' means he's going to throw a right-hand punch. So," Davis continued, pointing out the oddly shaped, multileveled, blue tile bathtub, "rather than embarrass them and myself, I just play on those shows and tell them not to say anything to me—I have nothing to say to them anyway."

Miles makes a good point. Intelligent, relevant questions are rarely directed to black guests on TV talk shows, and the media's handful of established hosts relate to his music about as well as Nixon's Silent Majority relates to the problems of Bedford-Stuyvesant residents. We stepped down into the circular bedroom. A TV set, dwarfed by the gigantic bed, silently radiated an afternoon ball game. "I just put it on because I have nothing to do," volunteered Miles, revealing at the same time a long row of flamboyant clothes and boots in dazzling colors. "I have these made for me," he explained. CBS flashed the image of its night host on the little screen, and it served as a cue. "Merv Griffin is embarrassing to me; I felt like yanking his arm off last year." Miles was referring to the 1970 Grammy Awards ceremony at Alice Tully Hall when, after a superb performance by Miles's group, Griffin—the evening's master of ceremonies—brushed him off with a remark that was disrespectful of his music. "The trouble with those cats is that they all try to come off to those middle-aged white bitches."

Such remarks don't exactly produce invitations to guest on late-night TV shows, but Miles aims his fire without such considerations. Even Columbia Records—with which he has enjoyed a good and fruitful relationship since the mid-fifties—has been the victim of his public candor. In a recently published statement to a black weekly, Miles, who refers to himself as the "company nigger," expressed a belief that his label was not affording black artists equal opportunities in terms of exposure. As we seated ourselves comfortably in the round, sunken living room, I asked if there had been any repercussions from Columbia. "No," he replied, "Clive [Columbia's president, Clive Davis] asked me why I had said that, and I said, 'Was I telling a lie, Clive? If you can say I'm a liar, I'll retract that

statement.' You see, all those records I have made with them have been a
bitch, and they come out being rich behind all this token shit."

"You would think that he's not grateful," says Clive Davis, "but I just
know he is. I'm not sure that it's his mind that he speaks; I'm not sure that
he just doesn't tell people what they want to hear, because it takes a certain amount of research before you go off making such statements. I'm
prepared for all of Miles's statements; none surprise me. I do mentally
treat him differently, not because he's black—because we have a tremendous number of black artists—but because he's unique among people,
and you expect the unexpected from Miles Davis."

Clive Davis admits that he is not totally unaffected by Miles's criticism.
"It bothers me because I think we have really done a tremendous amount
to be creative along with him, and we work very closely with him so that we
make sure that he sells not only to jazz audiences and to contemporary
rock audiences, but to R & B audiences as well."

Despite his complaints, Miles readily admits to having an unusually
close relationship with Columbia, and his long tenure with the label bears
this out; the forty-five-year-old giant of black music would have no problems finding another home for his recording activities. "The Internal
Revenue Service is always after me," says Miles, in this connection, "but I
just send their bills on to Clive. I got one for $39,000, but he took care of
it." When asked to confirm this, Clive Davis's reply was diplomatic: "Miles
is treated very well by Columbia Records. I think he's really appreciative of
it, too—we don't get Internal Revenue bills from Chicago or Blood, Sweat
and Tears."

The recent upsurge in Miles Davis's popularity is due mainly to an
album entitled *Bitches Brew*. Released in the spring of 1970, it was the
subject of a well-coordinated national promotion campaign aimed more at
the young rock fan than at the established Miles Davis follower. Of the
nearly thirty Miles Davis albums that have accumulated in Columbia's
catalogue over the past fifteen years, *Porgy and Bess*—with sales figures
approaching 100,000—had been the most successful; other albums
averaged around 50,000; recent releases barely crawled to the 25,000
mark, but *Bitches Brew*—a two-record set—has sold more than 400,000
copies in this country alone.

The sound of Miles's *Porgy and Bess* album and that achieved on *Bitches
Brew* reflect a disparity that is as great as the gap separating the sales figures
for the two releases, but it is not only the sound Miles has changed, he has
updated the appearance of his group as well: surrounded by young black

and white musicians sporting Afros, long hair, headbands, dungarees, and dashikis, Miles still wears tomorrow's fashions; and his group, positioned amid complex looking electronic paraphernalia, has all the visuality of a modern rock band. His new music is an abstraction of everything Miles has ever played before; it is as if he is summing it all up for us, and yet we know that he will not allow it all to end here. At the same time, it is a testimony to Miles's artistry and forward thinking that none of his past recordings—starting with the revolutionary 1949 Capitol sessions—sounds outdated in 1971.

If rock groups are not envious of Miles's musical accomplishments, they should be; many of them are just now reaching a poor approximation of the stage he and collaborator Gil Evans passed in the late fifties, and one can't help but wonder if, ten or twelve years from now, anyone will have more than a nostalgic nod for the current efforts of today's musical pop heroes. There is bitter irony in the fact that Miles has to take second billing—as was the case last year—to Blood, Sweat and Tears, which sells records in the millions and turns youthful audiences into a frenzy of excitement with musical ideas borrowed from Miles's past. "I can't be bothered with these groups," he says, recalling with amusement the time he turned down promoter Bill Graham's plea to have him retract a negative statement about Blood, Sweat and Tears. "If they can't stand constructive criticism, to hell with them. I'm honest in what I say, I don't lie, so I don't have to watch my words or take them back."

There are those who feel Miles's attacks on rock groups are unfair and that he, in an odd sense, owes them a debt of gratitude. They see his appearances last year at the Fillmores East and West—former meccas for the rock cult—as a turning point in his career, but they seem to lose sight of the fact that those concerts, as well as Columbia's promotional efforts, would not have sold the public on Miles Davis if he had not had something very special to offer. For more than twenty years, Miles has been pointing music in new directions, reaching unexplored plateaus, and forging ahead before others could catch up with him. "He has never been bound by convention," says Teo Macero, who has produced virtually all Miles's records since 1958. "You wouldn't expect Miles to go back and do something the way he did it years ago any more than you would expect Picasso to go back to what he was doing in his 'blue' or 'rose' periods."

One tangible result of Miles's recent commercial success has been the signing up by Columbia of several black musicians who last year would hardly have been able to get as far as Clive Davis's eleventh-floor office.

Explaining this change in policy, Clive Davis makes one momentarily forget that he is running a highly competitive commercial business: "I am very eager to allow Columbia to be used by the most forward-looking American jazz artists, to explore what kind of synergy can come out of jazz and rock. What do the jazz giants, the leading jazz figures of today, have to say? What is *their* reaction to the fact that, in attempting to fuse jazz and rock, Chicago and Blood, Sweat and Tears have reached millions of people all over the world while they, without such an attempt, only reach a few thousand with their music?"

Clive Davis mentioned that the label has signed Ornette Coleman, Jack DeJohnette, and Weather Report—an offshoot of Miles's group—and that it was recording Charles Mingus. "Just as Columbia sponsored a Modern American Composer series in classical music—not having any less reverence for Stravinsky, Mahler, or classical music performed by the New York Philharmonic or the Philadelphia Orchestra—so we are here exploring a very exciting new development in music to see where it will go. I don't know where it will go, but I think that by opening up the company to this kind of exploration of music by brilliant talent, we are providing a tremendous service."

Columbia's aims are obvious, and Miles is not fooled for a minute: "It's smart to be with the niggers sometimes. I know what made *Bitches Brew*, but they need guidance; Mingus needs guidance; Ornette needs guidance; nobody's going to tell them what to do because then they might call them white bastards, but they *have* to *tell* Mingus what to do, otherwise he'll do the same all over again, and they have to tell Ornette that he cannot play the trumpet and violin. Motown shows you where it's at, man."

It is difficult to imagine anyone telling Miles Davis what to do with his music, but he is just as receptive to constructive criticism as he is ready to give it. "Miles lets you be as creative as you want to be," says producer Teo Macero, "as long as it doesn't screw up his music. A lot of artists say, 'Man, don't touch my music, don't do this, I don't want any electronic sound, don't use a Fender bass,' and so forth, but Miles is so far ahead that he's on the same wavelength as you are, which makes for a great deal of excitement. When he plays, he does it with such intensity that every note is a gem. He doesn't make any mistakes. If he doesn't like something he did, it is usually because it didn't capture the right feeling. We never discuss the music or how things went in front of anybody else; he either calls me out into the hall or we sort of talk in the corner, and I try to refrain from talking about the piece over the studio talk-back system—that's something I've learned by working with him over the years. Like his private life, he keeps it to himself; I never ask because if he wants to tell me something, he'll do it."

The physical aspects of producing a Miles Davis album are as unconventional as his music. As Macero explains, there are no takes one, two, or three, "because there's something new that pops into the music every time, whether it's deliberate or just by accident, no one seems to know quite for sure. The group is constantly building toward a final goal, and we don't stop the tape machines like we used to do in the old days—they run until the group stops playing. Then we go back, listen, and decide between us what should be tacked to what—it becomes a search-and-find routine, and finally it's all there, it's just a matter of putting it all together."

Two albums, *Miles Davis at Fillmore* and the sound track for the documentary film *Jack Johnson* have been released since *Bitches Brew*, but neither shows signs of doing as well commercially. This of course provides an incentive to make the next release particularly interesting, and it looks as if *Live-Evil* (one word is the reverse spelling of the other) will be just that. Scheduled for a December release, it is the distillation of ten to fifteen reels of tape, selected from an original working pile of thirty reels. "The album is partly live, and it has an ethereal evil, where the mind is clouded and all these things are happening," says Macero; "it's like a wild dream." Artist Mati Klarwein, who was responsible for the unusual *Bitches Brew* cover, has been commissioned to give the new album a similar look.

If *Live-Evil* becomes another *Bitches Brew*, there will undoubtedly be more demands on Miles Davis's time, a commodity he values and likes to spend as a part-time pugilist working out in a midtown gym, swimming in some appropriate waters, sleeping in his oversized bed, or simply relaxing with friends amid the international decor of what has been termed "an architect's nightmare"—his house on West 77th Street. Unimpressed by critics ("I don't know any, because I never read what they say") and disc jockeys ("if we didn't make any records, they wouldn't have anything to do"), Miles periodically threatens to quit the music business so that he will no longer be the subject of exploitation, which, he says, is "the name of the game." Someday he will undoubtedly do just that, and the smile behind the mask may be seen by a public that never thought it existed.

Sy Johnson

An Afternoon at Miles's

Originally published in Jazz Magazine, *Fall 1976, 20–27. Copyright © 1976, Stites-Oakey, Inc. Reprinted by permission.*

Current pop psychology has reduced the term *vulnerability* to a borderline bromide. Nonetheless, I think it fair to say that this piece shows Miles Davis at his most vulnerable—at times astoundingly so.

That's all the introduction this moving article requires. Its author, Sy Johnson, is a fine musician—an arranger best known for his scores for Charles Mingus, the Lee Konitz nonet, the Terry Gibbs big band, Quincy Jones, and others, and a pianist who recorded with the fondly remembered Rod Levitt octet of the 1960s. He is also, as you will see, an accomplished writer, as well as an equally gifted photographer.—Ed.

In the summer of 1974, I was jazz editor of *Changes*, a tabloid of arts and letters edited by Susan Graham, manager and friend of Charles Mingus. I wanted to get a quote from Miles Davis for a jazz issue we were assembling, and when I called Neil Reshen's publicity office for access to Miles, an arrogant and angry male voice said, "How many times do I have to tell you—Miles Davis is not a jazz artist. Miles Davis makes his *own* music. Miles

Davis will have nothing to do with a jazz issue of *anything*. I don't ever want you to bother me again." Bang!!

Then, Bob Hurwitz, at that time with CBS publicity, called to say that Miles was seeing people and he could arrange an interview for the following week. I thought about it for a day and called to say okay, with reservations. If we could find something to talk about, then I would write a piece.

I had known Miles slightly in Los Angeles when he came out to the coast for the first time with Coltrane, Philly Joe, Paul Chambers, and Red Garland. I caught every night of a two-week engagement the band played at Jazz City, and I shot pictures by available light with my Leica whenever I could get close to the bandstand. That in itself was unheard of in the fifties, and when I made some prints, Philly Joe undertook to sell them to the customers.

When the band returned from two weeks in San Francisco, Miles sat down at my table late one night and began to talk about the Leica he got in Germany and how much he liked it. He said he had the clerk set the shutter speed and aperture at the store when he bought the camera and hadn't changed them since. I can't remember saying anything except to ask him what model Leica he had, which he didn't know. I was tongue-tied by the solemnity of the occasion.

From then on he would motion me into the kitchen of Jazz City with a nod, usually on the first intermission, when the club was crowded with people who wanted to talk with him. He'd stand with his back to the kitchen door, talking about his Mercedes, other players, women, and pointedly ignoring musicians and fans who wanted to say hello. They would wait patiently or try to say something over his shoulder, and finally drift away. I remember Benny Carter in line once and murderous glances at me from some of the younger black players.

When I came to New York in 1960, I saw Miles a lot at the Village Vanguard and one night took pictures from on the bandstand. When Miles saw the prints, he said, "I don't wantcha takin' no more pitcha's, ya hear," and walked away. He never said anything else, but he did frequently leave his trumpet on my table while he wandered around the club during solos by the rest of the band, and stub his cigarettes out in the ashtray. I always wondered if he remembered me from Los Angeles. When I agreed to the interview, I thought that at least I would find out.

I called Miles's producer, Teo Macero, and Teo said that Miles was recording the morning of the interview and that I should stop in for the last half hour when the likelihood of making Miles nervous was minimal.

The control room was full of thick Spanish funereal music and solemn men filling out W-4 forms when I arrived. Teo whispered that this was Miles's tribute to Duke Ellington.

"He Loved Him Madly," he said, waving his hand at the speaker.

Miles came out of the studio wearing a big jaunty hat, looking pinched and tired beneath it. He leaned against the console for a few minutes, lost in the music. Then, smiling wanly and touching a few hands, he slipped out the door.

I listened to the playback until it finished and was surprised to hear a warm strong statement from Miles emitting from the studio speakers. The band sounded sure of itself on the slow, treacly tempo. I was sorry I hadn't seen them record it.

My appointment with Miles was at Neil Reshen's office after lunch. When I arrived there, growing steadily more apprehensive, the receptionist told me that Miles was waiting for me at home and handed me a slip with the address. Michael Henderson and Al Foster from Miles's band were sitting in the tiny reception area, and I said to Al, "I'm off to see the master."

He said, "Do you call him that too? Some of the guys in the band call him the master."

I took the IRT to 79th Street and walked to Miles's corner. I could see him leaning on the wall in front of his house drinking a beer. He seemed relaxed and very much master of his own turf. I was sure Miles would remember me, but when I introduced myself, he gave me a disgusted look and said, "Might as well get it over with." I could see in my mind's eye the photograph I could make of Miles with beer and hat in front of the bas-relief carving on the front of his house, but he was inside the dark doorway before I could ask him.

There was a short hallway with another door on the right. I looked into it just in time to see Miles grab a black man just inside the room.

"I want you outside this door, motherfucker," he said. "You don't come inside unless I *invite* you inside." The man scrambled past me out the door, and I stepped into a cool, dark room. A pretty girl was threading tape onto a tape deck.

I noticed that the room had an elaborate circular structure built into it, giving a circle-in-a-cube motif that repeated throughout the house. The back room had a huge wooden table and glass doors leading out to a sunny garden.

Miles said something to the girl and, after a short conference that seemed about the garden, decided to go upstairs. He led me to another dark room with a circular upholstered seat built around the wall and a built-in piano overlooking the space. Poll-winner plaques hung on the walls.

Miles motioned to me to sit behind a long coffee table that had a heavy wooden cube with a three-foot, wire mobile on it. As I started to unpack my Sony, he stood on the other side of this huge table and began to adjust the mobile, moving a piece of it slightly, stepping back for a better perspective, stopping the movement at arm's length, moving in, taking a piece off, putting it back.

I thought he would sit down when he got it right, and when I finally could see that he had no intention of stopping, the house was suddenly flooded with music from downstairs. I recognized it from the morning session. It was loud enough to hear in New Jersey.

I thought, "I'll never hear a goddamned word he says. Should I ask him to have it turned off?" I could see the whole afternoon going down the drain, and I didn't know what to do about it.

Miles's lips moved. I shook my head, pointed to my ears. His mouth moved again. It looked like he said, "Ask me some questions so I can tell you some lies."

I shouted, "I can't talk with you standing over there."

He said, "Why should I have to sit down to talk to you? You're supposed to ask me questions so I can answer them."

He still hadn't taken his eyes off the mobile. Neither of us said anything. The music was suffocating, broken only by an occasional *clank* as he moved the pieces.

I swallowed hard and said, "Teo said this piece was dedicated to Duke Ellington."

"When did Teo say that?"

"This morning, after the session."

"I call it 'He Loved Him Madly,' " he said. "I'd like to do one-tenth of what Duke did."

I wondered for a second if he was serious.

"You've already done as much or more."

He looked at me for the first time since I arrived. I hoped I was making headway.

"How do you feel?" I asked. "How are your legs?"

"They get sore."

"Do you still get to the gym?"

"I have one in the basement. I can't use my legs. They're sore. They stay sore."

Miles finally seemed to get the mobile the way he wanted it.

"The guy who did this is a research chemist."

I asked, "How many ways does it go together?"

"Only one."

He gently began to touch life into the mobile with his fingers. Circles revolved inside of the other circles inside of other circles.

"Like this house." I thought.

"Damn you!! Ask questions. You're the one asked to be here."

I swallowed resentment.

"How's the band coming? Is it finally where you want it?"

The reply was muttered into the mobile.

"What?"

Miles gave me a withering look through the mobile.

"I *always* get a band where I want!"

I was finally fed up.

"Goddamn it, Miles, sit down."

"I can talk standing up."

"Bullshit! Between you and that music, I can't hear shit."

Miles came around the table and turned off an air conditioner, which I hadn't even noticed. The din diminished, and he sat down next to me.

"Come on, Sy, relax."

He handed me his beer. I took a swallow and then another.

Miles called out, "Loretta, Loretta."

The girl from the living room came up the stairs.

"Loretta, this is Sy. Bring us some beer."

Loretta smiled at me and went back down the stairs. I wished desperately that I had asked to have the tape turned down.

I told Miles I had known him in California. He didn't remember me. He was pleased that Benny Carter had come to see him. Encouraged by our truce, I decided to press on.

"Miles, I'd like to ask you about your new band. Since you started adding extra rhythm players at the Fillmore, I'm having a harder time following the music. I'm probably missing something. I'm not sure what to listen for."

Miles was immediately defensive.

"You can't understand me 'cause you're not me. In the second place, you're not black. You don't understand my rhythms. We're two totally different people. That's almost an insult to say you don't understand."

"I don't think it's an insult."

"You don't like my music."

"I'm *asking* you about it, not insulting it."

"I haven't mentioned *your* music."

"No, you've probably never been aware of my music."

"Why is that? Give me one reason. I listen to Stockhausen."

"Stockhausen and I have nothing in common."

"Yeah. I *know!!*"

Miles went to the mobile again, deftly setting it in motion.

"Just takes a touch. I bought it for fifteen hundred dollars. I like to sit up here and write music. If that guy can make that motherfucker like that, then I can use that fuckin' chord. You know what I mean?"

I *did* know what he meant. All those delicate arms moving independently and precisely inside of one another. Always changing, yet solidly anchored to the same base. It was like the new Davis music was supposed to function, in theory, anyway.

Miles went on. "White guys keep saying they don't understand my music."

"Do all black people understand it?"

"I don't even look at that shit."

"Miles, to my ear the band seems to keep rambling around. I can't find a center."

He is angry. "Who told you to *look* for a center?"

"I have to. For my own needs."

"Ooh—That's *your* problem."

"I haven't said that it wasn't. That's why I'm asking."

"Do you realize you got me up here listening to you? Telling me you don't like my music? I could be out in the sunshine." He looked out the window.

I could feel anger welling up in me again.

"What do *you* want to talk about?"

Miles looked over at me and his expression softened. He sat down beside me.

"Sy," he said, very softly, "I got into music because I *love* it. I *still* love it. All kinds."

My resentment vanished. It was the second time Miles had made an effort to ease the tension, and it directly contradicted my image of him.

"I think it's time people changed where they put the melody," he went on. "The melody can be in the bass, or a drum sound, or just a sound. I may write something around one chord. I may write something around a rhythm."

He looked at me.

"I always place the rhythm so it can be played three or four different ways. It's always three rhythms within one, and you can get some other ones in there, too.

"Do you know what I mean? It's almost like Bach. You know how Bach wrote."

We sat back and relaxed. Miles lit a cigarette. We listened to the tape from downstairs, which didn't seem so intrusive any more.

"White people don't like me."

I glanced over at him.

"I mean, a policeman grabbed me around the neck."

"Why?"

"'Cause I was black. I'm not gonna say what no white man wants me to say."

He reassured me, "I'm talkin' 'bout a policeman. 'Are you goin' peaceful, or am I gonna put handcuffs on you?' I'm supposed to say, 'Yes, I'll go down peaceful.' "

"That's what I would have said. Is it gonna be okay?"

He shrugs. We sit. Loretta comes up with two warm beers and glasses filled with ice cubes.

"We were out," she said. "I had to go to the store. I got you some cigarettes."

She left. I asked him about *Big Fun*, an album culled from tapes from his *Bitches Brew* period.

"I'll be tired of *this* music before today is over," he said, waving his hand in the air. "*That's* four years old."

I asked him about the many groups his former sidemen have spawned.

"Chick [Corea] has a nice band. He's so multitalented. He can play drums. He can play anything he wants to play, just like me. He's a music-*lover*, you know."

I mentioned some of Chick's compositions.

"He's written some pretty things," I said.

Miles made a face.

"Does it have to be *pretty* to be marvelous? I mean, the reason I don't go to the movies is that the music for the sex scenes is always so pretty. Strings and French horns. Sex isn't like that *all* the fuckin' time. Sometimes you hear some drums and shit. You want to get to the bitch in a *hurry!!* You're stumblin' over shit. You don't wanna hear no sweet shit, man."

"How do you keep it up?" I ask. "I mean, how do you keep changing the music all the time? You've left so many good musicians behind. I'm forty-four and I can count. . . ."

He cut me off.

"I'm forty-eight!! I never feel that shit. I'm not vain. As long as I'm not draggin' the musicians I'm with—and I pick the best ones I can find that are available to me—then I figure I'm pretty all right. That's the way *I* judge."

"They're probably worried about pleasing *you.*"

Miles sips his beer.

"Like sometimes I say, 'Al, don't get excited.' And I usually can control everything. Tell them to settle down. Or maybe they're overanxious, and if I see I can't do anything, I'll leave 'em alone. They know themselves.

"And Michael, fartin' around, showin' off, not being a group player. He'll do that shit two nights, and I'll tell him, 'Michael, you been fuckin' around for two days. Settle down!' And he'll say, 'I knew you were gonna say that!' And I'll say, 'Man, bitches make you act funny.'

"They get to think I'm their father! 'We don't see *you* fuck around on the road.' I say, 'I told you I used to have a bitch for every night I went to work, and one night I went to work and all seven of them were there. Shit!! *That's* why I don't fuck around.'"

Miles walked to the piano. It was a little spinet nestled under the circular structure. Some of the notes didn't play.

"When Chick joined my band, he used to play all this shit."

His hands flew over the keyboard.

"We used to talk about music until late every night. Pretty soon he was playin' like this."

Miles played something simple.

"That Chick is a bitch!!"

He shook his head in wonder.

I noticed a score of *Tosca* on the piano.

"I read in *Down Beat* that you were into *Tosca.*"

"Shit-it! Have you heard the record with Leontyne Price?"

I said I hadn't.

"What are you into besides Stockhausen and *Tosca?*"

Miles, very matter-of-factly: "Marvin Gaye, James Brown, Ann Peebles, Aretha, Roberta Flack." Obviously, a stock answer. After a pause, he went on. "I saw Artie Shaw. I said, 'Man, you knew when to quit.' He said, 'I got tired of that shit.' I said, 'I know, you got tired of fuckin' those bitches.'"

Miles chuckles to himself.

"Would you like to see the bedroom?"

He led the way past a small, open shaving area into a big room, gesturing toward a circular pit with an enormous wedge-shaped bed in it. The bed was unmade. I had heard stories about a big gong Miles kept at hand to summon reinforcements to his bed. I didn't see it.

Miles went into the bathroom and took a piss with the door open. I walked around, looking at the pictures, all of Miles, and at his famous wardrobe in disarray all over the room. There were shirts, pants, jackets, scarves thrown over everything. Gaudy platform shoes were underfoot everywhere, scuffed and clumsy.

We went back to the other room. A poster-sized concert picture of Miles leaned against the wall in the hallway, inscribed "for Loretta."

Miles said, "Policemen. They never change. They *stay* the same."

He was delighted at the insight.

He chortled softly, "Oh, shit. You know what I mean?"

He slapped his leg as he sat down.

I wanted to talk about his astonishing ability to adapt and grow with the times. I told him I couldn't think of any comparable examples in jazz.

"Hell, I was the best player in St. Louis. Clark Terry and I. He and I used to go out to jam, and in ten minutes the place would be crowded. He'd come over to my house and ask my father if I could go with him, you know, and he'd take me to a session. Man, we'd play from six o'clock to six the next morning. When I got to New York, I thought everybody knew as much as I did, and I was surprised. Wasn't nobody playing but Dizzy and Roy. The guys who *were* playing, you didn't even know or hear of. Same way in my home town. I was fifteen and guys would come to hear me play because they heard about me. Man, I didn't even know who they were."

"When did you join Bird?"

"Right away, as soon as he left Diz. Charlie Parker used to live with me. He used to talk to people about work, and they'd say, 'You don't have a trumpet player.' And he'd say, 'Here's my trumpet player right here.'"

"Is it true you used to quit once a night?"

"Once an hour."

Miles took deep delight in the recollection.

"Loretta!!"

Miles obviously can project his voice if he wants to. Miles met her at the head of the stairs for a whispered conference. They disappeared into the bedroom for several minutes.

"Had to drink some water 'cause I get dehydrated," Miles explained. "Loretta knows. Sometimes I'll say, 'Loretta, something's funny about me. What is it?' And she'll look at me and say, 'Fix your hair. It's sticking out over there.'"

Miles touches his hair behind his right ear.

"You know, Sy, chicks just *know* about you. Cicely [Tyson] knows when I don't feel good, and she'll call me up and say, 'What's the matter, Miles?'"

Miles's trumpet makes a sensual one-note entrance on the tape.

"Oooh," he says.

A long moody phrase follows.

"That's all I was gonna play on there, you know. Because it didn't lend itself to no more."

It was the passage that surprised my ear during the playback this morning.

"See what I mean," he says.

I asked him why he had begun to play organ.

"I can play it the way I want it. I know guys who can show their technique and all that stuff. I just play it for Dave [Liebman] and different little sounds and shit. Reggie [Young] can play the same things that I can play. I taught him to make the same sounds."

The drums can be heard making slow funereal snare drum patterns. Miles listened.

"That's nice. It kinda grows on you."

I told him I knew Al Foster and thought he was a nice guy.

"So nice I lent him my piano and he never did bring it back."

"What's more or less one piano to you," I tease him.

"A Rhodes-Fender!! You got to be kidding."

I poured the rest of the warm beer in my glass and wished I had some more ice cubes.

"Loretta!! Bring me a Band-Aid."

No response from downstairs.

"Look at that," he says.

He has his right shoe off. I could see a dime-sized hole on the knuckle of his middle toe. It is red and raw.

"Jesus Christ, how did you do that?"

"I don't know."

The bare foot is wheezed and old. I had the weird notion that Miles might be aging from the feet up. I remembered that he had broken his ankles when he smashed up his Ferrari earlier that year.

Miles let his injured foot drop.

"He's lost interest in it already," I thought. "Just another small hurt."

"Couldn't you feel that when you were walking around today?"

Miles shook his head abstractly.

I realized that the medication for his hip and legs was probably so strong that he really couldn't feel his feet.

We talked halfheartedly about a band Teo Macero had assembled. I told him I had arranged a piece of Teo's around a bass ostinato figure.

Miles came to life.

"See there. Now you're gettin' around to the bass. It's a *pleasure* to write around the bass."

He asked who was in the band. When I told him, he said, "All white guys."

I said, "Yeah, and he calls it 'Cotton.'"

Miles grinned. "Oh, yeah," he said.

I told him I had to write around the bass all the time working for Mingus.

He said, "Mingus is a *man*. He don't do nothin' halfway. If he's gonna make a fool of himself, he makes sure he makes a damn fool of himself. You know what I mean?"

He drank some beer.

"Mingus and I were really *close*. We used to rehearse all the time in California. I don't see enough of him.

"Sy, why don't somebody write an article about musicians who are really close friends and don't have time to see each other. You know, like Thad Jones, Elvin Jones, Hank. We're glad to see each other. We never see each other."

"Miles," I said, "Thad and I went to one of your Carnegie Hall concerts. We sat in the third row right under your nose."

"No kiddin'!"

"Yeah, and Thad got so upset that you kept spitting on the stage that he left."

Miles looked upset.

"Maybe it's because I didn't see him. I never see anybody when I'm onstage."

"No," I said. "He kept saying, 'Miles shouldn't spit onstage in Carnegie Hall.' And finally he said, 'I'm sorry, Sy, but if he spits one more time I'm gonna have to go.' And you spit, and he went."

Miles said, very softly, "Maybe it's a good thing we don't see each other. Didn't he know I just got over pneumonia?"

He shook his head sadly. I saw Loretta coming up the stairs.

"Loretta," I called out, "Miles needs a Band-Aid."

Miles said, gently, "She does what I tell her. She won't do what you say."

Miles hobbled off to talk to Loretta.

"You know," he said as he sat down again. "Roberta [Flack] called me from London, and she said, 'I went to hear Thad's band and nobody spoke to me.' She felt very bad."

Loretta came and knelt at Miles's feet. Some antiseptic cream and a Band-Aid were expertly put in place.

"Loretta, did you know Thad walked out on my concert?

"I take Loretta down to hear Thad, and I tell her, 'This is one of the greatest trumpet players you're ever gonna hear.' Don't I, Loretta?"

"Yes, Miles really loves Thad."

Miles sent Loretta to place an out-of-town call for him.

He continued, "When I go to hear a trumpet player, I've really gotta like him. I don't go to hear Freddie Hubbard only because I don't like him. I'd rather hear Thad *miss* a note than hear Freddie make *twelve*."

I told him that Thad told me how much he loves Miles's playing but that Miles's continual changing made him very threatening to older players.

Miles was silent for a minute and then said: "Thad should get that shit outta his head. That boy's a motherfucker. Has been for some years.

"You know, Sy, Thad's always around, and he doesn't come to see me. Nobody comes to see me. None of the guys, you know. All the young guys do, but Thad and all my friends like that never do. I like them, but they don't like me. Dizzy asks me to teach him. I say, 'Yeah, come by. I'll show you everything we're doin'. It'll be my pleasure.' And *he* don't come by."

Loretta: "Pick up, Miles."

The man he wanted was at another number. He asked, "How's he act-ing? Is he healthy? Huh? Is he thin? Is he drinking too much? Okay, Loretta, try this other number."

He comes back. His face is full of concern.

"One of my old gangster buddies. He ought to take care of himself. He gonna kill himself before I get to see him again."

"Miles, pick up."

"Hello, you old motherfucker. What!! Fuck him. If you think I . . .

"Good-bye!!"

He slammed down the phone. He was calm again before he even sat down. I asked him which of the younger guys came by to see him.

"Herbie [Hancock] does. He always comes by when he's in town. Chick does."

He stopped for a minute.

"No, Chick doesn't come to hear me."

I could barely hear him.

"Chick wouldn't be interested in my band."

Miles's eyes were moist.

I thought, "That's why he wears those huge glasses. His eyes give him away. The pain, the hurt, the vulnerability, forty-eight years, all there to see. But he puts those glasses on and it's the Black Prince, who knows no pain."

I said, "Maybe you have to come to them. Nobody's gonna knock on that front door."

I watched him put his shoe on again.

"Don't you wear socks? It's no wonder those fucking ridiculous shoes are tearing your toes off."

He went to a mirror and poked at his hair.

"It was those fucking policemen hurt my foot."

"What did they do, step on your toe?"

"It was a fucking policeman."

He walked over and slapped my foot.

"Damn it, Sy, I'm gonna throw a party. Do you think they'll come? Max, Mingus, Gil, Dizzy, Thad?"

I assured him they would if they were in town.

"That's what I'm gonna do. I'm gonna throw a party.

"Come on, Sy. I gotta get ready for a rehearsal at six."

He tried on another hat as I packed my Sony.

"I love this hat. Ain't it a bitch?"

He laughed all the way down the stairs. I said good-bye to Loretta.

Miles took my hand at the door.

"Come by tomorrow, if you want."

I stepped into the street. Sunlight blinded me. I remembered I hadn't taken my pictures.

I thought, "I bet it never happened. I'd better check the tape when I get home."

Bob Blumenthal

Miles Gloriosus

Originally published in the Boston Phoenix, *July 7, 1981. Reprinted by permission of the* Boston Phoenix *and the author.*

In fall 1975 Davis retired from public performances for nearly six years. His reasons for such a long hiatus included the need for a hip operation, general exhaustion, and an apparent desire—discussed candidly in his autobiography—to indulge some hedonistic proclivities. He slowly resumed recording in mid-1980 with a new, mostly young band, but his official return did not occur until June 26–29, 1981, with a nightclub engagement at Kix in Boston.

Bob Blumenthal reviewed this appearance in the *Boston Phoenix*, and his report is a colorful slice-of-life account of Davis's reemergence and the widespread interest that surrounded it. A seasoned jazz commentator, Blumenthal has written for the *Boston Phoenix, Rolling Stone,* the *Boston Globe,* and the *Atlantic Monthly.* Among his many liner notes have been ones for such Davis recordings as *Directions* (Columbia) and *The Complete Live at the Plugged Nickel 1965* (Columbia/Mosaic).—Ed.

A friend, wise to the ploys of lazy journalists, laid down the perfect challenge after the last of Miles Davis's eight sold-out performances at Kix a week ago. "What Miles Davis song title captures what's been going on here?" he challenged. Another companion offered, "So What," but even the most jaded and wary among us had to admit that the trumpeter's performance, and his new album *The Man with the Horn* (Columbia), were too intriguing to be dismissed with such indifference. After all, this was Miles, the Sorcerer, the Prince of Darkness, charisma incarnate, trendsetter, and talent scout supreme. At that intersection of aesthetics and hype, substance and stylishness, brash innovation and mass appeal—a junction most jazz musicians never approach—Miles Davis remains a monolith.

So the response to my friend's question could only be "Great Expectations" (from *Big Fun,* courtesy of Dickens), for it seems that the entire jazz community has been hanging on reports of Davis's return for the past five years. When he quit performing in 1975, rumors immediately began flying about his physical health and state of mind. Apparently he did undergo surgery (although the number and nature of the operations remain unclear), but the most alarming stories suggested that he had become an embittered recluse who no longer cared about music and rarely left his Manhattan brownstone. Former sidemen and Columbia Records insiders were quick to dispel such gloomy prognoses, and every six months or so one heard tantalizing hints that Davis was indeed headed back. Apparently at one point or another, Davis entered the studio with a band featuring Larry Coryell, commissioned arrangements from Paul Buckmaster, and considered fronting a band led by his nephew Vincent Wilburn. Other tales had him set to reunite with Gil Evans and eager to collaborate with Arthur Blythe. Finally, after the schedule for this year's Kool (né Newport) Jazz Festival had been announced, the trumpeter agreed to close the concert series with two sets at Avery Fisher Hall on Sunday, July 5. *The Man with the Horn* was completed, with a release date set to coincide with the New York concerts; and in the biggest surprise of all, old friend Fred Taylor booked Davis into Boston for four nights, a warm-up for Avery Fisher that marked his official return to action.

The jumbled reaction—part exhilaration, part annoyance—that I'm left with after several listenings to *The Man with the Horn* and three sets from Sunday and Monday night at Kix suggests that it is not easy being Miles Davis, yet at the same time that it is far too easy. On the one hand, history teaches us to expect that Davis will be the harbinger of changed directions and the herald of undiscovered genius. When he isn't, we feel shortchanged. Concurrently, the constants of Davis's sound and manner ensure that we will respond. Those for whom sound and manner are enough will no doubt gush over his return; those whose demands were too great will dismiss the whole episode as a media event. On such dichotomies are legends sustained.

It now seems silly that anyone expected Davis to return with either another radical departure or a reconsideration of his preelectric music. We should have known that he would pick up where he left off, with open-ended, vamp-driven, funky electric jamming. Refinements are detectable, and they augur more satisfying changes to come. There is now only one guitar in the band instead of two, thus lending a tauter edge to even the densest ensemble episodes. Davis also seems determined to employ a wider range of moods and rhythms than was heard in his last band; now reggae, ballad, and 4/4 swing are mixed amidst the various rock riffs. On the album each of the six tracks has a discrete groove, while at Kix the band was more likely to move in and out of competing attitudes. Even "My Man's Gone Now" was resurrected at the club, and a coy line was introduced that sounded like eight bars of an old "Walkin'" solo, though in each case the rhythm section's part carried crossover implications. None of the music at Kix, however, matched the obvious commerciality of the album's title track, a spacey MOR ballad with fawning lyrics sung by cocomposer Randy Hall. The purists are already howling about the song, which Columbia is releasing as a single (the company probably thinks the song is its best hope for protecting its substantial investment in Davis's comeback), but "The Man with the Horn" is too innocuous to get worked up about.

There never was anything wrong with early-'70s Davis that talented sidemen couldn't put right. The new band, however, is a mix of exceptional and merely acceptable musicians. In Fender bassist Marcus Miller and drummer Al Foster, Davis has a brilliant rhythm team, one that must be heard live—with Davis signaling impromptu dynamic shifts and breaks in the tempo—to be truly appreciated. Foster, with his tubby-sounding drum kit and incessant attack, did some particularly felicitous bashing, suggesting in the process that these high-energy, quasi-rock patterns are his true forte. The others played their parts well enough without showing enough individuality to set them apart. Mino, the showman of the band (after the leader), was functional in his role as miscellaneous percussionist. Saxophonist Bill Evans, the only member of nephew Wilburn's band whom Davis retained, is another member of the faceless contemporary crowd; he concentrated on soprano, which he attacks in elliptical Wayne Shorter fashion, and showed a fondness for early Coltrane in his tenor spots. Guitarist Mike Stern, the newest addition to the group (Barry Finnerty is heard on the album), showed more melodic daring in spots and clearly made a positive impression on Davis, who frequently stroked his long hair in mid-solo. Still, Stern relied on repetitive runs or heavy metal chording too often, and this diluted the impact of his better passages.

As for Davis, he retains the same aggressive, splintered approach to the trumpet that he has employed since the 1961 live recordings. His horn is now electric, with an attachment the size of a cigarette pack next to the valves and a small microphone suspended over the bell, but this seems primarily intended to reinforce a still-rebuilding embouchure. On the album, traces of weakness are audible in a few halfhearted tones, yet Davis's lip is now noticeably stronger. Although he is parsimonious with his playing time and seemed always displeased with his muted sound, his command of the trumpet was an indication that he takes his return seriously.

What Davis played was invariably familiar. The upper-register stabs, muttered conclusions at the bottom of the horn, squeezed tones, and abrupt shifts in intensity have become a bit too foreseeable over the past twenty years. That these clichés are Davis's own, and that his sound remains extremely affecting (especially at slow tempos), did not disguise the predictability of his solos. Since the sidemen remained relatively cautious while Davis blew yet opened up once he put down his horn and began directing them, the fireworks occurred when Davis wasn't playing.

It was then, as a stage presence, that Davis revealed his most substantial and unexpected evolution. In the early '70s he stopped walking offstage after his solos and began leading the rhythm section through its paces behind the other featured players. Now he seems to relish conducting and the results it elicits from the band. No longer aloof onstage, Davis is now openly responsive to his sidemen and the audience, and between patented glares he honestly seems to be having fun. Occasionally he gets carried away with the shenanigans, as in the last set Monday night, when he left the stage once too often to blow solos into good friend Cicely Tyson's lap. His interaction with the sidemen was more intriguing and inspired images of Davis as head of a musical clan, bestowing affection on favorite child Stern (a miniature Meatloaf), benign indifference on middle son Evans (Ozzie and Harriet's David with a soprano), wary approval on suave upstart Mino, casual respect on cousin Miller, and always one eye on cantankerous uncle Foster, who just might dip into the family liquor cabinet if left unattended.

Ah, you say, but this is show business, and we were talking about jazz. Perhaps, but Miles Davis has always been about more than music (Cicely Tyson doesn't travel to Boston for just anybody's gig), and at Kix the persona seemed to embellish and reinforce the sounds. Without excusing the unevenness of the music, or the shortness of sets that rarely stretched beyond an hour (hardly what one expected at $12.50 per ticket), the mere sight of Miles Davis onstage in this mood was satisfying. The man is enjoying himself, which is the most encouraging aspect of his resurgence. If this attitude can be maintained, if he continues to work on tightening the band and finds new ways to incorporate melodic and rhythmic material from his earlier work, he might really be something to hear by December. Excessive expectations, perhaps, but if Miles keeps smiling, anything may happen.

Gary Giddins

Miles's Wiles

Originally published in the Village Voice, *August 5–12, 1981, 27–28.*
Reprinted by permission of the Village Voice *and the author.*

Gary Giddins wrote "Miles's Wiles" during the same period that Bob Blumenthal did "Miles Gloriosus." The two pieces thus make an interesting complement, coming as they do from two critics of similar age and outlook.

Of all the jazz critics of the "baby boomer" (i.e., born just after World War II) generation, Giddins is among the best known and most prolific. He began writing for *Down Beat* in the early 1970s and joined the staff of the *Village Voice* in 1973. His criticism has been collected in three volumes: *Riding on a Blue Note* (1981), *Rhythm-a-ning* (1985), and *Faces in the Crowd* (1992). Giddins also is the author of biographies of Charlie Parker and Louis Armstrong, *Celebrating Bird* (1987) and *Satchmo* (1988). In addition, he was founder of the American Jazz Orchestra and its guiding force from 1985 to 1992.—Ed.

Five years in the life of Miles Davis can seem like a generation in the life of jazz. It's the distance, for example, between "Israel" and "Walkin'" and

Kind of Blue and *My Funny Valentine* and *Bitches Brew* and *Get Up with It.* The 1949 blues was heralded as the birth of the cool, and the 1954 blues as a return to the hot, but the distinction was to be found not so much in Davis's trumpet playing as in the settings he encouraged. This business of cool and hot is the jazz dialectic in a nutshell, and one reason Davis felt at home in both camps is that, more than any other instrumentalist of his generation, he knew that hot and cool could mesh without turning luke-warm; in fact, it is at that point where they are insoluble that we find the Prince of Darkness prancing on his eggshells. The bottom line of his cease-less innovating is to be found in his obsession with form and texture. His trumpet playing changed plenty in the course of thirty-five years, but his phases—first a brief apprenticeship in the shadows of Freddie Webster and Dizzy Gillespie, then the emergence of a thoroughly original style built on the acknowledgment of technical limitations, then a renewed assault on those limitations—might almost be an incidental by-product of his restless-ness. His evolution as a soloist is personal, a matter of the id; it's in the directions he sets for his cohorts, near and far, that his ego comes into full play. Which is why the four albums mentioned above seem less like sign-posts of one man's growth than measured attacks on the status quo.

The status quo in jazz is protected as much by obeisance to the pathfinders as by principled conservatism. Radicals are too much wor-shiped, their innovations shamelessly bled for new clichés to replace or supplement the old. Good musicians, justly proud of the individualism that is at the core of jazz, may invent new sounds and variations, but how many have addressed the fundamental issues of structure, instrumenta-tion, and repertoire? Miles Davis does, constantly, and every time he comes up with a new answer, the whole music shifts in its seat. He didn't originate all the directions that became associated with his records, but he found ways to make them palatable, even popular. His popularity probably accounts for the frequent omission of Davis's name from discus-sions of jazz radicals. We associate the avant-garde with privation, which Davis has never known, and with a specific approach to improvisational freedom, which he rejects. Still, he is a terribly conscientious avant-gardist, continuously remaking jazz in his own image, and often remak-ing himself in the process. Harold Rosenberg defined avant-gardism as an "addiction that can be appeased only by revolution in permanence." Davis's addiction has proven as unkickable as that of Coltrane or Coleman and perhaps more so than that of Taylor, and he's been in its throes longer than any of them.

I began by invoking the five-year cycle because of the five-year silence from which Davis has just emerged. His return is freighted with unique expectations: should Thelonious Monk return, we'd be delighted with new choruses of "Evidence" and "Straight, No Chaser," but we refuse to accept from Davis a mere continuation of where he left off. To this extent he's made good on his promise. But the comeback has also been taxed by his own silly arrogance. During his absence young zealots apotheosized him in a way that wasn't possible when he was actively performing, and although I don't think he actually bought their bill of goods, they may have convinced him he could get away with anything. His only New York interview was with a dilettante at the *Times* who was satisfied to reproduce his gibberish about money, women, and fast cars. His bumping of Blood Ulmer from his Kool concerts was widely attributed to competitive fear. Worst of all, he recorded a narcissistic sop to the airwaves with a title, "The Man with the Horn," that is scarifyingly close to Dorothy Baker's daydreams about trumpet players. Davis once told an interviewer that his hobby was "making fun of white folks on television." With this wilting performance, he appears to have expanded his field to black folks on radio.

The rest of Davis's new album is another story. *The Man with the Horn* (Columbia FC 36790) is hardly top-drawer or second-drawer Miles, but it's interesting in surprising ways, especially in tandem with his current concerts. In several important respects, Davis is surveying his past and expanding his options. Playing pure trumpet without benefit of electronic gimmickry, he has diversified his repertoire and put together his first homogeneous, studio-produced album since *A Tribute to Jack Johnson* in 1970. All the intervening records were either edited from concert tapes or collated from two or more widely divergent sessions. Although carefully edited to promote his continuing addiction to change, they were quite unlike the thematic statements that made Davis a major force in recordings in the late '50s and the '60s, when he produced the orchestral projects with Gil Evans, the pioneering essays in form *(Kind of Blue)* and texture *(Bitches Brew)*, and the incisive "in between" albums *(Milestones, Miles Smiles, Miles in the Sky)* that mapped out the steps leading to the major breakthroughs.

The degree to which Davis and producer Teo Macero have succeeded in making a varied album is all the more impressive given its two major drawbacks: the sidemen, excepting Al Foster, are faceless, and Davis is chopsless. He compensates for the failings of others by hiding them. Excepting guitarist Mike Stern, who mercifully plays on only one selection, the sextet's only soloist other than Davis is saxophonist Bill Evans. He compensates for his own deficiencies by facing them head-on, renouncing even the wah-wah machine that made his *Agharta* wimperings sound like deathly chortles. Indeed, *The Man with the Horn* is something of a tour de force for him, and there are moments, especially his two solos on "Aida," where he broaches the high register with nervous punctuating notes and pressing arpeggios, that put me in mind of the pride that animated some of Billie Holiday's last performances. I don't mean to make much of the comparison: Holiday was at the end of her rope, while Davis, judging from his concert, has already toughened his embouchure in the few months since this record was cut. The point is that he isn't cheating.

The album's big surprise is "Ursula," a swinging if monochromatic 4/4 jazz walk that could have been recorded in 1968. Because it consists exclusively of short, punching, middle-register phrases, much emphasis is placed on the triologue between Davis, Foster (who leans into some splashing Tony Williams stuff behind the sax solo), and a Fender bassist named Marcus Miller; it even ends with that ancient Milesian tradition of the trumpeter rasping, "Play that, Teo." Other ties to the past are explored in "Back Seat Betty," which has a good, simple theme strongly reminiscent of both "SHHH/Peaceful" *(In a Silent Way)* and the improvisation on, but not the theme of, "Petit Machins" *(Filles de Kilimanjaro)*. The rhythm section is discreet except for some psychedelic interludes, and Davis meanders nicely with a concatenation of mutters, tremolos, and shouts made cogent by his intensity and sound. Bill Evans enters with a squeaky, yearning cry and continues his solo in Davis's vein.

The conservatism elsewhere isn't so rewarding. "Shout" is tepid soul music by the threesome that crafted the noxious title selection, although it's no disgrace as a bid for the airwaves—at least Davis makes a yeoman try at a solo, and the saxophonist once again attempts to sustain the leader's mood. The uninvolving vamp on "Fat Time" undercuts the poignancy of Davis's tone; the orderly rhythms and modulations of the guitar solo sound antiquated compared with John McLaughlin's febrile work of ten years earlier, and I find the heavy-metal sonority as inappropriate here as it would be in a Beethoven quartet.

I don't think Davis sustains a single melodic idea on the entire record, but I suspect that had his chops been more in order, he might have displayed the ardent lyricism with which he once made cool hot and hot cool. The evidence was in his Kool concert performance, when he resurrected "My Man's Gone Now." It was the first time I'd heard him play something from the standard repertory since 1970, and it reminded me of

a rumor that was circulating shortly before he took his sabbatical: a musician talking to Davis backstage at a European concert said that Davis
expressed the desire to reinvestigate ballads, but added "they won't let
me." Oh, ominous apocryphal tales! For all the sludge that pervaded his
Kool recital, I find that two weeks later his two choruses of Gershwin's
melody remain fresher than most of what I heard at the festival. But I'd
better explain my use of the word "chorus," because it was in the restruc-
turing of that piece that Davis's impish radicalism returned. He didn't
play choruses per se; instead, the piece was poised over a scale or a pedal
point that allowed him to phrase with complete freedom, though this
didn't much affect his choice of notes. He followed the pattern of the
song with few deviations, but when he wanted to breathe, he didn't have
to concern himself with chords and measures and the way they relate to
each other. Here, Davis was working through an idea he'd been mulling
over for more than twenty years.

What made Davis radical in the '50s and '60s wasn't that he did away
with song form but that he opened it up. Even Duke Ellington, the
cleverest of all jazz radicals, who worked every variation imaginable on
traditional song and blues forms, never went beyond the basic parameters
of those structures. The challenge for Davis was illustrated unintentionally
in the second take of his 1954 recording of "The Man I Love": Monk plays
a piano solo in which he repeatedly bedraggles the six-note motif over the
bar lines, until finally he gets lost—Davis puts him back on the track by
playing the appropriate chord at the release. Monk subsequently settled
the issue for himself with subtly rubato, unaccompanied solos—an option
not open, or at least as appealing, to a trumpet player. Davis had to think
the problem through for his whole band. He had already worked to
simplify the harmonic labyrinth of bop as a soloist: he made an art of
choosing stimulating tempos and drew on his considerable knowledge of
harmony to choose the odd but tellingly right notes. This ability, added to
his painstaking development of a personal approach to timbre (abetted by
a Harmon mute), gave him the charismatic sound that forced the music
community to suspend its disbelief.

In the next few years, Davis adapted his regimen of simplification to a
band context by exploring modes and scales. The turning point was the
seminal *Kind of Blue,* that gorgeous, introspective collection of first takes so
smoothly executed that hardly anyone recognized it for the insurrection it
was. He revitalized the blues with "All Blues" and "Freddie Freeloader,"
introduced modulating tempos in "Blue in Green," replaced chords with

modes while retaining the traditional song form in "So What," and improvised form itself in "Flamenco Sketches." "So What" has always seemed the
most significant piece—a thirty-two-bar song based on the Dorian mode
with a second scale used for the release—because of its immense impact in
popularizing modality. But now, "Flamenco Sketches" appears more relevant. Its challenge was to play a series of five scales, the duration of each to
be improvised by the soloist. For the most part, Davis and his musicians
played it safe, modulating every four or eight bars, and telegraphing those
modulations by a mile. Within a few years, however, he was playing remarkable improvisations on standard tunes—"Autumn Leaves," "My Funny
Valentine"—which, though almost always cleaving to the metrical rules,
often gave the illusion of impromptu modulations, and of a structural freedom denied his sidemen.

At the same time, narcissism began to creep into this work. Fluffs
became marks of honor, even aesthetic signposts. It started subtly: there's
that magical moment during the "Strawberry" episode of *Porgy and Bess*,
when the trumpeter's technical failure seems preordained, as though he
were deliberately cracking his notes to convey the dolorousness of the
lament. By the time of "My Funny Valentine," which has one of the most
notorious fluffs ever released, one got the feeling that his every crackle
and splutter was to be embraced as evidence of his spontaneous soul. On
the other hand, his cavalier attitude toward mistakes was more than balanced by an astonishing ambitiousness in his overall performance: he
began increasingly to forage into the upper register at breathtaking tempos, the ideas spilling from his horn like leaves in October. This spiraling
aplomb, matched by a constant quest for new song forms (Wayne
Shorter's impact here can hardly be overestimated), resulted in some of
the most fiery playing of his career: "Country Son," "Petits Machins,"
"Right Off." And it is just at this point that he trades the bite and bril-
liance of his reclaimed virtuosity for the often mud-colored electronic
ensembles, which, for all their rhythmic excitement, vitiated his sound
before finally disguising it with gadgetry, limited his options, and substituted tribal chatter for the dagger-edged ego-play of his quintets. This time
when he remade the music in his own image the accent was almost entirely on texture, sometimes with notable results—for example, "Mtume," an
electrified Ellingtonian jungle in which Davis, gargling like a recently
spayed cat, provides compelling poignancy around which the churning
rhythms coalesce. But for the most part, his playing lost its charisma, and

even the "Interlude" solo on *Agharta*, with its urgent blues licks and pungent glissandos, suggests more of the pain than the grandeur in his music.

The new record and the concert I saw do make for an anticlimactic return, but they are promising nevertheless. He doesn't fudge notes on the record—maybe you can only do that when you're full of confidence, and he has reason to be guarded. Yet he's letting his own sound resurface. In editing down the band, he's cleaned away some of the sludge. In looking backward, he's opened up his repertoire. Gil Evans has also looked back to the *Porgy and Bess* triumph, and his current band plays a revised arrangement of "Here Come de Honey Man." A reunion between Evans and Davis may be the only hope of hearing the most lyrical soloist of our time collaborate with a peer. The last time they worked together, the evocative *Filles de Kilimanjaro* resulted, though Evans wasn't credited. That one can even imagine a sequel is the best news about Davis's return. Five years ago he appeared dead-ended; now, he seems cautious but open. After five years of silence, cautious but open is good news.

Max Harrison

Listening to Davis Live in London: The 1980s

Originally published in Music and Musicians, *August 1982;* Jazz Forum, *September 1983;* Jazz Express, *August 1984;* Hampstead and Highgate Express, *July 28, 1989. Revised in June 1994 and reprinted by permission of the author.*

During the 1980s Miles Davis regained his playing prowess and toured and recorded extensively with a succession of his own bands. While these ensembles retained the strong rock orientation of Davis's 1970s groups, their music was more formalized and structured, and Davis restored some elements of his earlier work, including the blues (as a song form, that is, not just as an element in his musical vocabulary) and a theme he had originally recorded in 1958 on the *Porgy and Bess* album, "My Man's Gone Now."

In a survey of Davis's London concerts during the 1980s, Max Harrison takes a careful look at both the music and the musicians. His largely sympathetic view of Davis's sidemen is especially noteworthy, since a number of these musicians took a critical beating in contemporary reviews.—Ed.

Nobody in this music shed stylistic skins so often, this mostly leading to an influential new synthesis of jazz essentials. And Davis's London performances, at the Odeon, Hammersmith, on April 20–22, 1982, suggested he had done it again. The circumstances were unusual. Ian Carr's program for "The South Bank Show" (Independent Television, April 25, 1982) reminded us that Davis had been inactive for several years and became virtually a recluse. This was due to illness, and although his 1981 tour indicated a partial recovery, his stage demeanor was far from the rather theatrical arrogance of former days. Yet this time, and on all three nights, the Hammersmith air was almost as electric as the music.

The band was pleasingly characteristic of jazz in the early 1980s in that it mixed Christian, Jew, and Muslim, was black and white, and spanned the generations. The two guitarists and two percussionists interlocked in a variety of ways, the dialogues of the former pair being inflected, sometimes blatantly, by electricity. The electronic modification of sound, indeed, sometimes distended the ensemble's diverse textures, and a sustained account of "My Man's Gone Now" has remained the most outlandish Gershwin performance I ever heard, setting Davis's austere lyricism in a startlingly new framework. This was produced by a variety of means.

Thus American reports of the band's 1981 appearances suggested that Mike Stern played only rock 'n' roll guitar, yet such accusations missed the point. Rather did he hold up a distorting mirror to Davis's melodic thoughts, this juxtaposition of two utterly different images of the same idea giving the music a most unexpected dimension. Obliquely related to this was the confrontation between stillness, typified by some of the leader's muted playing and by the soprano and flute solos of Bill Evans, and the violent, electronically heightened ensemble activity. Other factors, like the music's apparently irrational paragraphing, also gave us plenty to think about.

Some of us were still thinking about it when, almost exactly a year later, Davis returned to the Odeon, Hammersmith, on April 27–28, 1983. It was obvious from the moment he strode purposefully onstage that the past twelve months had treated him more kindly than the previous several years. He now dominated unmistakably, and this of course affected the music, a greater emphasis being placed on solos, especially his own. So much improved was Davis's health that throughout the long sets he gave us each night, he many times played in a single breath sequences that the previous year would have taken two, even three. Typical might be a phrase that began in middle register, soared to a sustained high note, and fluttered down in a quieter, imaginatively varied echo of the opening, and all this in an unbroken line.

It was more fluent than any playing I had heard from him live except—a long way back—during his first visit to Britain in September–October 1960. Davis yet again discredited the notion that however much he may have altered the style and personnel of his bands, his own playing remained the same. As he said during an interview with Richard Williams for *The Times* of London (April 28, 1983), having two guitarists featured so prominently in his current group was enough in itself to make him change yet again because their instrument obviously has such a different character from his own. Which is to say that one point of all the alterations he made to his music over the years was the stimulus they provided for *him*.

Still, Davis sounded like a man who would be lonely in any crowd, although the feeling of separateness was now strengthened by an impression of self-sufficiency. The previous year he mainly had played sitting down, whereas now he prowled the stage with his black suit and wide-brimmed black hat, only an unforgivable pair of brown shoes preventing him from looking like a flamenco dancer. And he actually waved his trumpet at the audience occasionally in acknowledgment of applause. Much more of these antics and he would be telling us the names of the pieces he played.

Another point was that, besides having stopped ignoring the audience, Davis had also stopped seeming to ignore his band. He punctuated solos by the others with high trumpet notes and sometimes gave further support with left-hand chords on his Oberheim synthesizer. Decisively controlled by the leader, each performance had a more lucid structure than a year earlier, and the overall use of the ensemble was still more interesting. He explained to *The Times* that he was now concerned with writing fragmentary melodies, six- or ten-bar thoughts that could move through a performance in a circular manner, without apparent beginning or end. Somewhat ironically, this was reminiscent of another great innovator, of whom Davis spoke contemptuously in 1959, for in the liner notes for his *Change of the Century* collection of that year, Ornette Coleman wrote that "in a certain sense there really is no start or finish to any of my compositions."

However, the sense of form, if elusive, was real in Davis's 1983 music, not only in each piece but in each set—the feeling of final and satisfying resolution in the closing moments of the April 27 performance being especially marked. A further point, and an aid to unification, was that this music was saturated with the blues—the blues via jazz, not via rock. That Davis still had two guitarists on board might seem to imply a further detour along the blind alley of populism. Yet *Bitches Brew* was now far in the past, and it seemed possible that Davis had molded his borrowings from rock into something sufficiently personal to silence questions about his initial, probably sales-conscious, motivations.

Apart from his own trumpet solos, the blues were most evident in Stern's playing, and by now he was no longer accused of trading in dog-eared rock 'n' roll clichés. The other guitarist, John Scofield, was closer to jazz in the traditional sense, having periods with Gerry Mulligan, Jay McShann, and Lee Konitz behind him. Although a full use was made of contrasts between these two, in this band matters were taken far beyond mere contrasts and juxtapositions. Rather did all elements interfuse, much that was only latent the previous year now emerging decisively, the result being music of extraordinary richness. Electronics having become fully integral, these performances had so many colors, textures, tempos, levels of volume, and, above all, so many voices.

Although more original on tenor, the instrument he played least, Bill Evans's soprano and flute solos once again provided interludes of calm, as did Scofield's contributions, and these balanced Davis's and Stern's more ardent declarations. Tom Barney's bass guitar and Al Foster's drums shifted smoothly between resounding and subtle pulses while Mino Cinélu's Latin American percussion fulfilled a role that at first seemed decorative but that, as the music grew less unfamiliar, emerged as essential. The paradox was that collectively all these voices, even when the music was at storm force, mirrored the irreducibly isolated sound of Davis's trumpet. The whole most potently reflected his vision in its unpredictability. Even the adept listener could never guess in which direction it would turn next, what the rhythm, the tempo, the colors would be. It appeared that the populist elements Davis had taken into his music really had passed through a purgatorial fire transmuting them back into jazz.

Another year on, and it was different again, providing less ground for optimism. The routine was now two concerts a day, and when the first of a Festival Hall pair (July 17, 1984) started a mere forty-five minutes late, Davis instantly hit us with a deafening and unsteady rock beat. This reassured a large part of what mainly was not a jazz audience, and yet he still played what he evidently wanted to play. Indeed he continued to offer great jazz trumpeting—and to double on PR more effectively than anyone else in the business. Witness his ironic flirtation at the edge of the stage with photographers who swarmed toward him like bees dive-bombing the proverbial honeypot—aside from one, wittier than the rest, who made himself conspicuous by ignoring Davis and photographing the other photographers.

Except in his youth, this trumpeter was never merely a soloist. His approach to the jazz ensemble lay near the heart of his creativity and his ability to continue making positive changes. But on this occasion we heard only two kinds of performance: blasting, heavily amplified ensembles and introverted, reticently accompanied solos from Davis. These sharply contrasting musics were linked in such ways as to indicate that he still thought of a concert as a single entity, and this related to his obvious concern with electronically manipulating the sound as a whole in the loud passages. These threw his own tortured lyricism into higher relief than ever, implying an increase of meaning. Despite, or perhaps because of, a context that had now begun to seem incongruous, it appeared that Davis's power to move sensitive listeners had actually grown.

It is not possible to deal with every year, but half a decade later (July 1989), still at the Festival Hall, it had all subsided into streetwise, high-tech, neon-bathed Muzak. And even this came a poor second to Davis's undignified Peter Pan-like need to cling to the trappings of youth. Not only had he lost all innovative drive, but his taste, not to mention his sense of form, had faltered to the point where his band, including a busier-than-thou anonymous tenor, a finger-busting, conservatory-groomed oriental keyboardist, a pony-tailed rock 'n' roll bassist, and a standard-issue deafening percussionist (I refuse to give the names), was egged on through routines that hardly would have passed muster halfway down the bill at a rock festival of the heavy metallurgical persuasion fifteen years earlier.

Davis had continued to renew himself for much longer than most people in jazz, and we should not complain. But listening to him in the 1980s showed how authentic achievements were finally overtaken by increasingly shabby compromises, how inner artistic compulsions were supplanted by dictates of the youth cult, fashion, and the market. The great nonconformist became the exact opposite, and it all ended as a rather typical story of the late twentieth century.

Larry Kart

Miles Davis Biography Fails to Unravel Strands of Art and Image

Originally published in the Chicago Tribune, *October 20, 1985. Copyright by the Chicago Tribune Company. All rights reserved. Used with permission.*

The springboard for Larry Kart's observations about Miles Davis was a review of Jack Chambers's *Milestones,* to date the most extensively researched biography of Davis. Kart goes on to make some unique points about the "most overtly theatrical jazz artist of our time."

Apart from a 1968–70 stint as assistant editor of *Down Beat,* Kart has spent most of his career on the staff of the *Chicago Tribune;* for a number of years he was that newspaper's entertainment critic. His often penetrating jazz criticism has yet to receive proper exposure in book form.—Ed.

If any jazz musician deserves a full-scale biography, it is trumpeter-bandleader Miles Davis.

A figure of major artistic importance for almost forty years, Davis also has become, in the words of drummer Chico Hamilton, "jazz's only superstar," a bona fide celebrity whose every move is news. And that side of Davis's career is not without meaning, both to Davis and to the public at large—a point reemphasized in 1981 when the trumpeter's emergence from six years of self-imposed retirement sent off shock waves that rippled through the world of jazz and even touched the shores of *Newsweek, Time,* and *People* magazines.

But as with any celebrity who also happens to be an artist, the art is what matters most, even when the party under discussion is as colorful and image-conscious as Davis. And if the image and the art have become entangled, as they surely have in Davis's case, it is the biographer's task to separate the strands.

But even though Canadian author Jack Chambers devotes more than 350,000 words to Davis's career in his *Milestones I: The Music and Times of Miles Davis to 1960* and *Milestones II: The Music and Times of Miles Davis since 1960,* Chambers seldom makes contact with Davis's music—describing key performances in vague terms and refusing almost throughout to rise to the level of judgment.

A particular Davis solo is said to be "bold." Another is "stunning." And when Chambers gets a bit more detailed, as in his account of "Boplicity" and "Moon Dreams" (two major recordings by Davis's *Birth of the Cool* band), the results aren't very helpful.

"'Boplicity,' " Chambers writes, "moves along through numerous shifts of texture as the various horns are rearranged into new alliances." As for "Moon Dreams"—while it is "a brilliant display of inimitable talents," the piece "is a kind of musical still life, easy to admire but impossible to love."

Itself virtually meaningless—why, and compared to what, is "Moon Dreams" impossible to love?—such stuff is even more annoying because the works that Chambers fails to discuss in any depth have been dealt with quite shrewdly by other writers. He makes little distinction between such tough-minded critics as Martin Williams and André Hodeir and the host of jazz journalists he quotes who essentially embroider variations on "I like it" or "I don't."

Chambers's fondness for the hands-off approach is particularly worrisome because Davis's career, with all its stylistic twists and turns, demands to be sorted out. But before one tries to do that, a few words about what Chambers's biography manages to accomplish.

An almost day-by-day account of Davis's life, *Milestones I* and *II* has its moments of tedium, as it delves into most of the many quarrels Davis has had with club owners, journalists, record company executives, and concert promoters. But Chambers does seem able to separate fact from gossip, and some of the facts are important.

For instance, it is not widely known that Davis suffers from sickle-cell anemia. In his case the side effects of this congenital disease became quite severe by the mid-1960s, leading to the deterioration of Davis's hip and wrist joints. Ever since, he has lived and played in near-constant pain.

Significant, too, is the story of Davis's mid-1950s battle with heroin addiction—a period that ended when, with typical grit, Davis kicked the habit by locking himself in a room and living through two weeks of withdrawal symptoms. But again, if a man is an artist, the art matters most—even when the life and the art are furiously intertwined.

Born in 1926 in Alton, Illinois (a satellite community of St. Louis), Miles Dewey Davis III received his most important early lessons from trumpeter Elwood Buchanan. The models Buchanan urged upon the boy were a pair of pure-toned, graceful players, Bobby Hackett and Harold "Shorty" Baker, not Louis Armstrong with his heated virtuosity. "Play without any vibrato," Buchanan told his student. "You're gonna get old anyway and start shaking."

It was solid, practical advice, and perhaps not too much should be made of it. But one wonders whether that was the point at which a link was made between two of Davis's key musical traits—his concern with sound for its own sake and his need to defeat the passage of time, his refusal to become boxed in to any way of playing that might be thought of as "old."

Davis certainly found himself in the midst of the new when he came to New York in 1944 and, within a short period of time, joined the quintet of alto saxophonist Charlie Parker—the most brilliant virtuoso of the music that had been dubbed bebop.

But not only did Davis's style lack the rhythmic and harmonic angularities of Parker and Dizzy Gillespie, when initially shaky technique improved, it also became clear that he had been following a different musical path all along—one whose suave symmetrical shapes were not that far removed from those of the better American popular songs of the 1930s and 1940s. In fact, for all the harmonic and timbral subtleties of its arrangements (the best of them written by Gil Evans), Davis's influential *Birth of the Cool* band amounted to a revamping of the pop song's aura of sophisticated romance—a way of deepening and purifying, but not dispensing with, prevailing notions of gracefulness and sentiment.

That approach, it should be noted, was firmly linked to the world of the musical theater—the home ground (along with the film musical) of the romantic popular song sensibility. And perhaps that link with the theater was crucial, for Davis was about to become the most overtly theatrical jazz artist of our time.

Consider the innate theatricality music of Davis's second great band, which he formed in 1955—the quintet that included tenor saxophonist John Coltrane, pianist Red Garland, bassist Paul Chambers, and drummer Philly Joe Jones. The soloists were excellent, but much of the effect of the Davis quintet was built upon the dramatic contrast between, on the one hand, the leader's brooding romanticism and Garland's swinging sweetness and, on the other, the hard-edged intensity of Coltrane, Chambers, and Jones.

And it could be argued that theatricality became even more important to Davis's art when he once more joined forces with Gil Evans and produced three celebrated big band albums, *Miles Ahead*, *Porgy and Bess*, and *Sketches of Spain*.

One had to admire the results, as Davis played with exquisite taste and Evans supported him with timbral subtleties that rivaled those of Ravel, but the music was very much a foreground/background affair, with Davis functioning as a kind of jazz Sarah Bernhardt, a "star" doing a turn in front of a mass of sumptuous sonic scenery.

Acknowledged by the late 1950s to be jazz's key style shaper, Davis now faced the first major challenge to that role, as Ornette Coleman, Cecil Taylor, and Coltrane began to move into the area known as "free jazz." And his initial response to this new and seemingly disruptive music was quite negative.

"If you're talking psychologically," he said of Coleman, "the man is all screwed up inside." As for Coleman's partner, Don Cherry, whose style was a fragmented offshoot of Davis's own music, he was "not a trumpet player—it's just notes that come out."

By the mid-1960s, however, Davis had formed a new band whose members (tenor saxophonist Wayne Shorter, pianist Herbie Hancock, bassist Ron Carter, and drummer Tony Williams) clearly had been affected by free-jazz styles. And in response to this, Davis himself began to change.

His solos tended to be less lyrical and more fragmented (at times, under the pressure of swift tempos, he even sounded a bit like Cherry). And especially in live performance, one felt that it was Davis's sidemen who were shaping the flow of the music, leaving the leader to function as a kind of musical counter-puncher.

If, indeed, Davis was no longer the dominant creative force in his own band ("We had," said Carter, of his fellow sidemen, "all decided on our groove before the band was formed"), the ostensible leader seemingly had only two ways to go. He could continue to counterpunch, fragmenting his essential lyricism more and more in response to Shorter's gaunt angularities and Williams's oblique rhythmic turmoil. Or he could, in effect, return to theatricality, abandoning the fierce but fruitful interactions of the Shorter-Hancock-Carter-Williams band for the foreground/background model of his collaborations with Gil Evans.

Davis chose the latter course, at first brooding over a static backdrop of guitars and electronic keyboards *(In a Silent Way)*, then adding more aggressive, rock-tinged percussion (*Bitches Brew*, etc.). But always the format was that of a showcase, a kind of musical stage set that was intended to leave one in suspense as to when, how, and even if the "star" would finally emerge.

Since his return from retirement, Davis has followed much the same plan—fiddling here and there with the scenery (the backdrops now owe a lot to the sounds of contemporary black pop music) and, so it would seem, shunning contact with any soloist who might elbow him out of the spotlight. But even though Davis's charisma lingers on, his music, for the most part, no longer justifies it—as though his self-cultivated image as an endlessly fruitful creator of new styles had broken free from any need to be more than "new."

But if that is the psychology of the fashion designer or the advertising man, not that of the artist, perhaps Miles Davis's career could have developed in no other way. As Paul Valéry once said, "It is impossible to impersonate, and at the same time really to be, the dominant intellect."

Gary Tomlinson

Miles Davis, Musical Dialogician

Originally published in Black Music Research Journal *11, no. 2 (Fall 1991): 249–64. Reprinted by permission of the Center for Black Music Research and the author.*

One would not expect that one of the most probing examinations of Miles Davis's controversial "fusion" oeuvre would come from a specialist in Renaissance music, but here it is. Gary Tomlinson, a professor of music at the University of Pennsylvania and author or editor of several volumes on the Renaissance period, wrote this piece as part of an extensive article called "Cultural Dialogics and Jazz." Tomlinson brings to this discussion considerable skills as musicologist and cultural historian.—Ed.

And then came the fall. *In a Silent Way*, in 1969, long, maudlin, boasting, Davis's sound mostly lost among electronic instruments, was no more than droning wallpaper music. A year later, with *Bitches Brew*, Davis was firmly on the path of the sellout. It sold more than any other Davis album, and fully launched jazz rock with its multiple keyboards, electronic guitars, static beats, and clutter. Davis's music became progressively trendy and dismal. . . . His albums of recent years . . . prove beyond any doubt that he has lost all interest in music of quality. (Crouch 1990, 35)

[On *In a Silent Way*] the solos are dissipated; the understated rock ostinato of the title piece turns at times into an enervated Chicago blues line. "SHHH/Peaceful" is even more precious, with electric pianos tinkling in and out. The impersonality of the guitarist is the finishing touch on a performance with all the enduring, debilitated stimulation of a three-day drunk on white port wine: sickly sweet and effective. . . .

The music [of "soul" jazz] was thoroughly blues-drenched; it emphasized the beat; people danced to it. The next kind of pop-jazz, the fusion music that grew out of the decadence of [the] modes, subdued and eventually eliminated these features.

As Miles Davis's music declined in the late 1960s, the sales of his records declined, too, and this was during the period when the new management of Columbia Records was raising sales quotas. Davis's bosses ordered him to make a hit record or else; *Bitches Brew* was his response. . . .

In general, what fusion music fused was the atmospheric tendencies of modal jazz with the rhythm patterns of rock. The gravitational pull of the modern rock beat upon soloists' accenting discourages any but the simplest kinds of linear development; as a result, other features—atmosphere, color, small variation of subsidiary detail—become primary among the values of a music in which decoration is raised to the essential. . . . Creating a coherent musical line even becomes dispensable. (Litweiler 1984, 126–27, 222–23, 227)

Strictly on the face of it, there is no reason why fusions might not have worked. Jazz has always been able to meet, absorb, and put to its own purposes almost everything in popular prospect. . . .

Nevertheless, I don't think jazz fusion worked very well . . . : the beat in jazz moves forward; it is played so as to contribute to the all-but irresistible momentum of the music: jazz *goes* somewhere. The beat in most rock bobs and bounces away in one place—like the kids on the dance floor these days. Rock *stays* somewhere. And to be a bit technical about it, "jazz eights," the implied "triplet feel" of jazz, is rarely heard in fusion, and can seem strangely out of place when it is. . . .

About Miles Davis and fusion, maybe I can be as blunt and outspoken as he usually is about everything and everybody. When I last heard Miles Davis he was stalking around a stage in what looked like a left-over Halloween fright-suit, emitting a scant handful of plaintive notes. . . .

Davis has always been one of those musicians who could come up with something so fresh, even on familiar material, as to make one forget, temporarily, all of his beautiful past. That evening everything I heard made me remember that beautiful past with pain. (Williams 1989, 47–49)

> We could credit Miles Davis for the mainstream creation of Fusion as a jazz-like trend. His Bitches Brew bands and Post-Bitches Brew bands read like a who's who of Fusion. . . .
>
> But so trendy and faddish was the Fusion mini-epoch that it was possible to trace its ebb very clearly. . . .
>
> There was by the downturn of the Fusion trend a reawakening, it would seem, of a neo-BeBop voice. . . . To me this was a healthy sign, concrete evidence that Fusion, for all its great sweeping trendiness which saw a few of our greatest musicians turn out a couple of new-style mood-music albums and bands, could not erase the deeper mainstream traditions of the music. (Baraka 1987c, 178)

What's eating these people? The coercive power of the institutionalized jazz canon is repeatedly evident in their rejections of the innovations Miles Davis introduced on *In a Silent Way, Bitches Brew,* and the albums that followed. The four authors represent the best writing from a wide spectrum of approaches to jazz: Litweiler, tending toward the academic and musicological; Crouch and Williams, journalistic from both black and white perspectives; and Baraka (How can he be categorized?), probing and poetically allusive, perhaps the most insightful and original voice on African American music over the last three decades. But however different their approaches, all four writers reveal the same stark inability to hear Davis's fusion music except against the background of what jazz was before it (and what it has since reverted to in the hands of some neo-bop jazz technicians). The rich dialogue of musical voices that went into the making of Davis's new styles around 1970—voices, as I will describe below, from outside as well as inside the walls of "pure" jazz—seems to carry no musical/cultural excitement for these writers. Far from it. Instead they hear only a departure from the canonized and thereby musically segregated jazz tradition. And this departure, the occasional vehemence of their tone makes clear, sounds to them like a betrayal.

It is worth pausing to analyze the rhetoric of these condemnations (and of many others, for the passages quoted are not unique in writing on fusion music). It is, first, a rhetoric of *absence*—absence, of course, conceived in tandem with the characteristic presence of earlier jazz. This rhetoric usually appears in descriptions of the musical features of fusion styles. Litweiler, for example, finds the solos on *In a Silent Way* dissipated (Compared to what?) and perceives in general that fusion music lacks "linear development" and melodic "coherence." (Whose development? What coherence? Armstrong's? Parker's? Davis's own in earlier works?) Williams, meanwhile, finds fusion music lacking in "jazz eights," the unequal and syncopated eighth notes prominent in most earlier varieties of jazz—and for Williams, apparently, a sine qua non of all possible music that would deserve the name. (We may leave aside Williams's specious distinction between a beat "going somewhere" and "staying somewhere," with its offhand dismissal of rock music.) The strategy operating here of chastising one music because it lacks the features of another, even though the two were conceived in decisively different cultural circumstances, is a familiar one in musicology—compare, for example, the continuing undervaluation of Verdi's operas in comparison to Wagner's. But the strategy is no more legitimate for its familiarity. And it does not gain in legitimacy, but only in teleological illogic, when the favored style precedes and even influences the rejected one.

The condemnations of Davis's fusion styles also invoke a complex rhetoric of *transgression*, one that cuts rather deeper than the rhetoric of absence. The transgressions involved take different forms in the hands of different writers. Some are matters of personal behavior: the hinted distaste in Williams's words at Davis's recent concert persona swells to self-righteous disgust in the similar description that opens Crouch's essay. Crouch is also particularly hard on Davis's personal foibles, although, strangely, he seems to voice this criticism only to reinforce the case against Davis's fusion (Crouch 1990, 36). The criticism of lifestyle is muted or disappears entirely in his reverential treatment of works like Davis's sessions with Thelonious Monk and Milt Jackson of 1954 (Crouch 1990, 32)—as if Davis treated women better or used drugs less in the 1950s than he did in 1970 or 1985.

By far the most often mentioned transgression of Davis's fusion is its commercialism. With *Bitches Brew* and later albums, the writers above and many others claim, Davis sold out, breached the rampart between the artistic integrity of jazz and the pimped values of pop. Fusion, Baraka (1987c, 177) writes and other writers agree, was mostly "dollar-sign music"; indeed, the very fact of *Bitches Brew*'s large sales seems for some writers to convict the music on the album without trial, discounting the artistic efforts that went into its production. This view, first, manifests a psychological naïveté that reaches a nadir in Litweiler's (1984, 223) recounting of Davis's docile acquiescence to his boss man's orders. Even a rough gauge of Davis's ambivalent psyche, we shall see, leads to stories of much greater complexity than this.

Second, the condemnation of fusion for its commercial success drastically underestimates the vitality, subtlety, and expressiveness of the pop traditions that influenced Davis. It is nothing more than an antipopulist chauvinism that turns from the unacceptable view that "what sells must be good" to the opposite and likewise unacceptable view that "what sells must be bad."

And finally, the contrast of commercial fusion with noncommercial earlier jazz amounts to elitism pure and simple, to a snobbish distortion of history by jazz purists attempting to insulate their cherished classics from the messy marketplace in which culture has always been negotiated. Those who advocate such a view should reread Ralph Ellison's review of *Blues People*. Ellison points out that even Bird and the other early boppers, musicians who were the ne plus ultra for many critics of esoteric jazz intellectualism, "were seeking . . . a fresh form of entertainment which would allow them their fair share of the entertainment market" (Ellison 1978, 59). Or, in a different connection, they should read recent nonhagiographical music histories that have Beethoven hawking the same opus to three different publishers or Mozart conniving, with a sad lack of savvy, at one music-business killing or another. Music created with an eye to eternal genius and blind to the marketplace is a myth of European romanticism sustained by its chief offspring, modernism.

One final transgression of fusion music offends Baraka and particularly Crouch: the transgression of the boundaries of pure ethnic expression. Baraka does not accuse Davis of this in his early fusion albums, at least not in so many words. But he does regard later fusion, from the late 1970s and early 1980s, as an aspect of a "*desouling* process" by which corporate powers whitened previously genuine black expression (see Baraka 1987b, 274); and, at times, as in the quotation above, he portrays all fusion music as an unfortunate departure from the "mainstream," black traditions of jazz (Baraka 1987c, 178).

Crouch goes much further. He seems to evaluate all jazz according to the purity of its blackness. Such a view could only inspire deep reservations about Davis's musical achievement, which always derived vitality from its disquieting perch in the middle of interethnic musical dialogues. Crouch, to give him his due, is at least consistent in his rejection of Davis's most overtly dialogical styles. He regards the famous *Birth of the Cool* sessions of 1948–50 as "little more than primers for television writing" that "disavowed the Afro-American approach to sound and rhythm" (Crouch 1990, 31). He sees the later collaborations with Gil Evans as a sign of Davis's seduction "by pastel versions of European colors"; for him "they are given what value they have . . . by the Afro-American dimensions that were never far from Davis's embouchure, breath, fingering" (Crouch 1990, 34). And, of course, he regards Davis's fusion music as the ultimate sellout to (white) corporate America, a mining of "the fool's gold of rock 'n' roll" (Crouch 1990, 30). This tendency to forsake the pure blackness of his origins, combined with his other personal shortcomings, led Davis in Crouch's narrative to a moral failure that is biblical in dimension: Crouch (1990, 30) talks of Davis's "fall from grace" and the "shriveling" of his "soul."

Another interpretation of Davis's fusion is more plausible than these. It recognizes in Davis's musical efforts from 1969 to 1974 a compelling expressive force created by his unflinching confrontation with the dialogical extremes of his background and environment. It recognizes, in other words, the Signifyin(g) power of Davis's music in this period. This interpretation gains credence from Davis's own remarks about his fusion and other music. It has been adumbrated in recent years by two prominent African American critics, Greg Tate and—I return to him, surprisingly, once more—Amiri Baraka. Tate's (1983) position, in a two-part *Down Beat* article, "The Electric Miles," is doubly significant, first for his sensitivity to Davis's new styles and the pop elements in them and second because he has elsewhere emerged as a nonacademic advocate of a black vernacular critical theory (see his remarks quoted in Gates 1989, 21, 27–28). Baraka's position seems to signal a deepening of his earlier views of fusion, an emotional coming to grips with tendencies in Davis's music that have long gone against his own black aesthetic grain; in this it reveals a healthy complexity and rich self-questioning in his thought. It emerged first in a moving profile of Davis that he wrote for the *New York Times* in 1985 and unfolded further in a later, expanded version of this essay (Baraka 1987a). This latter version ranks among the most psychologically astute writings on Davis.

> "White musicians are overtrained and black musicians are undertrained. You got to mix the two. A black musician has his own sound, but if you want it played straight, mix in a white musician and the piece will still be straight, only you'll get feeling and texture—up, down, around, silly, wrong, slow, fast—you got more to work with. There's funky white musicians. But after classical training you have to learn to play social music." (Miles Davis, as quoted by Amiri Baraka [1987a, 295])

> Miles Davis's music, like African-American culture generally, originates as a specific reflection of African-American life and perception in the still mostly

segregated black communities of the society, but it, like Miles, reaches in all directions within the whole of that society and transforms them. . . .

But interracial bands are nothing new to Miles. So talk of Miles's eye to the buck as being the principal reason for using white musicians doesn't really wash. Though it is my own feeling that Miles knows always almost exactly what he is doing around the music—form and content, image and substance.

There is something in the mix Miles *wants* [us] to hear. It might be commercial, to some extent, but it is also social and aesthetic. . . .

Miles's special capacity and ability is to hold up and balance two musical (social) conceptions and express them as (two parts of) a single aesthetic. . . . By *Miles Ahead,* Miles understood enough about the entire American aesthetic so that he could make the *cool* statements on a level that was truly *popular* and which had the accents of African-America included not as contrasting anxiety or tension but as an equal sensuousness! (Baraka 1987a, 289–90, 294, 304)

Behind Miles Davis's frequent stereotyping of white and black musicians, behind all the color generalizations he voiced over the years that led many to accuse him of racism, stands an acute fascination with *difference.* The refutation of the charge of racism—of the kind, at least, that leads to segregation—has always been easy: Davis's bands, since his first collaboration with Gil Evans in 1948, featured white musicians more often than not. The issue is not simple racism. Instead Davis's insistent matching of musical to ethnic differences over the years bespeaks the collaborative musical variety that he felt compelled to seek by merging various approaches. There is, indeed, something in the *mix* he wanted us—all of us, whites as well as blacks—to hear. Perhaps more than any other contemporary musician, Davis made this stylistic, cultural, and ethnic mix the stuff of his music.

It is hard not to see in Davis's musical expression of difference a reflection of his own ambivalent background, situated between the marginal status white America accorded him because of his skin color on the one hand and the middle-class or upper-middle-class affluence in which he was raised on the other. His values were shaped by two contradictory statuses, a disenfranchised ethnic one and an empowered economic one; this was the first mix Miles Davis learned. He grew up with the contradictory messages that come with such mixed status. His situation was, from the first, a situation *between*—between mainstream bourgeois aspirations historically identified in America as white aspirations and the deep tributary of the proud and angry selfhood of a marginalized ethnos.

By virtue of his relatively secure and even privileged economic status, his background was unlike that of most earlier jazz greats. What must the boppers at Minton's, Parker and Gillespie and the others, have made of him when he first arrived in New York in 1944? He, a precocious eighteen-year-old with an enrollment at Juilliard and a generous allowance from his father? (Parker, at any rate, was not one to overscrutinize a gift horse: he soon moved into Davis's digs.) More generally, how did his affluence set him apart from the very musicians he idolized? And, later, how did the many of Davis's close associates, who, like him, struggled with drug addiction, view his good fortune of having a supportive father and a 300-acre farm to retreat to while he kicked his habit? Few of them were so lucky. The affluence of Davis's family was simply not a typical background for a black jazz musician—or perhaps any jazz musician—in the 1940s and 1950s.

Davis's (1989) recent memoir, *Miles: The Autobiography*, provides little insight into the difference and distance that must have conditioned his relations with the great boppers and many of his later black collaborators. Davis portrays his acceptance among them as a simple matter of mutual artistic respect growing in some cases into friendship. But the disparity in backgrounds suggests that the emotional bonds between Davis and a musician like Parker must have been tinged with ambivalence on both sides. And for Davis, I think, this kind of ambivalence quickly grew to be a defining trait of his musical personality. It was an uneasiness at sitting on the fence, between worlds, that impelled him always to seek out distinctive middle voices, stylistic mediations, and compromises between differing idioms. This is the source of his special capacity, so well expressed by Baraka, to meld two musical/social conceptions into a single way of making music. And the capacity revealed itself early on: by late 1948, a scant three years after his first recording sessions with Parker, Davis was already following his ambivalent star, leading an ethnically mixed nonet in the new, cool style that was in important respects an antibop reaction. "The mix" was on; it was already beginning to saturate Davis's musical thought.

Almost from the beginning, then, Davis's musical achievement was an acutely dialogical one, reveling in the merging of contrasting approaches and sounds, highlighting the awareness of difference that seems so crucial a part of Davis's own personality. This is indubitable whether or not we accept Davis's facile generalizations (as quoted in Baraka 1987a, 295) about the differences between black and white musicians. It does not deny, of course, the blackness of Davis's music, its origins, in Baraka's words

(1987a, 290), "as a specific reflection of African-American life and percep-tion"; rather it affirms the wide-ranging variety of African American percep-tions themselves. As Baraka (1987a, 306) sums up: "Miles went to Juilliard. Miles's father was a medium-sized landowner and dentist. All that is in his life and to a certain general extent is in his art." ("But Miles is still tied to the blues," Baraka continues; I will return to this point below.) Davis's per-ceptions of African American life differed from Parker's just as surely as they differed from Armstrong's, Jelly Roll Morton's, or Leadbelly's. His per-ceptions were, especially, a product of the particular matrix of ethnic marginalization and economic assimilation that characterized his youth. From this cultural ambivalence, refracted through the unique lens of Davis's psyche, arose a powerfully synthetic Signifyin(g) voice. From ambivalence—or, better, from multivalence—arose musical dialogue.

Davis's fusion music from 1969 to 1974 represents the culmination of this dialogue, a logical outgrowth of his earlier musical development and the mediating concerns expressed in it—whether in the cool style, in his orchestral collaborations with Gil Evans, or in the laid-back blues of his extraordinary work with Bill Evans, John Coltrane, and Cannonball Adderley in the late 1950s. Taken as a whole, Davis's fusion music is a melting pot into which he stirred an ever-changing mélange of ingredi-ents from his (our) fragmented and dizzyingly varied musical environ-ment. Each new recording session, from as early as those of *Filles de Kilimanjaro* (June and September 1968) and *In a Silent Way* (February 1969) on, seems to add ingredients to the mix with increasing relish, greater abandon. Sometimes the new ingredients float on top of the earli-er mix, like oil on water, and seem incapable of successful blending with it. But more often Davis succeeds in dissolving the new elements in the old to create a novel and effective brew. The old ingredients are hardly ever discarded. They may be chemically altered by the new, perhaps even almost unrecognizable, but they remain to make their contribution.

The fusion mix as a whole challenges, with an aggressiveness matched only by some of the free jazz of the early and mid-1960s, the "verities" of earlier jazz. The famous—notorious among jazz purists—expanded rhythm section or "bottom," which on *Bitches Brew* involves as many as ten players (three drummers, a percussionist, three electric pianists, an electric guitarist, an electric bass player, and an acoustic bass player), no longer functions either in the traditional supporting manner of postbop ensemble jazz or in the liberated manner of free jazz. Instead it usually fulfills enhanced versions of both functions at once. It is a thick web of simultaneous solos, radically loosed from subjugation by the treble soloists; at the same time it lays down, in the form of insistent ostinatos suggesting static or repetitive harmonies, an uncompromising metric framework borrowed from such sources as African and Brazilian polyrhythms and James Brown–style rhythm and blues.

At times this functional balance of the bottom swings to one extreme or the other. In the strain of Davis's fusion style that remains closest to traditional jazz formal procedures, such as that heard on most of *On the Corner* (1972), the bottom simply provides intricate rhythmic support for a succession of treble solos. It is characterized usually—and in this, of course, it departs from jazz precedent—by funky rhythm-guitar riffs and percussive polyrhythms governed by an insistent backbeat. At other times the bottom beat dissolves into nonmetrical collective soloing, as in the recurring echo-trumpet passages of the title track of *Bitches Brew.*

Most intriguing are the moments, especially prominent on *Bitches Brew* and a number of works recorded soon after it (for instance, those later collected on *Big Fun*), when the traditional functions of treble soloists and rhythmic bottom seem almost to be reversed. In these passages Davis, perhaps along with Wayne Shorter on soprano sax or Bennie Maupin on bass clarinet, states a melodic fragment over and over, with minimal variation, which serves paradoxically as a sort of cantus firmus "bottom" for the collective improvisations below. In nonmetrical or irregularly metrical contexts—for example, the opening section of "Lonely Fire" on *Big Fun*— this cantus firmus-like riff not only serves as a structural anchor but simultaneously directs attention away from itself to the intricate web of collective soloing around and beneath it (in "Lonely Fire" the web consists of electric bass guitar, electric pianos, sitar, and a variety of percussion). Something of a functional reversal of top and bottom results. When the cantus firmus technique appears in a metrical context, on the other hand, both bottom and top share in traditional rhythm section functions; but the anchor of Davis's repeated riff allows individual instruments from the bottom to depart from supportive roles and take off at will on solo flights.

In general this functional freedom of the rhythm section is what Greg Tate (1983, 22–23) hears when he describes Herbie Hancock as "break[ing] down on electric keyboards like solo and rhythm parts were one and the same" on the album *A Tribute to Jack Johnson,* or when, on "Calypso Frelimo" from *Get Up with It,* he characterizes Pete Cosey's guitar as "a second set of congas to Mtume's, a second rush of cymbals to Al Foster's, a second steel drum simulacrum to Miles' Gnostic organ, a second rhythm guitar to Lucas', and . . . one of three solo voices." Other earlier examples of this multivalent effect are "Spanish Key" from *Bitches Brew* and "Great Expectations" on *Big Fun;* listen especially to John McLaughlin's electric guitar.

Indeed, McLaughlin's role in Davis's ensembles from *Bitches Brew* on is emblematic not only of the functional flexibility of the fusion bottom as a whole; its breadth of expression suggests also some of the varied influences Davis gradually incorporated into his fusion music. Departing from his more traditional and lyrical jazz guitar style, which harkens back all the way to Charlie Christian and is evident on *In a Silent Way,* McLaughlin moved in two directions in his later work with Davis. The first of them to emerge was a syncopated, offbeat, sometimes wah-wah rhythm-guitar comping indebted more to the funky rhythms of James Brown and Sly and the Family Stone than to any jazz predecessors. The second was a psychedelic, fuzz-toned, bad-axe virtuosity indebted to Jimi Hendrix. This style begins to take shape on *Bitches Brew* and the earliest cuts of *Big Fun,* all recorded late in 1969; it explodes into the works recorded in the first sessions of 1970: "Gemini/Double Image," later released on *Live-Evil,* "Go Ahead John" on *Big Fun* (where McLaughlin's funky comping is also prominent), and others. It is carried on by the later guitarists Davis used after McLaughlin left the band (especially by Cosey; on his role see Tate [1983, 23–24]). And, most intriguingly, Davis himself adopted the style by the end of 1970, playing his muted trumpet through an amplifier with a wah-wah pedal on works such as "Sivad" and "Funky Tonk" (both on *Live-Evil*) to achieve an acid-rock solo style combining the Hendrix/McLaughlin sound with the characteristic Davis articulation, phrasing, and melodic figures.

Davis's adoption of the electrified sounds of psychedelic rock and the complex rhythm-guitar offbeats of funk is one of the developments in his fusion music most sorely lamented by jazz purists. A more comprehending view would regard it as another of the dialogical moves to achieve an interethnic sound that recurred across his career. Both Sly and Hendrix, the most important influences on these aspects of Davis's fusion, were musicians mediating between two worlds much in the manner of Davis himself. Sly's achievement in his early music with the Family Stone (roughly 1967–69) was to merge black funk and white counterculture in an unprecedented and peculiarly Bay Area amalgam. Hendrix's wrenching, acid-singed virtuosity moved along a parallel path. His merger of authentic blues with psychedelia spoke mainly to middle-class, white audiences of the late 1960s—audiences who had moved through *Sgt. Pepper's* and *Magical Mystery Tour* and the Rolling Stones, through the early head-rock of the

Jefferson Airplane and the folk-acid of the Grateful Dead, and were looking for higher thrills. Hendrix answered the needs of the mainly white
listeners at Monterey and Woodstock for a mediated, "whitened" rock-
blues.

Baraka (1987a, 309), though he mentions Sly only in passing,
captures eloquently the significance of Davis's affinity for "the white or
'integrated' media-ubiquitous rebellion Hendrix represented." It reflected
Davis's position at the "other side of the social and musical equation"
from musicians such as John Coltrane and Pharaoh Sanders, his partaking
of the "coalition politics of the Panthers rather than the isolating national-
ism of the cultural nationalists." Baraka's reading is on the money. Davis's
thoroughgoing electrification of jazz allowed it to incorporate rock 'n' roll
styles that were in themselves coalitions reaching across ethnic lines. The
music of *Bitches Brew* captured a huge audience—by jazz standards, at any
rate—made up in large part of venturesome white rockers willing to try
something new. (I was one of them, I should acknowledge, a fledgling
jazz-rock trumpeter who turned on to *Bitches Brew* and its predecessor *In a
Silent Way* when they emerged during my first year of college; my own
commitment to engage with Davis's fusion music stems from this forma-
tive musical/cultural experience.)

But it does not follow from all this interethnic dialogue and coalition
politics that in *Bitches Brew* and his later albums Davis renounced or sold
out his black artistic self, anymore than Crouch's accusation follows from
Davis's cool jazz or his collaborations with Gil Evans. In all these styles—in
Bitches Brew just as surely as in *Birth of the Cool*—Davis's distinctive, blue
plangency remains at the heart of his achievement. He is still tied to the
blues, as Baraka says. His trumpet contributions to his fusion works vary
from minimalist utterances—which he tended toward especially in the
early fusion works in order, I think, to purge his style of the postbop
phrasing that lingers, sometimes incongruously, on *Filles de Kilimanjaro*—
to amplified, virtuosic assaults. But all his fusion work sings the blues, its
melodies pivoting again and again on ♭VII or playing subtly on ♭III/♮III
exchanges. Indeed, Davis speaks the blues rather more plainly here than
in many of his earlier styles; Tate (1983, 18) is right to say that Davis
turned from "post-bop modernism" to funky fusion "because he was bored
fiddling with quantum mechanics and just wanted to play the blues again."

And Davis's bluesy fusion lines *swing* in his inimitable manner: fuzzy,
arch, suspicious of the listener's motives, sometimes almost offhanded,
sometimes angrily spat out, always from the heart. Listen to how he plays

the straightforward modal ruminations of "SHHH/Peaceful" on *In a Silent Way* or the repeated (and sometimes transposed) I to ♭VII scalar riff that makes up much of his role in "Spanish Key." Even such simple material exhibits Davis's personal vision of the freedoms of pitch, timbre, and articulation that have marked the great jazz trumpeters from Armstrong on. It is these freedoms that constitute Crouch's "Afro-American dimensions" of embouchure, breath, and fingering. They represent the technical revolution brought to the trumpet by black Americans, a revolution that toppled the prim Arban methods and military precision of Victorian cornet virtuosos and broke wide open the expressive range of the instrument. As for Davis himself, the power of his vision was such that it could embrace as a convincing expressive aspect even his famous cracked and fluffed notes.

The dialogical dimensions of Davis's fusion, then, are numerous. This music opened lines of communication between traditional jazz, with its blues background and improvisational impetus, on the one hand, and rhythm and blues, funk, and white acid rock on the other; these communicative channels are enriched all the more since the nonjazz musics involved in them were ultimately blues-based as well. The dialogics of fusion involved also an extraordinary freedom of colloquy within the ensemble, a freedom of exchange wherein the complex bottom and any of its constituents could function as top and vice versa. This far-reaching democratization of the ensemble has an obvious antecedent in various versions of free jazz, but it came to Davis's music also from pop sources—specifically Sly and the Family Stone, whose vocal and instrumental arrangements featured all the musicians with an equality rarely heard in earlier rhythm-and-blues styles. And the democratic, multiple improvisations of much of Davis's fusion music took encouragement also from European avant-garde trends— specifically the structural indeterminacy sometimes explored by Karlheinz Stockhausen, whose music and thought Davis came to know around 1970.

The fusion dialogue reached in other directions as well. Davis's self-conscious incorporation of extra-American sounds in his fusion albums looks back to various precedents: to the Spanish accents of his earlier efforts (especially *Sketches of Spain* with Gil Evans) and to bossa nova influences on him and other jazz musicians. But his transmutation of these borrowed sounds in the new mix moves further than those precedents and qualifies his fusion as a legitimate ancestor of some recent international pop idioms. The Brazilian and African percussionists and the Indian musicians of his ensembles contribute not so much full-fledged styles as raw sound materials. More flavors for the mix.

And even when a full-fledged style is borrowed, it is transformed in arresting ways. The haunting, nonmetric "Selim" on *Live-Evil,* arranged by Brazilian musician Hermeto Pascoal, takes over melodic and harmonic inflections from the samba or bossa nova but leaves behind their most salient features—their rhythms. "Maiysha," on both *Get Up with It* and *Agharta,* juxtaposes its primary theme, a well-behaved samba, with a hard-driven, guitar-dominated blues; the grinding gearshift that results is repeated over and over on the (superior) *Agharta* version. And in "Calypso Frelimo" the calypso is sublimated, reduced to Davis's recurring theme fragment on organ, stated usually against Mtume's furious conga drumming. This constructive technique, involving repeated, wispy allusions to tamer styles, is a frequent one in Davis's fusion works. It looks back to such cuts as "Mademoiselle Mabry" from *Filles de Kilimanjaro,* whose long, freely formed theme is punctuated by two cadential figures, a modal/chromatic one borrowed from Hendrix's "The Wind Cries Mary"—even Crouch (1990) likes this "elevation" of "pop material"—and a keyboard interjection in the protofunk style of Joe Zawinul's "Mercy, Mercy, Mercy."

It may not be too farfetched to suggest that the opening of one more dialogue is signaled in the title of *Bitches Brew.* This is the dialogue of equality between woman and man, which—to judge from his autobiography—Davis always found extremely difficult to sustain. The title *Bitches Brew* at first seems no more than a tired play on Davis's demeaning and obsessive epithet for women, all women. Then we look more closely and discover that there is no apostrophe in it: *Bitches Brew,* not *Bitches' Brew.* "Brew" is a verb, not a noun, and the title does not describe the music on the album so much as the musicians and their activity in making it. The musicians themselves are the bitches; the separate linguistic realms of "bitch" as demeaning epithet and "bitch" as admiring title, akin to "motherfucker" in Signifyin(g) talk, are joined. It is as if the title hints at Davis's hesitant coming to grips with the bitch within himself, his recognition of his own most mysterious otherness, and his desire to enter into a meaningful, nondemeaning colloquy with it. At the deepest level, this desire might even subsume all the other dialogical axes of his fusion: black and white, American and non-American, top and bottom, pop, jazz, and avant-garde.

The four condemnations of fusion I quoted at the beginning of this essay demonstrate the fundamental difficulties that the dialogics of culture pose for us. They are a microcosmic expression of the abiding threat that the recognition of difference carries with it. Their intolerance of fusion music reflects the discomfort of both black and white critics with the *mix* Davis created. It amounts to a dismissal of Davis's complex and eloquent Signifyin(g) on the many musical idioms around him.

At a more general level, their intolerance stems from Davis's breaching of too many walls of the kind we habitually set up to order and make sense of the world. So I have not cited the views of Crouch, Litweiler, Williams, and Baraka to condemn them for an atypical narrowness and intolerance, but rather to exemplify in a particular musical situation an aversion that we all share to the dialogical complexity of our construal of the world around us. Without struggling against this aversion, we will construct, as they constructed in their accounts of fusion, solipsistic, monological values and meanings.

Henry Louis Gates (1988, xxiv) wrote, "Anyone who analyzes black literature must do so as a comparativist." I have tried to extend the reference of this maxim beyond black literature to embrace African American music and expressive culture in general, and beyond that to embrace all culture of any variety. African American texts may well have a particularly salient dichotomy of formal antecedents on which they Signify. But this does not set them qualitatively apart from all other texts and indeed all other products of culture, for all of these arise from multivalent colloquy with earlier cultural acts. The condition of African American culture and its theory, once again, provides a compelling instance of the dialogical condition of all culture and cultural theory.

Dialogical knowledge, as I said above, is the building of a precarious discourse that never fully displaces the other discourses around it. It is unsettling precisely because it defeats our natural impulse to be settled in the complacency of our own rules and terms. It threatens because it refutes the comforting idea of mastering a fully cleared space with open horizons in order instead to scrutinize the mysterious others crowding in on it. Mastery is no doubt the easy route to follow. But the path of mystery, if steeper, will surely lead to more humane rewards.

Acknowledgments

Many people have assisted in the preparation of this essay. For their readings, criticisms, and suggestions, I would like particularly to thank three of my colleagues at the University of Pennsylvania: Houston Baker, Jeffrey Kallberg, and the cicerone of my exploration of jazz studies, Ralph Rosen.

Thanks are also due to Samuel Floyd for the initial invitation to write on a subject distant from my more usual Renaissance haunts.

References

Baraka, Amiri [LeRoi Jones]. 1987a. "Miles Davis: 'One of the Great Mother Fuckers'—P. J. Jones in Conversation." In *The Music: Reflections on Jazz and Blues*, 286–316. New York: William Morrow. (Revised version of interview with Miles Davis, *New York Times*, June 16, 1985)

———. 1987b. "The Phenomenon of *Soul* in African-American Music." In *The Music: Reflections on Jazz and Blues*, 268–76. New York: William Morrow.

———. 1987c. "Where's the Music Going and Why?" In *The Music: Reflections on Jazz and Blues*, 177–80. New York: William Morrow.

Crouch, Stanley. 1990. "Play the Right Thing." *New Republic*, February 12, 30–37.

Davis, Miles, with Quincy Troupe. 1989. *Miles: The Autobiography*. New York: Simon and Schuster.

Ellison, Ralph. 1978. Review of *Blues People*, by Amiri Baraka. In *Imamu Amiri Baraka (LeRoi Jones): A Collection of Critical Essays*, edited by Kimberly W. Benston, 55–63. Englewood Cliffs, N.J.: Prentice-Hall.

Gates, Henry Louis, Jr. 1988. *The Signifying Monkey: A Theory of Afro-American Literary Criticism*. New York: Oxford University Press.

———. 1989. "Canon-Formation, Literary History, and the Afro-American Tradition: From the Seen to the Told." In *Afro-American Literary Study in the 1990s*, edited by Houston A. Baker Jr. and Patricia Redmond, 14–39. Chicago: University of Chicago Press.

Litweiler, John. 1984. *The Freedom Principle: Jazz after 1958*. New York: Da Capo.

Tate, Greg. 1983. "The Electric Miles." *Down Beat* 50, no. 7 (July): 16–18, 62; no. 8 (August): 22–24, 54.

Williams, Martin. 1989. *Jazz in Its Time*. New York: Oxford University Press.

Gary Giddins

Miles to Go, Promises to Keep

Originally published in the Village Voice, *October 15, 1991, 83, 94–95. Reprinted by permission of the* Village Voice *and the author.*

Gary Giddins wrote "Miles to Go, Promises to Keep" only days after Davis's death on September 28, 1991. Giddins manages two difficult tasks: he gives us a concise—and at times revelatory—survey of the trumpeter's career, and he reminisces in a heartfelt and personal way without cloying.—Ed.

The rumor was abroad for three or four weeks: He was in intensive care in Santa Monica and fading fast. Cancer? AIDS? He had played so well at JVC in June it seemed impossible. Reports of July's Miles Plays Gil concert in Montreux were glowing. On the other hand, I remembered he wore a curly, shoulder-length wig and looked perilously thin, and regretted my reference to his "Mariah Carey waistline." To be sure, at sixty-five, still decked out in the chameleonic silks and satins of superstar jazzdom (dreaded oxymoron), he no longer resembled Miles the gymnast, Miles the boxer. But the power was there, the ennobling ache, the audacious humor.

It wasn't cancer or AIDS that did him in September 28, but a stroke coming on top of pneumonia, his health already compromised by years of drug abuse, the hip surgery that changed him irrevocably in the mid-'70s, not to mention diabetes and sickle-cell anemia. The warning did nothing at all to alleviate the immense sadness that attended the confirmation of his death. Someone I hadn't spoken to in years called to reminisce: the end of an era, she said. The thing is it was our era—not the swing era or bop era or cool jazz era. At his last New York concert, I jokingly asked his most vociferous detractor why he came. "I keep hoping," he said. And that explains part of the sadness, too. Miles kept us hoping, and now there is no more hope that he will do once again what he managed to do at least four times in four decades, which was to change and enliven our musical attitudes, tastes, and perceptions.

After the news broke, I had the sudden desire to hear "He Loved Him Madly," which I hadn't heard in twelve or thirteen years but had played to distraction when it was first released on the 1975 *Get Up with It* album. Unlike the dozens of conventional tributes to Ellington, that record had captured the holy calm and fear that ought to attend the passing of a man of Ellington's stature. It's a thirty-minute dirge based on an organ drone in which nothing seems to happen, yet a mood that suggests echoes in a medieval cathedral is advanced straightaway and sustained for several minutes. Strongest when mysteriously still, "He Loved Him Madly" falters during the flute solo—a solo of any kind would be too decorous for the occasion's deep solemnity. And it's too long, a reflection of the minimalist trance music ubiquitous in the mid-'70s. Listening to it now, and to the entire album, which was recorded over four years, I'm as puzzled as ever by the intangible form but more certain than before that the jury has yet to return a verdict on the prolific and complicated "directions" Davis attempted to forge in that period. The assumption, pervasive then, that Miles's records were constructed in the editing room, sometimes by a producer in his absence, was taken as proof that they represented a cynical concession to Mammon. That bias is hardly borne out by a thirty-minute dirge or a thirty-two-minute "Calypso Frelimo," with its mockingly elliptical calypso strain, or the crushing keyboards-sitar-rhythm novelty of "Rated X." But there is dire filler as well—the inanity of "Mtume," which sounds like a razor job, and the empty-headedness of "Red China Blues."

In 1947 Miles, at twenty-one, recorded as a leader for the first time at Savoy Records. He had been on the Street for two years, and participated in Charlie Parker's breakthrough "Ko Ko" session, though not, pace the *New York Times,* on "Ko Ko" itself for the crucial reason that he did not have the necessary chops to play the furious eight-bar arabesques Dizzy Gillespie was called upon to supply. But on "Billie's Bounce" and, more cogently, "Now's the Time," Davis showed that even though he might be confined to the middle register and incapable of nudging every passing chord implied in the harmonic sweep of bop, he brought something vital to the new music. His timbre, influenced by Freddie Webster, was personal, if not yet achingly personal, and he could fashion a melodic variation by skimming chords for the storytelling notes. So in 1947, with his idol Charlie Parker serving humbly as his sideman on tenor sax (Parker's sideman instrument), the Juilliard dropout and his doctorate-seeking friend John Lewis were in a mood to show off. Miles brought out "Sippin' at Bell's," a twelve-bar blues with an inverted melody and such a flurry of chords that it hardly sounds like a blues. Here lies the true beginning of cool jazz. As a gift to Miles, Lewis presented his friend with "Milestones," a line with so many harmonic bottlenecks that Parker insisted he'd play just the bridge because the tune was too hard for a country boy like him. This gave Davis and Lewis something to ponder.

In 1949 Miles, at twenty-three, demonstrated for the first time his legendary strength as a visionary and persistent organizer. He assembled some of the finest writers and players in New York to explore things they'd been hearing and discussing and that Gil Evans, at thirty-seven the senior conspirator, had been working on in his arrangements for Claude Thornhill. They all met at Gil's pad, but Miles was in charge. He formulated the nine-piece instrumentation (heavy on brass) and secured an isolated club gig and three record dates—subsequently collected as *Birth of the Cool.* John Lewis and Max Roach from the Parker quintet were there along with Lee Konitz, Gerry Mulligan, J. J. Johnson, Kai Winding, and Al McKibbon, plus four guys alternating on French horn and tuba. A perfectly integrated ensemble, and not just racially: the more profound integration configured improvisers and writers, soloists and ensemble, hot and cool. Not many records were sold; still, the nonet went straight from cult to classic. The key sides—"Boplicity," "Israel," "Move," "Rocker," "Godchild," "Rouge"—remain a superb achievement, utterly uncontaminated by the musty imitations that came to be associated with West Coast jazz.

The first Miles Davis album I bought was *In Europe,* recorded in Antibes in 1963, a single platter that plays about sixty-two minutes, longer than most CDs. Since it was also the first Miles Davis album I had ever heard, I had no way of knowing that the selections were mercuric versions of pieces Davis had originally conceived at slow and medium tempos. The record remains a shocker, the debut of a tenacious new quintet, though it didn't sell well and is usually out of catalogue. Davis plays a staggering, high-powered solo on "Milestones," the opening notes fired at a clip; Herbie Hancock gives a new lift to block-chord solos (something Red Garland excelled at with Davis) on "Autumn Leaves"; and George Coleman, on that piece and others, enters with an authority that makes incomprehensible the unremitting criticism he had to endure in those years, his punishment for succeeding—as did the equally underrated Charlie Rouse in Monk's quartet—John Coltrane. But the biggest news about this record, short of the explosive energy generated by Davis, was the brushfire in the rhythm section, ignited by Ron Carter and the seventeen-year-old drummer Tony Williams. The emotional high point came near the end, on "Walkin'," when Williams finally burst free in a solo that was greeted in some circles as the big bang of jazz drumming.

Perhaps because "Walkin'" is such a heartstopper, the second Davis album I bought was the 1954 Prestige classic of that name. I listened to the title track late on the evening I brought it home, then drove over to one of the few people I knew who was also finding his way into jazz. We listened to it a couple of times and were giddy with excitement, for three reasons. One, the theme is performed with a rare sense of drama and deliberation; not unlike Ellington's "Such Sweet Thunder," the 1954 "Walkin'" has the strutting grandeur of a blues march. Second, the rhythm section is a thing of rare, glowing, erotic beauty; in the period between the years when Jo Jones tattooed the hi-hat for Basie and Tony Williams's ride cymbal shivered like autumn leaves with Miles at Antibes, nobody ever made metal resound with more colorful, emphatic hues than did Kenny Clarke on this record—in meticulous accord with the stout bass of Percy Heath and the hungrily inspired piano of Horace Silver. Third, and most of all, it was a revelation to us, at sixteen, to be held spellbound by a long improvisation that unwound without recourse to pyrotechnics, but worked its magic with the smart, dark, penetrating logic of an impeccable fable impeccably told.

Later, from books, I learned that the 1954 "Walkin'" helped trigger and codify the new counterreformation in jazz known as hard bop. Much, much later it occurred to me that those warring subcultures—West Coast jazz (cool) and East Coast jazz (hard bop)—that occasioned prolonged debate over so many years had the same midwestern parent, Miles Dewey Davis of Alton, Illinois.

None of those records made much money at first. And Davis, who had successfully cold-turkeyed smack and whose throat had healed from an operation that left his voice little more than a menacing rasp (fueling the Prince of Darkness legend, especially after his producers included snippets of it on his albums), knew the only way he could cross beyond the coterie audience was to sign with the best network label, CBS's Columbia Records, where the canny head of A and R was George Avakian. Davis had been introduced to Avakian in 1947, at the Deuces, where Dizzy was playing; all three posed for a picture.

Miles later told George that he decided that night he was going to maneuver his way to Columbia. He asked Avakian to sign him up in 1954, but with three years remaining on his Prestige contract, they decided to wait. After Miles triumphed at the 1955 Newport Jazz Festival as the added guest to an all-star quintet (Gerry Mulligan, Zoot Sims, Thelonious Monk, Percy Heath, and Connie Kay), Avakian's brother Aram convinced him he'd better not wait any longer. Davis wanted an advance on signing of $4,000, which was considered a fortune, especially for someone who had been a junkie and might prove unreliable. But the executives at Columbia were impressed by what Avakian described as his "quiet perseverance," and they agreed. Avakian convinced them, "He may be as big as Dizzy."

Prestige made the most of Davis's limbo status by recording in three marathon sessions his first and greatest quintet (Coltrane, Red Garland, Paul Chambers, Philly Joe Jones)—enough to fuel a series of albums, with seductive one-word titles. When Columbia was allowed to release a Davis album, in early 1957, they issued another quintet session, *'Round About Midnight* (for some reason, the publisher of the title song insisted they insert *About*, which was never used again). They needed something different for the follow-up. Avakian suggested an expansion of the nine-piece band and asked Davis who he would like to work with. "Gil," he said. So during the quintet's long engagement at the Café Bohemia, the three men met at Lindy's to map out the instrumentation; they came up with a nineteen-piece ensemble for *Miles Ahead*. Evans had the idea of composing links between the selections, something never done before. (He did it again in an album with Cannonball Adderley; the Beatles popularized the idea ten years later with *Sgt. Pepper's*.) It was the first time Miles explored the possibilities of splicing and dubbing that became central to his music in the '70s.

The only problem was the cover—a sailboat against a blue sky, intended to express the idea of Miles forging ahead, with a blond model on the boat. Davis protested, "Why'd you put that white bitch on there?" But the company wasn't about to burn the 50,000 copies of the jacket already printed. *Miles Ahead* was a commercial and critical landmark in the music of the '50s. Possibly no other album in that era, outside of the work of Duke Ellington, did more to awaken the affluent society, in and out of the academy, to the range of progressive (a regressive term) jazz. Dave Brubeck—whom Davis championed and whose "The Duke" was included on *Miles Ahead*—sold many more records and had a clamorous following on campus, but Miles's albums and Miles's ascension represented a new and dangerous sexiness that would have a far more durable impact here and abroad.

At thirty-one he was the representative black artist. People wanted to hear what he had to say—he was the subject of *Playboy*'s first interview. People were obsessed with the way he dressed—he was featured in fashion magazines. People who didn't buy jazz records except maybe Ella singing Cole Porter would buy something by Miles. He defined the era's stance and tone, its irreverence, its style, its daring introversion, its brusque belligerence. When Louis Armstrong attacked Eisenhower and segregation in 1957, he was harassed by a right-wing columnist who demanded a boycott as well as scrutiny from the FBI. When Davis stood up to the cops who bloodied him in front of Birdland a few years later, he became a hero of the civil rights era. In no time, he had the clout to kill the offensive *Miles Ahead* cover (now a collector's item): for *Someday My Prince Will Come*, he made sure the cover model was black. A breakthrough, that, in 1961.

One of the arrangements that didn't make it on to *Miles Ahead* was a particular favorite of Gil's, "Summertime." From that seed, however, grew the second and most enthralling of the three key Davis-Evans collaborations, *Porgy and Bess*. Never before had Miles's emotional range, from the chillingly stark laments to the unexpected closing splash of big band euphoria, been so compellingly displayed. But for many people the third album, *Sketches of Spain*, struck deeper. Here the arrangements were scaled down to minimal scrims, drunk with color. Davis seemed to stand naked before the ensemble, the jazzman as confessional poet, working out a timbre that had never been heard on trumpet, that was in fact virtually the reverse not only of conventional jazz intonation but of the robust Spanish style the album celebrated. Although inadequately rehearsed and marred by clams, the sheer power of the spectacle overwhelmed reservations. If the overall effect is less rich, even less persuasive than *Porgy*, the unparalleled "Saeta" remains a taunting solitary cry from the heart, an isolated peering into the dark before the expressionistic deluge of New Things and electronic dinosaurs.

Sketches of Spain was originally intended to represent a more capacious response to Third World music, an exploration of the sounds coming from Asia and Africa. Avakian had been collecting records from Columbia's international division, which he headed, and had turned many of them over to Evans. But Evans got hung up on Spain, and by the time they were ready to record, Avakian had long since left the company and Teo Macero became Miles's producer. One of the rejected tunes from the original concept was Cyril Scott's fin-de-siècle "Lotus Land," which neither producer nor arranger could shake. Avakian produced "Lotus Land" for the Calvin Jackson Quartet, and Evans arranged it for Kenny Burrell's *Guitar Forms*. Something else about *Porgy* and *Sketches:* The relatively simple two-session sextet album that Davis squeezed exactly midway between those behemoths had a far more profound influence on the future of all music because it actuated a logical, irresistible blending of modal or scalar improvisation and the familiar forms that have long been the framework for jazz—*Kind of Blue*.

One evening on a midwestern campus in 1968 or 1969, half a dozen undergraduates blissed-out on lysergic acid diethylamide paused before a huge oak on center campus as a breeze rustled the leaves. One of us, probably the one who now works at the *Times*, said, "It sounds like Tony Williams's cymbals." Someone else detected the chords of Herbie Hancock in the branches. Others ascertained Ron Carter in the trunk and Wayne Shorter in a peal of thunder. After a properly dramatic pause, the Sorcerer himself came along by means of a lightning streak. For a few minutes we stood transfixed by this spontaneous performance by the Miles Davis Quintet in a giant oak tree—a really fine performance. I indulge in this recollection primarily for auld lang syne, and secondarily to pursue the point about Miles representing the era of those of us who came of age in that most charring and exhilarating of modern epochs, the '60s.

It is probably not unfair to characterize the last forty years in jazz as the Miles Davis era if for no other reason than that more than anyone else he kept us guessing, debating, pondering. It is undoubtedly true that he recorded his greatest achievements in the '50s and his most popular works in the '70s. Yet it was only in the '60s that he and three other musical entities achieved an oddly suspenseful relationship with the audience that I believe was unprecedented then and remains unequaled since. The transformations of Bob Dylan from folkie to rocker, of the Beatles from rockers to art-rockers, of John Coltrane from hard bopper to New Thing prophet, and of Miles Davis from cool bopper to jazz-rocker-prophet were played out inch by inch on records. And each of the changes transcended the specifics of music to irradiate the culture itself. Of the four, Davis has thus far had the longest career and largest capacity for change.

Yet at the time, he was surely the least attended. His records sold miserably and were often chided. A rock critic accused him of stagnating. This came as a surprise to those of us in the dwindling jazz audience who lived for his every new release, no matter how weird (like the Bob Dorough vocal tacked onto *Sorcerer* or the narcoleptic arrangement of "Nefertiti"). From the time Wayne Shorter joined the band, every Miles album seemed to wrestle with the frustrations of conventional form. Davis accelerated, deconstructed, and finally jettisoned standard songs. He reduced new pieces to serial repetition or fragmented riffs. He added electric keyboards and on one track guitarist George Benson. The trip from *Nefertiti* to *Miles in the Sky* to *Filles de Kilimanjaro* (an unbilled collaboration with Gil Evans, though nobody knew it at the time) to *In a Silent Way* generated countless debates, fights, recriminations, doubts, celebrations, ulcers. When he finally busted through the rock barrier with the sometimes impenetrable *Bitches Brew*, worries no longer counted for much. The beast came slouching toward Bethlehem, and its name was fusion. The atmosphere was so disconcerting that many of us overlooked the far superior *A Tribute to Jack Johnson,* issued in its shadows.

Then came the onslaught of double albums and the six-year hiatus and the return, in 1981. Finally, he effected a rapprochement between the old Miles, wailing recognizable blues and ballads on an acoustic trumpet, and an electronic band that sometimes postured more than it played. In his exasperating but indispensable autobiography, he makes it clear that the bands of the '40s, '50s, and '60s continued to hold for him far more glory than most of what followed. Yet from the '80s, we have the obvious joys of Miles's incomparable sound and effective writing on such diverse comeback-era albums as *We Want Miles, Star People,* and *Aura.*

Looking back at the prehiatus period, including *Agharta,* which elicited an overkill from me (an anonymous reader delivered a box to the *Voice* after my piece appeared, containing industrial steel wool, Q-Tips, and the advice that I clean out my head before reviewing Davis again), I find in the best selections the promise, if only rarely the fulfillment, of an open-ended form that escapes the tyranny of chords and regulation eight- or twelve-bar phrases. Throughout the stuff from the dizzyingly complex period of 1974 and 1975, there is the allure of a new form, something that remains jazz's most elusive grail. The drawback with many of those sessions is that Miles himself sounds so bad, his timbre mottled by an electronic attachment. The '80s Miles came closer to satisfaction because he seemed restored, even when the rhythms were repetitious or cloying.

Through all those years when he pointedly refused to play with the musicians he came up with, his equals, Davis always kept alive the possibility of working with Gil Evans again. In interviews and at press conferences, he would insist that he wanted to work with Gil but that Gil was too busy, which didn't make much sense but at least left the door open. For a time, they discussed the possibility of adapting themes from *Tosca.* And then, in 1988, Evans died. Yet at Montreux last summer, Davis finally reunited with the remains of the Gil Evans orchestra. But while that union suggests something of a closed circle, I don't think Miles's legacy ends with the gorgeous masterpieces that represent his late-'50s/early-'60s style. Some of the '70s records are going to come back, too, not to fuel a revival of the facile hyphenated musics of that period but to instruct a new generation in some of the possibilities of fusing acoustic and electronic instrumentation, free form and song form, jazz improvisation and multiple rhythms. I can't get it out of my head that Miles is still the future. He is for damn sure a glorious past.

Marc Crawford

Memorial for Miles, and the Friend Who Couldn't Make It

Originally published in Swing Journal, *June 1994. Copyright © by Marc Crawford. Reprinted by permission of the author.*

Marc Crawford and Miles Davis were friends for more than thirty years, and therefore Crawford's farewell is even more personal than Giddins's. But Crawford, typically, does not draw attention to himself. Rather, he tells about a friendship of even longer duration: that of Davis and another great trumpeter, Clark Terry.—Ed.

Trumpeter Miles Dewey Davis III will be gone three years on September 28. He died on that day in 1991 at St. John's Hospital and Health Center in Santa Monica, California, from pneumonia, respiratory failure, and a stroke. He was sixty-five.

In an October 1 editorial titled "Miles Ahead," the *New York Times* said: "Mr. Davis' genius emerged in his 20's, with the *Birth of the Cool* recordings. He recorded prolifically and changed constantly, breaking fresh ground with his revolutionary bands in the 1960's, then forging adventurously into the 70's and 80's—when, in sequins and enormous dark glasses, he looked and occasionally sounded like a rock star. His work spoke at once to old and young, though what the old relished as classic Miles, the young might consider square. . . . One of his albums was called *Miles Ahead.* And he was: an American original, as cool as they come."

But October 5, at Saint Peter's Church in New York, Miles had seemed as dominant in death as he had ever been in life. His unflinching eyes stared out from a huge color photograph set on the altar at the hundreds of invited and uninvited musicians, friends, and industry functionaries who streamed down the aisles. They filled every seat in the sanctuary and in the hastily requisitioned auditorium beyond.

They had come to sit and eulogize the memory of "the Black Prince," Sir Miles Davis, Knight of Malta, Chevalier of the French Legion of Honor, that incomparable jazz master who had lived so much of his life as a legend.

Dizzy Gillespie was there, and Max Roach. So was Quincy Jones. He showed the film he made on Miles at Montreux. And there was Gerry Mulligan, Herbie Hancock, Ron Carter, Barry Harris, Donald Byrd, Tony Williams, Jimmy Cobb, comedian Bill Cosby, actor Wesley Snipes, producer George Wein, and on and on.

But the only music played was Miles Davis recordings.

The streets of Midtown Manhattan glistened under a cold autumn rain, but inside the Reverend Jesse Jackson's appreciation of Miles was warm: "He was our music man, leaning back, blowing out of his horn, out of his soul, all the beauty and pain and sadness and determination and wishful longing of our lives. He would growl his independence and ours out of his horn. And sometimes by turning his back as he played a solitary song, he would only let us hear him talking to God."

David Dinkins, then mayor of New York City, called Miles's music "a profoundly African American form" and expressed the gratitude of eight million New Yorkers.

In Paris, on July 18, Miles was knighted and made a Chevalier of the Legion of Honor. Minister of Culture Jack Lang told him: "France has a special kind of love for you." And now the cultural attaché of the French embassy in Washington had come to repeat Lang's words.

But the friend who couldn't come was Clark Terry, who grieved alone with a cracked spine in Helen Hayes Hospital, forty miles to the northwest in the wilds of Rockland County. And none of his impressive credentials could bring him a whit closer. It was of no consequence that his was among the most original and enduring trumpet voices in all of jazz or that he was a Kansas City Jazz Hall of Famer, chairperson of the Thelonious

Monk Institute of Jazz's academic council, an advisory board member of the International Association of Jazz Educators, a National Endowment of the Arts Jazz Master, or that no other musician had ever played in the bands of Charlie Barnet, Count Basie, and Duke Ellington, who rated Clark's playing "beyond category."

"There's something wrong with any man who can't get along with Clark Terry," says drummer Louis Bellson. Which explains why his peers chose Terry to break the color bar in 1960 by joining the NBC-TV Tonight Show Orchestra where he remained for fifteen years. He has also played at the White House for four American presidents. Most recently Japan's Teikyo University conferred yet another honorary Ph.D. upon him and appointed him head of its Clark Terry Institute of International Jazz Studies at the Westmar Campus in LeMars, Iowa.

Who can say how that upper-middle-class Davis boy might have differed had fate chosen a role model other than Clark Terry, who was born and reared in abject poverty.

Recalling his late teen years before coming to New York at eighteen in 1944, Miles wrote: "Clark Terry was the one who really opened up the St. Louis jazz scene for me, taking me with him when he would go sit in. . . . All through [that] period I loved Clark Terry—still do to this day—and I think he felt the same way about me."

In the early 1950s Miles was strung out on heroin. One day Clark found him on the streets in New York homeless and hungry, bought him a meal, and put him up in his hotel room before leaving for an out-of-town gig. Miles promptly stole everything of value that wasn't nailed down and sold it to buy dope. Without it, Miles knew the familiar sickness he faced would tie his body up in knots.

"I avoided anyplace I thought Clark was going to be," Miles wrote. "When we did finally run into each other, I apologized and we went on like nothing had ever happened. Now, that's a good friend. A long time after that every time he caught me in a bar drinking with my change on the counter, he'd take it for payment on what I had stolen. Man, that was some funny shit."

"I made up my mind I was getting off dope," Miles once told me, remembering those early 1950s. "I was sick and tired of it. You know you can get tired of anything. You can even get tired of being scared.

"I laid down and stared at the ceiling for twelve days, and I cursed everybody I didn't like. I was kicking it the hard way. It was like having a bad case of flu only worse. I lay in a cold sweat, my nose and eyes ran. I threw up everything I tried to eat. My pores opened up, and I smelled like chicken soup. Then it was over."

"It had to put a crust on him," Dr. Davis, Miles's father, told me. "There was always somebody trying to get him back on dope. He had an iron will that broke it, and that will applied to everything he did as a result. I'm proud of him."

For two weeks in September 1991, Miles lay in a coma in that California hospital. A couple of days before Miles regained consciousness, Clark Terry underwent surgery for a cracked spine back east in the Long Island Jewish Medical Center. Doctors told him he would be unable to play or make a living for five months. They put him in a body cast. One doctor told Clark, then seventy, he might not walk again.

Clark's hands were full wrestling with his own pains and problems and the sickening side effects of medications. But he worried most about Miles even as they transferred him to a hospital in Rockland County. Miles had emerged from the coma with his hearing intact but had lost the ability to speak.

Telephoning was a painful chore, but each day Clark placed a call with messages to be whispered in Miles's ear. He would not hang up until assured his message had been delivered and was told how Miles reacted.

"Miles smiled." Then Clark hung up and began to pray.

What memories those messages must have triggered in Miles. Perhaps he wrote what he best remembered: "One of the most important things that happened for me in high school—besides studying under Mr. Buchanan—was when one time the band went to play in Carbondale, Illinois, and I met Clark Terry, the trumpet player. He became my idol on the instrument. . . . I had on my school band uniform and Clark had on this hip coat and this bad, beautiful scarf around his neck. He was wearing hip butcher boy shoes and a bad hat cocked ace-deuce. I told him I could also tell he was a trumpet player by the hip shit he was wearing. He kind of smiled at me."

And later: "But him telling me I was bad and could really play at that time did a lot of good. I already had confidence, but Clark telling me this just gave me more. . . . [W]e hung out all over the St. Louis area, sitting in and going to jam sessions, and when people heard that Clark and I were going to be sitting in on a particular night, the place would fill up quick. . . . I learned a lot from listening to him play the trumpet. He introduced me to the fluegelhorn. . . . [A]nd he's still playing it today and is one of the best in the world . . . if not *the* best."

Miles further recalled: "Every time I got a new horn back in those days, I would go looking for Clark to fix up my horn, get the valves to working, and he would fix it up like nobody else could. Man, Clark had a way of twisting and lightening the spring action of the pumps of a trumpet, just by adjusting the springs around, that would make your horn sound altogether different. It made your horn sound like magic, man. Clark was a magician with that shit. I used to love for Clark to fix my valves."

There was a terrible hurt in Clark's eyes when I entered his hospital room that Saturday afternoon September 28. The impossible had happened. Miles was gone—his eyes closed for keeps. Clark resembled nothing so much as a helpless little boy who had tried as hard as he could to make things all right and failed.

Red Holloway held his hand. The tenor saxophonist had flown in from California to be with him. "You're not going to die," he assured Clark. "You're going to get well." He might have been talking to a small child.

"There was always somebody trying to get me to say mean things about Miles," Clark said to no one at all. "But I wouldn't even know how to fix my mouth to do that."

Index

Page numbers in italics indicate music examples. Album titles appear in italics; song titles appear within quotation marks.